Invitation to Reading and Writing

JACK O'KEEFE

*Daley College,
City Colleges of Chicago*

PRENTICE HALL, Upper Saddle River, New Jersey 07458

This book is dedicated to Phyllis, Jack, Kevin, and Denis,
who make possible all the good things in my life

Library of Congress Cataloging-in-Publication Data

O'Keefe, Jack.
  Invitation to reading and writing / Jack O'Keefe.
    p. cm.
  Includes index.
  ISBN 0-13-079774-X
    1. College readers. 2. English language—Rhetoric—
  Problems, exercises, etc. 3. Report writing—
  Problems, exercises, etc. I. Title.

PE1417.O45 2000
808′.0427 21—dc21

99-043022

Editorial Director: Charlyce Jones Owen
Editor-in-Chief: Leah Jewell
Editorial Assistant: Joan Polk
AVP, Director of Manufacturing
  and Production: Barbara Kittle
Senior Managing Editor: Bonnie Biller
Production Liaison: Fran Russello
Project Manager: Linda B. Pawelchak

Manufacturing Manager: Nick Sklitsis
Prepress and Manufacturing Buyer:
  Mary Ann Gloriande
Cover Director: Jayne Conte
Cover Design: Joe Sengotta
Marketing Manager: B. Schait
Copy Editing: Lynn Buckingham
Proofreading: Maine Proofreading Services

Acknowledgments begin on page 285, which constitutes
a continuation of this copyright page.

This book was set in 10/12 Bookman by Lori Clinton
and was printed and bound by R.R. Donnelley and Sons, Inc.
The cover was printed by Phoenix Color Corp.

©2000 by Prentice-Hall, Inc.
Upper Saddle River, New Jersey 07458

Printed in the United States of America
10 9 8 7 6 5 4 3 2 1

ISBN 0-13-079774-X

Prentice-Hall International (UK) Limited, *London*
Prentice-Hall of Australia Pty. Limited, *Sydney*
Prentice-Hall Canada Inc., *Toronto*
Prentice-Hall Hispanoamericana, S.A., *Mexico*
Prentice-Hall of India Private Limited, *New Delhi*
Prentice-Hall of Japan, Inc., *Tokyo*
Pearson Education Asia Pte. Ltd., *Singapore*
Editora Prentice-Hall do Brasil, Ltda., *Rio de Janeiro*

CONTENTS

UNIT I:
Personal Achievement in Education

UNIT II
The Immigrant Experience in America

UNIT III
Living with Disabilities

UNIT IV
Laugh So You Don't Cry

UNIT V
Overcoming Racism

PREFACE

This book encourages and invites students to read and write. Students improve as learners only when they get involved in reading and writing—about topics and ideas that are interesting to them. On this interaction between reading and writing, David Bartholme believes that a course in reading must necessarily be a course in writing and vice versa. From reading, students learn ideas and patterns of thought and organization called *genre schemes*. Much grammar, punctuation, and vocabulary are learned vicariously through practicing reading and writing. In *Joining the Literacy Club*, Frank Smith points to this involved, nonconscious learning; it is from "reading that the writers learn all the intangibles they know." (17)

This text is arranged around thematic units of readings and writing—and assignments built on them—that will, I hope, catch students' interest: Personal Achievement in Education, The Immigrant Experience in America, Living with Disabilities, Laugh So You Don't Cry, Overcoming Racism, and Defining Family in Modern America. These themes provide students with several different views on each topic. With this deeper context, students can write more intelligently about them.

In the early parts of this book, the writing assignments call for expressive writing, in which students write about themselves and their families in relation to the themes for each unit. James Britton explains how such expressive writing later leads to other kinds of writing: "In developmental terms, the expressive is a kind of matrix from which differentiated forms of mature writing are developed" (*Language and Learning*). Later, once students have acquired some fluency and confidence in writing, this text encourages them to write essays and the synthesis paper—with explanation of how to use sources. Interest is the key—because students will write well about things that matter to them. Students should write about the readings in a separate journal, the reading response journal, which will be explained in Unit I.

Several of the thematic units explore excerpts from longer autobiographical works: Angelou's *I Know Why the Caged Bird Sings*, McBride's *The Color of Water*, Rose's *Lives on the Boundary*, Least Heat Moon's *Blue Highways*, and Simon's *Bronx Primitive*. We encourage students to read the full texts by providing an introduction or a "teaser" for each of them. It's so important for students to be "immersed" in reading—whether newspapers, magazines, or books—that any hook—like extra credit, or even class reading sessions—can be very helpful. We want students to like reading.

For each reading, in addition to vocabulary, prereading, and work in a reading response journal, students are given a choice of writing assignments and a collaborative learning activity that will help them write and learn together, with other students forming an "audience" for each writer. There is a sense of excitement and a feeling of community when students work together—as well as valuable lessons in learning how to get along with other group members.

All of the writing in the "Writing from Reading" assignments lends itself to work in the computer lab—for discovery and final drafts. For the prewriting and collaborative work, I suggest first writing in the classroom and then moving to the lab. With the completed draft, students can staple their prewriting and earlier drafts to the back, giving them a sense of process, as well as the stages necessary to arrive at the printed paper. This lab work has the additional benefit of helping students to become computer literate (if they are not so already). When students have completed the final draft, they can read it out loud to another student for a sense of audience, or they can listen while another student reads it back to them. Frank Smith emphasizes the need "for an interested reader for anything that students write, whether it is the teacher personally, other adults, or other students" (*Joining the Literacy Club*). This sharing again fosters a sense of community.

As for the always sensitive matter of writing evaluation, I suggest putting only positive comments on papers, no grades; too often students care only about the grade, not the writing. Teachers and students in conference can later give the papers a portfolio grade at midterm and at the end of the semester. For those final drafts that need much more work, the teacher can ask the students to correct the papers on the computer and return them. Regarding the problems with fragments and run-ons so common to beginning writers, I advise teachers to note on papers where these errors occur, but not to identify or rewrite them for students. Let students retain ownership of their own papers by making *them* attempt to rewrite and correct. This can be a painful process—for both students and teacher—but may be more effective in the long run.

The readings and the writing assignments in this text have been developed and field tested in my own developmental reading and writing classes and in those of my colleagues, Corinne Allen, Jim Kozicki, and Carlene Hyrams. I'm thankful both to them and to their students. Not everything works, of course, with all students and all teachers. Teachers have to pick and choose what they feel comfortable with because they know their students best. In a nutshell, what this text hopes for is what all teachers hope for: to help students enjoy reading and writing. As theorists like Frank Smith and Stephen Krashen have pointed out, writing practice is not enough; acquiring the "code" of writing "happens only via comprehensible input, reading" (Smith *Joining the Literacy Club*). We work and teach with the hope our students will acquire that code.

ACKNOWLEDGMENTS

I am thankful beyond words to great teachers in my life: Dr. Robert Coogan, Robert C. McMullen, Dr. Bernard F. Dick, and Edward L. Surtz, S. J. At Daley College, I have been blessed with great friends and colleagues who have buoyed me more than they will ever know: Jim Kozicki, Dr. Beverly Tinsley, Corrine Allen McArdle, Emma Smith, Janet Mroczek, Carlene Hyrams, Shirley Carpenter, and Cheri Lynn.

In addition, the following reviewers made helpful suggestions: Kelly Belanger, Youngstown State University; Lisa Berman, Miami-Dade Community College; Kate Gleason, Interboro Institute; Karen Patty-Graham, Southern Illinois University–Edwardsville; Mary Helen Holloran, University of Wisconsin–Milwaukee; Harvey Rubinstein, Hudson County Community College; and Gary Zacharias, Palomar College.

Jack O'Keefe
Daley College, Chicago

STRUCTURE OF THIS BOOK

This text is organized in two ways: first, by thematic readings and, second, by the development of writing skills.

A cluster of readings focuses on specific themes such as achievement in school, triumphing over racism, the immigrant experience, overcoming disabilities, and humor. The study of each of these topics in some depth will provide ideas and opportunities for students to discuss and to write about their own lives.

The second organizing principle in this text is the development of writing skills: following the steps in the writing process, constructing a thesis, writing an argument essay, and finally writing a brief synthesis paper with several sources. Each step in the development of writing skills is tied to one or more of the chapter readings, so that students progress from writing about themselves to more objective writing at the end of the book, such as constructing argumentative essays and synthesis papers.

Interspersed at points in the book is work on sentence style, sentence combining, punctuation, and commonly confused words (word demons).

Each reading selection is the focal point of several reading and writing opportunities, arranged as follows:

1. Vocabulary in Context: word definitions and vocabulary development.
2. Prereading: predicting meaning from the title and a small portion of the reading.
3. Reading the selection itself.
4. Reading Response Journal: summarizing and practice in comprehension and writing skills.
5. Writing from Reading: suggested writing activities based on the reading and the students' response to it.
6. Collaborative Learning Activity: designed for those teachers and students who do group work.
7. Writing Tips: work on a specific skill linked to the reading and writing.
8. Review: a brief review of the main reading and writing principle(s) for each chapter.

TO THE STUDENT

You are in charge of your own education. No one is as important for your success as you. If, in the past, you have not done as well as you would have wished, it's time to forget about that and focus on what you *can change*: your present and your future. In school, as in life, attitude is everything. Keep your attitude positive.

This book invites you, indeed, encourages you, to make yourself a better reader and writer. These two skills are intimately tied together: through reading you develop vocabulary and ideas; at the same time, you absorb a sense of structure and writing style. While the readings in this book are short, you are encouraged to read the full-length texts from which the selections are taken—for example, Rose's *Lives on the Boundary*, Angelou's *I Know Why the Caged Bird Sings*, Silko's *Yellow Woman*, Least Heat Moon's *Blue Highways*, McBride's *The Color of Water*, and others. Through reading you are invited to enter a world larger than your own. We hope your response will be a strong "Yes."

UNIT I

Personal Achievement in Education

> Your success in school is tied to the development of your reading and writing skills. In this section of the book, you will read some personal success stories in education that may inspire you to become a better student. In addition, you will study the writing process, which will enable you to explore ideas for your own education.

THE DARE

Roger Hoffmann

Roger Hoffmann's story relates a frightening adolescent adventure caused by peer pressure. As you read it, try to think of a similar experience in your life—something that you foolishly dared to try.

VOCABULARY IN CONTEXT

"glass *shards*"—pieces, fragments of glass
"*guerrilla* act"—acts done by nonprofessional soldiers, volunteers
"his smile *evaporating*"—leaving, going away
"*ambiguous* phrases"—unclear, with more than one meaning
"*silhouette*"—outline or shadow
"*implicit* I-dare-you's"—unspoken
"one *convulsive* jerk"—shaking, trembling

PREREADING

Prereading is a technique for improving reading comprehension. Read the title and the first and the last paragraphs of the selection. Then write a prediction of what the full reading will reveal. Predicting meaning will keep you focused. Writing about the reading helps you to understand and remember it as you record your thoughts. The place for this writing is your reading response journal.

The format for the "Prereading" will be kept simple and clear, standard for each reading in this textbook.

1. Usually for your prediction, you read the title and the first and last paragraphs. For "The Dare," read the title and the first and second paragraphs, because in this essay the last paragraph has a surprise ending. After you have done your prereading, write what you predict the full reading will say.

The Dare

Roger Hoffmann

1   The secret to diving under a moving freight train and rolling out the other side with all your parts attached lies in picking the right spot between the tracks to hit with your back. Ideally, you want soft dirt or pea gravel, clear of glass shards and railroad spikes that could cause you instinctively, and fatally, to sit up. Today, at thirty-eight, I couldn't be threatened or baited enough to attempt that dive. But as a seventh grader struggling to make the cut in a tough Atlanta grammar school, all it took was a dare.

2   I coasted through my first years of school as a fussed-over smart kid, the teacher's pet who finished his work first and then strutted around the room tutoring other students. By the seventh grade, I had more A's than friends. Even my old cronies, Dwayne and O.T., made it clear I'd never be one of the guys in junior high if I didn't dirty up my act. They challenged me to break the rules, and I did. The I-dare-you's escalated: shoplifting, sugaring teachers' gas tanks, dropping lighted matches into public mailboxes. Each guerrilla act won me the approval I never got for just being smart.

3   Walking home by the railroad tracks after school, we started playing chicken with oncoming trains. O.T., who was failing that year, always won. One afternoon he charged a boxcar from the side, stopping just short of throwing himself between the wheels. I was stunned. After the train disappeared, we debated whether someone could dive under a moving car, stay put for a 10-count, then scramble out the other side. I thought it could be done and said so. O.T. immediately stepped in front of me and smiled. Not by me, I added quickly, I certainly didn't mean that I could

do it. "A smart guy like you," he said, his smile evaporating, "you could figure it out easy." And then, squeezing each word for effect, "I . . . DARE . . . you." I'd just turned twelve. The monkey clawing my back was Teacher's Pet. And I'd been dared.

4   As an adult, I've been on both ends of life's implicit business and social I-dare-you's, although adults don't use those words. We provoke with body language, tone of voice, ambiguous phrases. I dare you to: argue with the boss, tell Fred what you think of him, send the wine back. Only rarely are the risks physical. How we respond to dares when we are young may have something to do with which of the truly hazardous male inner dares—attacking mountains, tempting bulls at Pamplona—we embrace or ignore as men.

5   For two weeks, I scouted trains and tracks. I studied moving boxcars close up, memorizing how they squatted on their axles, never getting used to the squeal or the way the air felt hot from the sides. I created an imaginary, friendly train and ran next to it. I mastered a shallow, head-first dive with a simple half-twist. I'd land on my back, count to ten, imagine wheels and, locking both hands on the rail to my left, heave myself over and out. Even under pure sky, though, I had to fight to keep my eyes open and my shoulders between the rails.

6   The next Saturday, O.T., Dwayne and three eighth graders met me below the hill that backed up to the lumberyard. The track followed a slow bend there and opened to a straight, slightly uphill climb for a solid third of a mile. My run started two hundred yards after the bend. The train would have its tongue hanging out.

7   The other boys huddled off to one side, a circle on another planet, and watched quietly as I double-knotted my shoelaces. My hands trembled. O.T. broke the circle and came over to me. He kept his hands hidden in the pockets of his jacket. We looked at each other. BB's of sweat appeared beneath his nose. I stuffed my wallet in one of his pockets, rubbing it against his knuckles on the way in, and slid my house key, wired to a red-and-white fishing bobber, into the other. We backed away from each other, and he turned and ran to join the four already climbing up the hill.

8   I watched them all the way to the top. They clustered together as if I were taking their picture. Their silhouette resembled a round shouldered tombstone. They waved down to me, and I dropped them from my mind and sat down on the rail. Immediately, I jumped back. The steel was vibrating.

9   The train sounded like a cow going short of breath. I pulled my shirt-tail out and looked down at my spot, then up the incline of track ahead of me. Suddenly the air went hot, and the engine was by me.I hadn't pictured it moving that fast. A man's bare head leaned out and stared at me. I waved to him with my left hand and turned into the train, burying my face into the incredible noise. When I looked up, the head was gone.

10   I started running alongside the boxcars. Quickly, I found their pace, held it, and then eased off, concentrating on each thick wheel that cut

past me. I slowed another notch. Over my shoulder, I picked my car as it came off the bend, locking in the image of the white mountain goat painted on its side. I waited, leaning forward like the anchor in a 440-relay, wishing the baton up the track behind me. Then the big goat fired by me, and I was flying and then tucking my shoulder as I dipped under the train.

11   A heavy blanket of red dust settled over me. I felt bolted to the earth. Sheet-metal bellies thundered and shook above my face. Count to ten, a voice said, watch the axles and look to your left for daylight. But I couldn't count, and I couldn't find left if my life depended on it, which it did. The colors overhead went from brown to red to black to red again. Finally, I ripped my hands free, forced them to the rail, and, in one convulsive jerk, threw myself into the blue light.

12   I lay there face down until there was no more noise, and I could feel the sun against the back of my neck. I sat up. The last ribbon of train was slipping away in the distance. Across the tracks, O.T. was leading a cavalry charge down the hill, five very small, galloping boys, their fists whirling above them. I pulled my knees to my chest. My corduroy pants puckered wet across my thighs. I didn't care.

READING RESPONSE JOURNAL

What follows are sample directions for the "Reading Response Journal," which will appear after each reading:

1. After finishing the reading, write a one-paragraph summary of the reading *in your own words*. Writing the summary will help you remember the reading and make sure you understand it.

2. Write about how you can relate the reading to anything similar in your own life or in the lives of those around you.

3. If number two doesn't work for you, think about another topic from the reading that you can write about.

After the summary and ideas to write about, comprehension questions like these will help you grasp and recall the ideas in the reading:

4. At the end of the story, the boy should be embarrassed by wetting his pants, but he's not. Why?

5. Looking back on his experience, the writer thinks that childhood dares may influence the way adult males respond to challenges. What do you think? Any examples?

6. Do you think there is a "reckless gene," as some doctors have suggested, that causes some children to be accident and injury prone?

7. Among challenges that adults take, the writer mentions "tempting bulls at Pamplona." Explain this.

8. Roger tells us his "I-dare-you's" escalated, advancing from shoplifting and pulling pranks on teachers to vandalizing mailboxes. Try to recall some lesser dares or goofy stunts that you tried before the scariest one.

9. Roger does his dare because of peer pressure. Write of some good and bad things peer pressure has caused you to do.

WRITING FROM READING

"The Dare" and the Writing Process

"The Dare" can be a story that gets your attention. Perhaps it can inspire you to write about yourself, to describe the attractions and dangers of your own dares. We will use what's called the writing process to assist you in developing a paper of several paragraphs or more about your dares.

As a guide for your writing, consider using the Reporter's Questions that journalists try to answer in their writing: *who, what, when, where, why* (and sometimes *how*):

> *Who* was with you?
> *What* did you dare to do?
> *When* was your dare?
> *Where* was your dare?
> *Why* did you attempt your dare?

Look back at Hoffmann's article to see how *he* answered the five W's:

Who: narrator (Hoffmann) and buddies (Wayne, O.T.) and three eighth graders
What: dive under and out beneath a moving railroad car
When: seventh grade
Where: Atlanta lumberyard
Why: peer pressure, trying to overcome image of "teacher's pet"

Once you have answered the five W questions, you should be able to prewrite more about your "dare" experience.

Brainstorming List

First, try to brainstorm, a type of *pre*writing that helps get your writing to flow. Write a *list* as fast as you can about different dares you attempted in childhood, perhaps the first time you stole a drink of beer or tried smoking or did anything that was stupid.

Freewriting

Second, look back at your list and pick one dare or one foolish act that strikes you as particularly dangerous. Write nonstop about this dare—this is called freewriting—for ten minutes. Don't stop writing, don't correct or cross out, and don't worry about sentence structure or spelling. Keep going forward.

Discovery Drafts

Using either or both of these types of prewriting is the first step of the writing process. After prewriting, you then write discovery drafts of your paper using what you have already written. With your prewriting as a start, write a rough draft or discovery draft of several paragraphs or more.

Final Draft

You have completed your prewriting and one or more discovery drafts. It's time now to write a final draft, the last copy of your paper—though your teacher may ask you to make more changes later. Have you learned anything about yourself from looking back on your dare? Roger Hoffmann says that "at thirty-eight, I couldn't be threatened or baited enough to attempt that dive." How about you? Would you ever repeat your dare?

Read your paper out loud to yourself and to another student. Does it sound okay? Is it clear to your listener?

Staple all your prewriting and discovery drafts, no matter how sloppy, to your final draft, with the oldest material on the bottom and the final draft on top.

COLLABORATIVE LEARNING ACTIVITY

Peers as Audience

Some writing you do is for yourself, for example, notes for a class or a list of reminders. However, most writing demands an audience. You need to read to, talk with, and share ideas with other writers and readers—your fellow students. You shape your writing with an audience in mind. As an illustration of how a sense of audience determines what you will write, think about how you would describe a recent party you attended to one of your friends away at school—and how you would describe that same party to your parents or your grandmother.

To help you to develop a sense of audience, your instructor might have you work in groups, a method of teaching often called collaborative or cooperative learning. In this structure, students share their prewriting, discovery drafts, and final drafts with other students. Groups of three or four students are best. There are a few simple rules: First, move together so that your desks touch and you will be able to hear better; then, introduce yourselves to one another. After getting acquainted, take turns reading your papers out loud, slowly and clearly, to the group. After a student has read, make positive comments about his or her paper; in time, you may be able to make some constructive criticism as well.

WRITING TIPS

Clear Transitions

In telling a story, the writer must keep a clear chronology, or time order, of events. Hoffmann tells us at age thirty-eight of a dare when he was twelve: "*Today, at thirty-eight*, I couldn't be threatened or baited enough to attempt that dive. But as a *seventh grader* struggling to make the cut in a tough Atlanta grammar school, all it took was a dare."

Notice the words telling time: *Today, at thirty-eight* and *as a seventh grader.* These are called transitions, connecting words, that give us the chronology of the story.

Hoffmann uses other transitional words and phrases, too, such as *For two weeks* and *The next Saturday.* Make a list of other transitional words and phrases Hoffmann uses to indicate time.

Application to Writing

Look back over the dare story you wrote to check whether or not the time sequence is clear. See if you need to add transitions to signal each part of the story. Do you have a clear beginning, middle, and end? Some other transitional words or phrases you can use include the following:

first	then
second	soon
third	before
next	later
another time	meanwhile
finally	at the end

REVIEW

Writing is a messy process that should include brainstorming and/or other prewriting to get you started. Writing quickly is a technique that forces you to get your thoughts down on the page. Writing slowly may prevent your thoughts from flowing.

After your prewriting, use the five W's to give yourself more information.

Use your prewriting and answers to the five W's to write your final draft. Read your paper out loud to yourself and to another student. Staple the brainstorming and/or freewriting to your final draft to see how you have progressed from start to finish and to demonstrate to your instructor how hard you've worked.

I WAS A REMEDIAL STUDENT, from *LIVES ON THE BOUNDARY*

Mike Rose

Mike Rose's *Lives on the Boundary* describes the education he received as the son of Italian immigrants in Los Angeles. Rose tells of his struggles as a dreamy, shy adolescent mistakenly placed in the remedial track at his Catholic high school because he was confused with another student who had the same last name. Despite some personal and family problems, Rose battled to attend college and, later, graduate school, training to become a teacher and finally a professor of English at UCLA.

If you have had ups and downs in your education, you can learn a lot from Mike Rose—he's been there.

In this excerpt from *Lives on the Boundary*, Mike Rose describes his struggles as a remedial math student. As you follow his words, try to think of troublesome times in your own schooling.

VOCABULARY IN CONTEXT

"*Voc. Ed.*"—abbreviation for vocational education or non–college prep classes

"*restive* Ken Harvey"—impatient under restriction

"*laryngectomize*"—remove the larynx, so the person can't talk

"*platitudinous* melee"—conversation full of meaningless statements

"*disorienting* place"—disturbing, upsetting

"*dissonant* notions"—unsettling

"*elite*"—the special students

"*constrained*"—limited

"*diffuse* them"—put them off

"*pedagogy*"—teaching method

"*finessing* the rest"—faking, pretending

"*flaunt* ignorance"—show, display openly

"*attribute* their difficulties"—point to a cause

"*shroud* of hopelessness"—burial covering

PREREADING

1. Read the first paragraph about Ken Harvey and the last one about what remedial students go through. There is some difficult vocabu-

lary in this reading but try to make your way through it. Do your best
to predict what Rose will say about Ken Harvey and about himself
in remedial classes.

2. After you have done your prereading, predict what the full reading
will say.

I Was a Remedial Student

Mike Rose

1 And then there was Ken Harvey. Ken was good-looking in a puffy way
and had a full and oily ducktail and was a car enthusiast . . . a hodad.
One day in religion class, he said the sentence that turned out to be one
of the most memorable of the hundreds of thousands I heard in those Voc.
Ed. years. We were talking about the parable of the talents, about achievement, working hard, doing the best you can do, blah-blah-blah, when the
teacher called on the restive Ken Harvey for an opinion. Ken thought
about it, but just for a second, and said (with studied, minimal affect), "I
just wanna be average." That woke me up. Average?! Who wants to be
average? Then the athletes chimed in with the clichés that make you want
to laryngectomize them, and the exchange became a platitudinous melee.
At the time, I thought Ken's assertion was stupid, and I wrote him off. But
his sentence has stayed with me all these years, and I think I am finally
coming to understand it.

2   Ken Harvey was gasping for air. School can be a tremendously disorienting place. No matter how bad the school, you're going to encounter
notions that don't fit with the assumptions and beliefs that you grew up
with—maybe you'll hear these dissonant notions from teachers, maybe
from the other students, and maybe you'll read them. You'll also be
thrown in with all kinds of kids from all kinds of backgrounds, and that
can be unsettling—this is especially true in places of rich ethnic and
linguistic mix, like the L.A. basin. You'll see a handful of students far
excel you in courses that sound exotic and that are only in the curriculum of the elite: French, physics, trigonometry. And all this is happening
while you're trying to shape an identity; your body is changing, and your
emotions are running wild. If you're a working-class kid in the vocational
track, the options you'll have to deal with this will be constrained in

certain ways: You're defined by your school as "slow"; you're placed in a curriculum that isn't designed to liberate you but to occupy you, or, if you're lucky, train you, though the training is for work the society does not esteem; other students are picking up the cues from your school and your curriculum and interacting with you in particular ways. If you're a kid like Ted Richard, you turn your back on all this and let your mind roam where it may. But youngsters like Ted are rare. What Ken and so many others do is protect themselves from such suffocating madness by taking on with a vengeance the identity implied in the vocational track. Reject the confusion and frustration by openly defining yourself as the Common Joe. Champion the average. Rely on your own good sense. Fuck this bullshit. Bullshit, of course, is everything you—and the others—fear is beyond you: books, essays, tests, academic scrambling, complexity, scientific reasoning, philosophical inquiry.

3   The tragedy is that you have to twist the knife in your own gray matter to make this defense work. You'll have to shut down, have to reject intellectual stimuli or diffuse them with sarcasm, have to cultivate stupidity, have to convert boredom from a malady into a way of confronting the world. Keep your vocabulary simple, act stoned when you're not or act more stoned than you are, flaunt ignorance, materialize your dreams. It is a powerful and effective defense—it neutralizes the insult and the frustration of being a vocational kid and, when perfected, it drives teachers up the wall, a delightful secondary effect. But like all strong magic, it exacts a price.

4 My own deliverance from the Voc. Ed. world began with sophomore biology. Every student, college prep to vocational, had to take biology, and unlike the other courses, the same person taught all sections. When teaching the vocational group, Brother Clint probably slowed down a bit or omitted a little of the fundamental biochemistry, but he used the same book and more or less the same syllabus across the board. If one class got tough, he could get tougher. He was young and powerful and very handsome, and looks and physical strength were high currency. No one gave him any trouble.

5   I was pretty bad at the dissecting table, but the lectures and the textbook were interesting: plastic overlays that, with each turned page, peeled away skin, then veins and muscle, then organs, down to the very bones that Brother Clint, pointer in hand, would tap out on our hanging skeleton. Dave Snyder was in big trouble, for the study of life—versus the living of it—was sticking in his craw. We worked out a code for our multiple-choice exams. He'd poke me in the back: once for the answer under *A*, twice for *B*, and so on; and when he'd hit the right one, I'd look up to the ceiling as though I were lost in thought. Poke: cytoplasm. Poke, poke: methane. Poke, poke, poke: William Harvey. Poke, poke, poke, poke: islets of Langerhans. This didn't work out perfectly, but Dave passed the course,

and I mastered the dreamy look of a guy on a record jacket. And something else happened. Brother Clint puzzled over this Voc. Ed. kid who was racking up 98s and 99s on his tests. He checked the school's records and discovered the error. He recommended that I begin my junior year in the College Prep program. According to all I've read since, such a shift, as one report put it, is virtually impossible. Kids at that level rarely cross tracks. The telling thing is how chancy both my placement into and exit from Voc. Ed. was; neither I nor my parents had anything to do with it. I lived in one world during spring semester, and when I came back to school in the fall, I was living in another.

6   Switching to College Prep was a mixed blessing. I was an erratic student. I was undisciplined. And I hadn't caught onto the rules of the game: Why work hard in a class that didn't grab my fancy? I was also hopelessly behind in math. Chemistry was hard; toying with my chemistry set years before hadn't prepared me for the chemist's equations. Fortunately, the priest who taught both chemistry and second-year algebra was also the school's athletic director. Membership on the track team covered me; I knew I wouldn't get lower than a C. U.S. history was taught pretty well, and I did okay. But civics was taken over by a football coach who had trouble reading the textbook aloud—and reading aloud was the centerpiece of his pedagogy. College Prep at Mercy was certainly an improvement over the vocational program—at least it carried some status—but the social science curriculum was weak, and the mathematics and physical sciences were simply beyond me. I had a miserable quantitative background and ended up copying some assignments and finessing the rest as best I could. Let me try to explain how it feels to see again and again material you should once have learned but didn't.

7   You are given a problem. It requires you to simplify algebraic fractions or to multiply expressions containing square roots. You know this is pretty basic material because you've seen it for years. Once a teacher took some time with you, and you learned how to carry out these operations. Simple versions, anyway. But that was a year or two or more in the past, and these are more complex versions, and now you're not sure. And this, you keep telling yourself, is ninth- or even eighth-grade stuff.

8   Next it's a word problem. This is also old hat. The basic elements are as familiar as story characters: trains speeding so many miles per hour or shadows of buildings angling so many degrees. Maybe you know enough, have sat through enough explanations, to be able to begin setting up the problem: "If one train is going this fast . . ." or "This shadow is really one line of a triangle. . . ." Then: "Let's see . . ." "How did Jones do this?" "Hmmmm." "No." "No, that won't work." Your attention wavers. You wonder about other things: a football game, a dance, that cute new checker at the market. You try to focus on the problem again. You scribble on paper for a while, but the tension wins out and your attention flits elsewhere. You crumple the paper and begin daydreaming to ease the frustration.

9   The particulars will vary, but in essence this is what a number of students go through, especially those in so-called remedial classes. They open their textbooks and see once again the familiar and impenetrable formulas and diagrams and terms that have stumped them for years. There is no excitement here. *No* excitement. Regardless of what the teacher says, this is not a new challenge. There is, rather, embarrassment and frustration and, not surprisingly, some anger in being reminded once again of longstanding inadequacies. No wonder so many students finally attribute their difficulties to something inborn, organic: "That part of my brain just doesn't work." Given the troubling histories may of these students have, it's miraculous that any of them can lift the shroud of hopelessness sufficiently to make deliverance from these classes possible.

READING RESPONSE JOURNAL

1. Having completed the reading, write a one-paragraph summary of it. A summary condenses a reading in your own words. It's a way of understanding and remembering what you read. What follows is a sample summary of this reading from *Lives on the Boundary:*

Sample Student Summary

    The reading by Mike Rose describes his being mistakenly placed in vocational classes in high school. For Rose and fellow student Ken Harvey, these classes were boring and meaningless. Brother Clint, the biology teacher, discovered that Rose should have been assigned to the college prep program and had him transferred. The change brought Rose new problems, such as difficulties with more challenging math.

    Now write *your* summary of the reading.

2. Write a few sentences explaining how this reading might relate to your life or the lives of those around you.

3. Are there any other connections of the ideas in this reading to your world? If so, write about them.

4. Why does writer Mike Rose give Ken Harvey's story before his own?

5. What did Ken Harvey mean by saying, "I just wanna be average"?

6. What does Rose mean by asserting that to make Ken Harvey's self-defense work "you have to thrust the knife in your own gray matter"?

7. How was Rose finally able to go from voc. ed. classes to college prep?

8. When Rose switched to college prep classes, what subject was especially hard for him?

9. How did Rose distract himself from the algebra problem?

10. Why does Rose feel some anger in his remedial classes?

11. What does Rose mean when he says that some students point "to something inborn, organic" as the cause of their problems in school?

12. Paraphrase the following sentence from the selection. Paraphrasing is another technique for better reading: changing the words of a quotation while keeping the thought. In contrast to a summary, which is for longer readings, a paraphrase is only for a key sentence or two that you wish to put into your own words. Paraphrasing clarifies the meaning of difficult and important sentences. Remember to replace the words of the original with your own words (some students use a thesaurus, or dictionary of synonyms, for this). You may also wish to change the order of words from the quotation, that is, reverse the order. Make sure that your paraphrase reads smoothly.

    Here is Rose's last sentence: "Given the troubling histories many of these students have, it's miraculous that any of them can lift the shroud of hopelessness sufficiently to make deliverance from these classes possible." Following is a sample paraphrase of Rose's sentence: "That any students are hopeful enough ever to raise themselves from vocational classes is astounding because of their poor educational background."

    Notice that the order of words has been changed. Getting out of vocational class has been moved from last to first. The reference to their troubled history now comes last.

    The vocabulary is changed: "can lift the shroud of hopelessness" becomes "hopeful enough"; "miraculous" is rendered as "astounding."

WRITING FROM READING

Mapping or Clustering

In the previous section of this unit, we studied brainstorming and freewriting as two ways of prewriting, getting your writing started. Let's now look at another prewriting method, called mapping, or clustering, in which you draw connections between ideas. For example, using question 1 from "Prereading," place the phrase "remedial classes" in the center of the page and then try to connect other ideas to it.

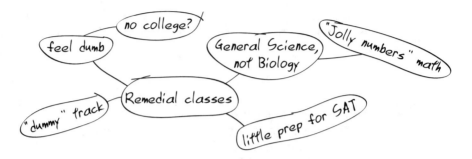

For some students, this mapping can help visualize connections and relationships between ideas, providing a way to start their writing.

Which prewriting method should you use? The best advice is to try all three methods of prewriting—brainstorming, freewriting, and mapping—to see which works best for you. Once you find a prewriting method you like, you can stick with it.

1. Were you ever (or are you now) in any remedial classes? Prewrite about any frustrations you have felt in remedial classes. Write about how you dealt with those feelings and about how you feel looking back at that time.

2. Mike Rose, now a Ph.D. and professor of English at UCLA, was a remedial student who was able "to lift the shroud of hopelessness" and overcome being classified as a remedial student. Do you know anybody like Rose who triumphed over adversity to become a success in school? What about yourself? First prewrite about your school hero and then write a longer paper about him or her. Be sure to tell what this person did to become a success.

3. Were you ever in a class or subject that was over your head? Write about your feelings in that situation and how you dealt with them.

4. Students are always told to stay in school, not to drop out. But what if, like for Ken Harvey, school is boring and meaningless. If you had been a teacher or friend of Ken Harvey's, write what you would have said to him.

COLLABORATIVE LEARNING ACTIVITY

Listening for Transitions

After you've done your prewriting and your first draft, share your paper with the other students in your group and listen well to theirs. Turn your paper face down, so you can concentrate on your listening. Remember first to introduce yourselves again and read slowly, loudly, and clearly.

Transitions are connecting words and phrases such as *first, next,* and *in conclusion.*

For this activity, listen to each paper for transitions between paragraphs and sections. Transitional words and paraphrases help a paper "hang together." Suggest specific transitions for those papers that need them.

WRITING TIPS

Giving Examples

It's important to give examples. Describing being frustrated and bored in school, Rose says, "Your attention wavers. You wonder about other things: a football game, a dance, that cute new checker at the market." Rose gives three examples of his daydreaming. Now you try creating your own example. Give two or three specific things you think about as you daydream.

VOCABULARY DEVELOPMENT

For college students, encountering new or difficult vocabulary words interferes greatly with their reading process, especially when these new words come thick and fast. In meeting vocabulary for the first time, try to guess the meaning of the new words and keep reading; *do not stop your reading* process to look in the dictionary. After finishing a section of the reading, then stop to look up the new words in a dictionary. Some students set aside part of their reading response journal for such new vocabulary. Once you learn the meanings of the new words, go back and read the section again. For an example, we'll study in depth one paragraph that is thick with difficult vocabulary from Mike Rose's *Lives on the Boundary.* You probably would not have time to go through every paragraph like this, but you can learn the method.

We will look at a way to guess the meaning of new words from their context, the surrounding words, and then we will turn to dictionary study.

The *context* of a word refers to its meaning as it is used in a particular instance; for example, the abbreviation *Voc. Ed.* in Mike Rose's sentence, "One day in religion class, he said the sentence that turned out to be one of the most memorable of the hundreds of thousands I heard in those Voc. Ed. years." The abbreviation *Ed.* we know has to do with Rose's discussion of school here, so we might guess that it means "education." So what of the abbreviation *Voc.?* There are very few words that begin with *voc.,* like "vocal" or "vocabulary." Both of these words seem too narrow for the context here. "Vocational" education does fit the meaning here. If you have no good guess, no clue, about what "vocational education" means, you have to use the dictionary. The dictionary says the abbreviation *voc.* means "vocational" and *ed.* is the common abbreviation for "education." The first definition of *vocational* in the *American Heritage Dictionary* is "Of or relating to a vocation." This first meaning is followed by a second, which fits here, "Relating to, providing, or undergoing training in a special skill to be pursued in a trade: vocational students."

The context of Rose's sentence is his discussion of his high-school education—"in those Voc. Ed. years," the early years of his high school work when he took classes that were not college prep. In his next paragraph, Rose defines "Voc. Ed." in a more personal way: he says that in a vocational track "you're defined by your school as 'slow'; you're placed in a curriculum that isn't designed to liberate you but to occupy you, or, if you're lucky, train you, though the training is for work the society does not esteem." So, Rose's personal definition is not neutral like the dictionary definition ("relating to a vocation"); instead, Rose sees "Voc. Ed." as limiting, boring, and mind-numbing.

Now you can't do all this work every time you meet a new word because you would never finish your reading, but it is important to try to guess what new words mean from their context.

Let's consider another example from Rose's same paragraph: "Ken was good-looking in a puffy way and had a full and oily ducktail and was a car enthusiast . . . a hodad." Here, set off by the periods (a comma or dash would also have sufficed) is the meaning of *hodad,* "a car enthusiast." In this case, Rose has defined the word for us.

Later in the same paragraph, Rose describes the "restive" Ken Harvey who thought about the teacher's question "just for a second." This last phrase tells us that Ken Harvey responded very quickly, so we might guess from the context that "restive" means "hurried" or "impetuous"—and that would be pretty close because the *American Heritage Dictionary* definition of "restive" is "Uneasily impatient under restriction." The restrictions of school lie heavily on Ken Harvey.

In this same class discussion that Rose is describing, he has a long, hard sentence: "Then the athletes chimed in with the clichés that make you want to laryngectomize them, and the exchange became a platitudinous melee." What does he mean in this one sentence that has four fairly difficult words? If we know that a cliché is an overused phrase like "smart as a whip" or "fit as a fiddle," we have a start. Because the athletes are mouthing clichés, Rose wanted to "laryngectomize them." What does the larynx have to do with their talking and what does the verb form "laryngectomize" mean? What he wants them to do is shut up, which would be accomplished by removing their larynxes or voice boxes, so the word "laryngectomize." Perhaps we know that *melee* is a "fight or a brawl," but what about "*platitudinous* melee"? The root word of *platitudinous* is *platitude,* which means what? A platitude is similar to a cliché, a somewhat meaningless, too-general phrase. So, the "brawl" was simply the jocks batting these empty generalizations back and forth across the classroom.

This is a lot of work for one short paragraph, but the idea is to try first to figure out what words mean from their contexts. If that doesn't work, then it's dictionary time.

REVIEW

For a while in doing your writing, try out the three different kinds of prewriting—brainstorming, freewriting, and mapping—we have studied. Later, you may settle on one method, but first try them all.

LAURA, from *LIVES ON THE BOUNDARY*

Mike Rose

What follows is a brief description of a young Hispanic student at the University of California at Los Angeles (UCLA) and her troubles there. As you read the passage, try to think of hard times you've had with school.

VOCABULARY IN CONTEXT

"*serpentine* path"—snaky, winding

"*by dint of* remarkable effort"—by force of, because of

"blond *apparitions*"—ghosts, appearances

PREREADING

1. Read only the *first sentence* of paragraph 1 and only the *first sentence* of paragraph 2. Predict what the two paragraphs will say.

Laura

Mike Rose

1 Her name is Laura, and she was born in the poor section of Tijuana, the Mexican border city directly south of San Diego. Her father was a food vendor, and her memories of him and his chipped white cart come back to her in easy recollection: the odor of frying meat, the feel of tortillas damp with grease, and the serpentine path across the city; rolling the cart through dust, watching her father smile and haggle and curse— hawking burritos and sugar water to old women with armloads of blouses and figurines, to blond American teenagers, wild with freedom, drunk and loud and brawny. She came to the United States when she was six, and by dint of remarkable effort—on her parents' part and hers—she now sits in classes at UCLA among those blond apparitions.

2 She has signed up for and dropped the course I'm teaching, remedial English, *four* times during this, her freshman year: twice in the summer before she officially started, once in each of the quarters preced-

ing this one. This is her fifth try. She is with me in my office, and she is scared to death: "I get in there, and everything seems okay. But as soon as we start writing, I freeze up. I'm a crummy writer, I know it. I know I'm gonna make lots of mistakes and look stupid. I panic. And I stop coming."

READING RESPONSE JOURNAL

1. Briefly summarize the reading.

2. What meaning does the reading have for you? Is it something to write about?

3. Are there any other ideas, related to the reading, for you to write about?

4. What name do we give Laura's inability to write?

5. Why does Mike Rose give such a strong image of Laura's father's job as food vendor?

6. Why is remedial English so terrifying for Laura?

WRITING FROM READING

Organization from Prewriting and the Tentative Topic Sentence

In the first two sections of this unit, you studied different types of prewriting—brainstorming, freewriting, and mapping. In this section, you will see how students find tentative topic sentences from their prewriting and get organized enough to write their papers.

In this reading, Laura had problems with writing. Here is a student paper on that same topic—with the steps in the process, from prewriting to final draft, beginning with a brainstorming list about "Writing Problems":

Writing Problems

Handwriting hard to read

Where do commas go?

Run-on sentences

Spelling hard even with spellcheck

Slow on writing lab computer

Leave words out of sentences

Scared I'll make mistakes

Can't think of anything to write

Red marks all over papers

Fragments

What do teachers want?

Teachers put me down

Never look over work when finished

Use only simple words

Don't write enough

Don't understand apostrophes

What's possession?

Can't always tell sentences

Makes sense when I write it, but not when I read out loud

Afraid to use new words

Scared to read my paper in class—won't be any good

Teachers tell me I write poorly

Reviewing his list, the student looks for anything that *repeats* or connects to something else on his list. He notices that he often mentions specific errors or specific problems:

What follows is the student's paragraph developed from his prewriting.

```
Run-on sentences          Use only simple words
Fragments                 Leave words out
Spelling errors           Never reread, look over
What's possession           when finished
Don't understand          Can't tell sentences
apostrophes               Makes sense when I write
Handwriting hard to read   it, not when I read it
Where do commas go?       Don't write enough
```

Another pattern he sees in his list is his concern with teachers:

```
Red marks all over papers
What do teachers want?
Teachers tell me I write poorly
Teachers critical of me
```

Another theme that runs through the student's list is his negative attitude:

```
Scared to read my papers in class
Scared to make mistakes
Afraid to use new words
```

His list is organized into three categories: (1) specific problems, (2) his view of teachers, and (3) his negative attitude. The student can focus on one or all three of these areas to write about. Each category suggests a topic to write about:

```
My problems in writing
My concerns with my English teachers
My negative attitude toward writing
```

The student decides to write about his attitude toward writing, the shortest of his three lists. He scans his list, trying to come up with a tentative topic sentence, a main idea. He comes up with a possible topic sentence, "My attitude toward writing has always been negative," and uses this as a starting point for a paper.

Sample Student Paper from Prewriting

My attitude toward writing has always been
negative and can be summed up in one word—fear. I am
so scared that I will make mistakes that it takes me
a long time to write. Also, I am afraid to use new
words because I might get them wrong. My worst fear is
to read in front of class because I know my paper
will sound stupid, and I'll be embarrassed in front of
everyone.

For another paper, the student looks to his list of writing problems to see if there are any connections to help him write a tentative topic sentence or even a main idea, what's called a tentative thesis statement, for a longer paper.

As he reads his list, he thinks to himself, "I have a lot of writing problems. This is overwhelming." These thoughts lead him to a tentative topic sentence: "My writing problems are very serious."

Then the student sees a way to organize his list and his paragraph: from his *most serious* problems to his *least serious.*

Don't write enough
Can't tell sentences
Leave words out
Fragments
Run-on sentences
Spelling mistakes (even with spellcheck)
Where do commas go?
What's possession—when do I use apostrophes?
Never makes sense when I reread

The student omits from his list the point about his bad handwriting because now he works on computers. He combines the problem of possession and apostrophes because they're related and leaves out the lack of rereading because he's now going to read his papers over once they're done.

Here is the student's longer paragraph from his list:

My writing problems are very serious. First of
all, I don't write enough, maybe because I write too
slowly. Now with this prewriting, I can speed things
up. Another difficulty I have is that I don't always
know what a sentence is, causing me to write lots of
fragments and run-ons. Perhaps if I read my sentences
out loud to myself and the other students in my group,

```
I can get better at this. Also, where do commas go? I
can get help for this by studying the rules in the
book. The same with the rules for possession and
apostrophes, I have to look them up and study them. I
think my problems with spelling and with leaving words
out will get better now that I am going to reread my
papers and share them with my group. I know that my
writing problems are serious, but I also realize that
now I have some ways to improve myself.
```

In addition to the student's prioritizing of his problems, he hits on a natural problem-solution pattern as he tries to find a remedy for each problem.

Here then are two ways to organize: first, make a priority order from most important to least important (or the opposite); second, try to suggest a solution for every problem.

1. Prewrite about some of the roadblocks you have had to overcome to reach college. They may not be as hard as Laura's—poverty and language problems—but they affected you personally. After you have finished your prewriting, write a longer paper about your struggles to make it to college.

2. Talking with Rose, Laura describes her problems with writing:

   As soon as we start writing, I freeze up. I'm a crummy writer, I know it. I know I'm gonna make lots of mistakes and look stupid. I panic. And I stop coming.

   Why do you think Laura has this attitude about her writing? What kind of English teachers did she have in her previous schooling? Do you share any of Laura's feelings about writing? Whether or not you do, think back to the English teachers you have had in elementary and high school. How did they like your papers? What attitude about writing did they help you form? First, prewrite about these questions, making a priority order and then later write a longer paper about your writing education. What was good and what was bad? Tell how you feel about your writing today. Suggest solutions for any writing problems you need to work on.

COLLABORATIVE LEARNING ACTIVITY

Shared Problems

In your groups, read your prewriting about "My Attitude toward Writing" (question 2) to each other. Do you notice any problems that you share? As a way to help you get organized, try to make a group list of the problems and prioritize them, that is, rank them from most serious to least serious.

Also, discuss some "self-help" solutions that you can use to work on these problems.

WRITING TIPS

Use of the Senses

In Rose's description of Laura's father as food vendor, notice how he uses the senses: "the odor of frying meat, the feel of tortillas damp with grease, and the serpentine path across the city; rolling the cart through dust, watching her father smile and haggle and curse." We smell the meat, feel the grease and the dust, see and hear Laura's father go through a food vendor's range of emotions.

Is there a street food you find unappetizing? Pick some food you don't like and describe it in a sentence or two by what you see, feel, taste, hear.

REVIEW

Don't be discouraged about the number and kinds of writing problems you have. They all can be fixed—if you read and write a lot more. You don't get better by wishing to—you have to practice.

EPILOGUE: LILIA, from *LIVES ON THE BOUNDARY*

Mike Rose

An epilogue is an added ending, similar to a P.S. (postscript) in a letter. This section at the conclusion of Mike Rose's book shows hope. Here is Lilia, born in Mexico and first saddled with remedial classes, who overcame her obstacles to become a success.

VOCABULARY IN CONTEXT

> "*neurophysiology*"—physical aspects of the nervous system
> "*genetically* coded"—determined by genes, inborn
> "you sometimes can't *articulate* what you know"—tell, express
> "gaps and *discordances* in the terrain"—disagreements, clashes

PREREADING

1. Read the first paragraph and last paragraph. Write your prediction of what the whole article will say.

Epilogue: Lilia

Mike Rose

1 I sit with Lilia, the tape recorder going. "We came from Mexico when I was four years old. When I went into school, I flunked the first grade. The first grade! I had to repeat it, and they put me in classes for slow learners. I stayed in those classes for five years. I guess there was a pattern where they put me in those really basic classes and then decided I would go through my elementary school years in those classes. I didn't learn to read or write. My parents got my cousins—they came here prior to us, so they knew English really well—and they had me read for them. I couldn't. They told my parents I didn't know anything. That's when my parents decided they would move. They moved to Tulare County. My aunt was there and told them that the schools were good and that there was work in agriculture. I picked grapes and cotton and oranges—everything—for six straight summers. I kinda liked it, out there with all the adults, but I knew it wasn't what I wanted for the future. The schools *were* good. The teachers really

27

liked me, and I did very well. . . . Between the eighth and ninth grades I came to UCLA for six weeks in the summer. It was called the MENTE program—Migrants Engaged in New Themes of Education—I came here and loved the campus. It was like dreamland for me. And I made it my goal to come here."

2   The school that designated Lilia a slow learner is two miles from my old neighborhood on South Vermont. She arrived as a child about eight years after I left as an adult. The next generation. We make our acquaintance in an office of the University of California at Los Angeles. Lilia is participating in an unusual educational experiment, one developed by some coworkers of mine at UCLA Writing Programs. Lilia and fifteen other freshmen—all of whom started UCLA in remedial writing courses themselves—are tutoring low-achieving students in Los Angeles area schools. The tutoring is connected to a special composition class, and Lilia and her partners write papers on their tutorial work and on issues of schooling. Lilia is writing a paper on the academic, social, and psychological effects of being placed in the remedial track. Her teacher suggested she come to see me. I can't stop asking her questions about growing up in South L.A.

3   Desire gets confused on South Vermont. There were times when I wanted so much to be other than what I was, to walk through the magical gate of a television cottage. But, strange blessing, we can never really free ourselves from the mood of early neighborhoods, from our first stories, from the original tales of hope and despair. There are basic truths there about the vulnerability and power of coming to know, about the way the world invites and denies language. This is what lies at the base of education—to be tapped or sealed over or distorted, by others, by us. Lilia says the tutoring makes her feel good. "Sometimes I feel that because I know their language, I can communicate. I see these kids and I see myself like I was in elementary school." Lilia stops. She asks me what it was like in South L.A. when *I* was there, when I was going to school. Not much different then, I say. Not as tough probably. She asks me if I've ever gone back. I tell her I did, just recently. . . .

4   The place was desolate. The power plant was still standing, smaller than I remembered it, surrounded now by barbed wire. All the storefront businesses were covered with iron grating; about half of them, maybe more, were shut down. The ones that were open had the grating pulled back the width of the door, no further. The hair and nails shop was closed. The Stranger's Rest Baptist Church was closed. Teddy's Rough Riders—an American Legion post—was battered and closed. The Huston Mortuary looked closed. My house had been stuccoed over, a dark dirty tan with holes in the walls. 9116 South Vermont. My old neighborhood was a blighted island in the slum. Poverty had gutted it, and sealed the merchants' doors. "It's worse now," I tell Lilia, "much worse. No one comes. No one goes." At Ninety-sixth Street two men were sitting on the curb outside a minimart. East on Ninety-first a girl sat in the shadows of steps tucked back from the pavement. At Eight-ninth Street, a woman walked diagonally in front of me, moving unsteadily in a tight dress, working the floured paper off an X-L-NT burrito.

As I drove back by my house, I saw a little boy playing with two cans in the dirt. Imagination's delivery. Fantasy in cylinders and tin.

5   Lilia is telling me about one of her fellow classmates who had also been designated a slow learner. "She said it was awful. She had no friends because everyone called her dumb, and no one wanted to be seen with a dumb person. . . . Because they were calling her dumb, she started to believe she was really dumb. And with myself and my brother, it was the same thing. When we were in those courses we thought very low of ourselves. We sort of created a little world of our own where only we existed. We became really shy."

6   What we define as intelligence, what we set out to measure and identify with a number, is both in us and out of us. We have been socialized to think of intelligence as internal, fixed, genetically coded. There is, of course, a neurophysiology to intelligence, but there's a feeling to it as well, and a culture. In moving from one school to another—another setting, another set of social definitions—Lilia was transformed from dumb to normal. And then, with six powerful weeks as a child on a university campus—"opening new horizons for me, scary, but showing me what was out there"—she began to see herself in a different way, tentatively, cautiously. Lilia began the transition to smart, to high school honors classes, to UCLA. She could go back, then, to the schools, to the place where, as she says, she "knows the language."

7   The promise of community and equality is at the center of our most prized national document, yet we're shaped by harsh forces to see difference and to base judgment on it. The language Lilia can speak to the students in the schools is the language of intersection, of crossed boundaries. It is a rich language, filled with uncertainty. Having crossed boundaries, you sometimes can't articulate what you know, or what you know seems strange. What is required, then, is for Lilia and her students to lean back against their desks, grip the firm wood, and talk about what they hear and see, looking straight ahead, looking skyward. What are the gaps and discordances in the terrain? What mix of sounds—eerie and compelling—issues from the hillside? Siting with Lilia, our lives playing off each other, I realize that, finally, this is why the current perception of educational need is so limited: It substitutes terror for awe. But it is not terror that fosters learning, it is hope, everyday heroics, the power of the common play of the human mind.

READING RESPONSE JOURNAL

1. Read the entire selection and write a summary of it in one paragraph.

2. Tie in the ideas of the reading to your life or that of others.

3. Can you think of anything else to write about from this reading?

4. What are some of the links between Mike Rose and Lilia?

5. How did her parents recognize Lilia's needs and help her with her education?

6. How does Rose come to meet and to interview Lilia?

7. Lilia inspires Rose to go back and visit his old neighborhood. What does he find?

8. Lilia explains how dumb one of her classmates "who had also been designated a slow learner" felt. How does this reflect the experiences of Lilia and her brother?

9. What does Rose mean when he says, "The promise of community and equality is at the center of our most prized national document"?

10. We have already learned that a paraphrase is your "translation" of an author's sentences. Remember to keep the idea, but change the words. Paraphrase the last two sentences of Rose's book:

> This is why the current perception of educational need is so limited: It substitutes terror for awe. But it is not terror that fosters learning, it is hope, everyday heroics, the power of the common play of the human mind.

WRITING FROM READING

More Work on the Topic Sentence

The topic sentence is the main point, the main idea, of a paragraph. This topic sentence is very often—but not always—written at or near the beginning of a paragraph.

Sometimes called the controlling idea, the topic sentence sets up the rest of the paragraph. Consider the first sentence of Rose's fourth paragraph: "The place was desolate." The rest of the paragraph stems from that topic sentence:

> "The power plant was still standing."
> "All the storefront businesses were covered . . ."
> "The hair and nails shop was closed."
> "The Stranger's Rest Baptist Church was closed."

These sentences illustrate the desolation referred to in the topic sentence. Every paragraph does not begin with the topic sentence first. The topic sentence can go later in the paragraph. In fact, in some paragraphs the topic sentence is not directly stated at all, but implied.

1. What follows are some topic sentences. See if you can write a short paragraph elaborating on each one.

   My early schooling was boring.
   OR
   My early schooling got me excited about learning.

   My old neighborhood was a source of many adventures.
   OR
   My old neighborhood was dangerous.

2. Describing her own and her brother's experiences in remedial classes, Lilia explains, "When we were in those courses we thought very low of ourselves. We sort of created a little world of our own

where only we existed. We became really shy." Did this ever happen to you or to somebody in your family—that you felt dumb and began to withdraw? These are painful experiences, but you can learn from them. Prewrite about these feelings, their causes, and their effects.

3. Write a longer paper based on your prewriting from the preceding assignment and include how you feel now looking back at that time. Here are two topic sentences you can choose from if you wish:

My early years in school made me feel dumb.

OR

My early school days inspired me.

4. Rose's own story and Lilia's are success stories. What successes do you yearn for in your own life? Lilia became a successful student and tutor to low-achieving students. Prewrite about your hopes and dreams for yourself. Then write a longer paper about them. Consider starting your paper with one of these two sample topic sentences:

From my early days in school, I learned _____, and I am now working toward my dream _____.

OR

My early schooling made me feel _____, and I have spent years trying to overcome that early experience.

COLLABORATIVE LEARNING ACTIVITY

Sentence Combining for Style

Sentences should be not only correct but also interesting. One way of adding some zest to your writing is through sentence combining, merging shorter sentences into longer, more graceful ones.

ORIGINAL: (1) The school day was over. (2) The students joyously rushed through the halls to their lockers. (3) They sped to the bus stop or to their cars. (4) They left the building deserted. (5) They scurried home to pursue the pleasures of a long weekend.

These sentences are short and choppy. Here are some of these same sentences combined:

REVISED: (1) When the school day was over, the students joyously rushed through the halls to their lockers and sped to the bus stop or to their cars. (2) Leaving the building deserted, they scurried home to pursue the pleasures of a long weekend.

There are three simple changes here: The first original sentence is changed to a *when* clause and added to the second sentence.

Also, sentence 3 is added to sentence 2 with *and* and with *students* as the subject for both *rushed* and *sped.*

Finally, sentence 4 is made into an *-ing* phrase—*leaving*—and placed at the beginning of sentence 5.

Now you try it by combining the following short sentences:

> ORIGINAL: (1) Students arrived at school. (2) Students clambered out of their cars. (3) Others jumped out of buses. (4) They all dragged their bodies to their lockers. (5) They trudged to class.

As in the earlier example, try to use a *when* clause, connect two verbs with *and,* and use an *-ing* phrase. There are many other correct ways to combine these sentences, but these are three useful methods: (1) using subordinate (*when*) clauses; (2) joining verbs with a conjunction (e.g., *and*); (3) using participial phrases (beginning with *-ing* words).

Again, there are many different, correct ways to combine these sentences. A sample answer follows:

> REVISED: (1) *When* students arrived at school, they climbed out of their cars *and* jumped out of buses. (2) After *dragging* their bodies to their lockers, all the students trudged to class.

(Note that the transition *after* is used here before *dragging* to put the sentences in sequence.)

Let's try some more examples. At this point remember we are using three methods of sentence combining:

1. *when* clauses (*after, before,* and other time clauses work well too)
2. verbs joined with *and*
3. *-ing* phrases

More Exercises

> ORIGINAL: (1) Students came into classrooms. (2) They found their teachers ready and waiting. (3) They opened their books. (4) They opened their notepads. (5) They geared up for the first of many classes. (6) They would repeat the same steps many times during the day.

REVISED:

ORIGINAL: (1) Students filed into the cafeteria. (2) They unstacked the chairs. (3) They placed them under their tables. (4) They sat down. (5) They ate quickly. (6) They rushed out for their open air break.

(Note: Use *after* here with *eating*.)

REVISED:

WRITING TIPS

Transitional Sentences

Transitions can be more than just words like *then, next,* and *finally.* A writer will sometimes use a sentence or two as transition: "The school that designated Lilia a slow learner is two miles from my old neighborhood on South Vermont. She arrived as a child about eight years after I left as an adult. The next generation." These sentences link Lilia with Rose. In your paper about your schooling, see if there is some tie between your educational past and your present. Is there some person or place that links the old and the new? Try to write a sentence or two about that connection in your paper.

REVIEW

Try to think of a topic sentence as a road map or sign pointing to where your paragraph is heading. Be clear and you won't get lost. You may find after finishing your paragraph that you have wandered a bit. That's OK, but see if you can rewrite your topic sentence to fit better.

FENCES AGAINST FREEDOM, from *YELLOW WOMAN AND A BEAUTY OF THE SPIRIT: ESSAYS ON NATIVE AMERICAN LIFE TODAY*

Leslie Marmon Silko

In this excerpt from an essay about her schooling on a Native American reservation, Leslie Marmon Silko describes the racist attitudes Native American children had to overcome. Silko survived this treatment and achieved status as one of today's best-known Native American writers.

VOCABULARY IN CONTEXT

"Laguna"—Pueblo Indian tribe of New Mexico

PREREADING

1. Read the first sentence of paragraph 1 and tell what the rest of the paragraph will be about; then, do the same with the first sentence of paragraph 2. Write the answers in your reading response journal.

Fences against Freedom

Leslie Marmon Silko

1   I learned about racism firsthand when I started school. We were punished if we spoke the Laguna language once we crossed onto the school grounds. Every fall, all of us were lined up and herded like cattle to the girls' and boys' bathrooms, where our heads were drenched with smelly insecticide regardless of whether we had lice or not. We were vaccinated in both arms without regard to our individual immunization records.

2   But what I remember most clearly is the white tourists who used to come to the school yard to take our pictures. They would give us kids each a nickel, so naturally when we saw tourists get out of their cars with cameras, we all wanted to get in the picture. Then one day when I was older, in the third grade, white tourists came with cameras. All of my playmates started to bunch together to fit in the picture, and I was right there

with them maneuvering myself into the group when I saw the tourist look at me with a particular expression. I knew instantly he did not want me to be in the picture; I stayed close to my playmates, hoping that I had misread the man's face. But the tourist motioned for me to move away to one side, out of his picture. I remember my playmates looked puzzled, but I knew why the man did not want me in his picture: I looked different from my playmates. I was part white and he didn't want me to spoil his snap-shots of "Indians." After that incident, the arrival of tourists with cameras at our school filled me with anxiety. I would stand back and watch the expressions on the tourists' faces before trying to join my playmates in the picture. Most times the tourists were kindly and did not seem to notice my difference, and they would motion for me to join my classmates; but now and then there were tourists who looked relieved that I did not try to join in the group picture.

READING RESPONSE JOURNAL

1. Now read the full two paragraphs. Is there anything in these two paragraphs that you can relate to your life or that of your loved ones?

2. Can you find anything else in these two paragraphs to write about?

3. Why does Silko have such a detailed memory of racist treatment imposed on her at school?

4. What feeling does Silko have as a third grader when the white tourist didn't want to include her in his picture of the Native American girls?

5. Why do you think this third-grade girl "knew why the man did not want me in his picture"?

6. How did this snub affect Silko later when other tourists asked for the Native American children to pose?

WRITING FROM READING

The Topic Sentence Revisited

In her essay, Leslie Marmon Silko explains the crippling attitudes that she learned to triumph over. Notice that the first sentence of each of these two paragraphs is a topic sentence, one that announces what the rest of the paragraph will say. Silko supports her topic sentence, "I learned about racism firsthand when I started school," with two examples: the use of insecticide on the Native American children and their vaccinations.

In paragraph 2, Silko's topic sentence, "But what I remember most clearly is the white tourists who used to come to the school yard to take our pictures," introduces her traumatic story about being excluded from the picture because of her mixed race. The topic sentence sets the content of these two paragraphs, the first by examples, the second by a powerful story. Here are some other topic sentences that could lead to well-developed paragraphs about school attitudes:

1. My school days were spent trying to impress my classmates.
2. Because my high school was strict, I learned self-discipline to survive.

Now try to write a topic sentence about events or attitudes you learned from in school. Remember, it must be a sentence that will allow you to say more about the topic. Next, write a paragraph based on your topic sentence.

Here are sample paragraphs developed from the suggested topic sentences:

1. *My school days were spent trying to impress my classmates.* I was the class clown bugging my teachers by talking out in class and smarting off. Once I shook eraser dust on the teacher's chair, so she would dirty her skirt. My grades were always terrible. After all, guys didn't want to date smart girls.

2. *Because my high school was strict, I learned self-discipline to survive.* Homework always had to be turned in before school; late work was not accepted. Also, if I didn't do my chemistry lab correctly, I had to attend school on Saturday to finish it.

COLLABORATIVE LEARNING ACTIVITY

Improving Topic Sentences

Share your topic sentences with other group members and see if they can help you to write better ones.

WRITING TIPS

The Implied Topic Sentence

In this chapter, we have reviewed the use of the topic sentence, very important for student writers. We must understand, however, that not all paragraphs have topic sentences. At times, writers construct paragraphs with implied, or suggested, topic sentences that are not written out but left unstated.

Read this paragraph by Silko about her Grandma Lily:

My Grandma Lily had been a Ford Model A mechanic when she was a teenager. I remember when I was young, she was always fixing broken lamps and appliances. She was small and wiry, but she could lift her weight in rolled roofing or boxes of nails. When she was seventy-five, she was still repairing washing machines in my uncle's coin-operated laundry.

In this paragraph there is no written topic sentence. Read it through again and try to come up with a topic sentence, one that says something about Grandma Lily's mechanical skills that lasted all her life.

The topic sentence in Silko's paragraph is implied, something like "Grandma Lily's interest in and skills with mechanical objects persisted her whole life." The point is that as a writer it is good to have a strong topic sentence, but as a reader you must recognize that not every paragraph will have one.

REVIEW

Look back at the selections from Silko's writing in this chapter, and recognize her strong topic sentences in powerful writing about racism.

SCHOOLS MAY HAVE PROBLEMS, BUT THEY OFTEN BEGIN AT HOME

Mike Royko

Mike Royko's article is an argument for looking at the real root problem of education today in America.

VOCABULARY IN CONTEXT

> "*warranted*"—justified
>
> "*dysfunctional*"—not working, ineffective
>
> "*stark* difference"—dramatic, clear

PREREADING

1. Read the title and the first and last paragraphs to make your prediction about this article.

Schools May Have Problems, but They Often Begin at Home

Mike Royko

1 The people who run the Evanston school system are reported to be scratching their heads over why their white students do so much better in the statewide tests that measure reading, math and other skills.

2   Overall, Evanston does very well. But there is a stark difference in the academic records of black and white students, the administrators say.

3   But why? They say they don't know.

4   Can they be that nearsighted? Is it possible that while dealing with this kind of problem, day in and day out, they don't understand it? Don't the administrators talk to the teachers or the students?

5   Or are they, as I suspect, taking pains to be politically correct and trying to avoid some shin-kicking controversy.

6   Well, my shins are callused and no longer sting when kicked. So I'll risk the scorn of the politically correct crowd and offer some suggestions as to what's behind this strange problem.

7   Let's start by looking at a few of the usual suspects:

8   The Evanston school system itself? No, the system can't be at fault. Evanston has always had an admirable school system. It's why many

people bought homes to that close-in suburb, although fewer are now doing so for that reason.

9   The teachers? While it's easy to point fingers at teachers, in this case it isn't warranted. The teachers must be pretty good if they get such excellent results out of about half of the students—the half who are white. Are we to believe that they don't bother to try to teach the black students those things they teach the whites? If so, we'd have heard about it by now.

10   The physical facilities and other resources? Some of the physical plants are kind of old, but so what? Some of the oldest school buildings in America are at Harvard, which doesn't prevent the students there from getting enviable educations.

11   Spending? Evanston isn't tight-fisted. It spends more per pupil than many blue collar suburbs that get results just as good.

12   So what does that leave us?

13   The students, obviously. And a racist would say that the explanation is obvious: Black kids just aren't as smart as the white kids; it's some kind of genetic thing.

14   Which is nonsense. A black kid is as capable of learning as a white kid. Colin Powell and Jesse Jackson (Senior and Junior) didn't just recently start taking some wondrous smart pills.

15   Where does that leave us? We've just about run out of suspects. So I guess I should get to the point.

16   Let's try parents, family, home. These are words you seldom hear when the media's education experts, the administrators, and politicians talk about schooling. They prefer talking about new programs, new taxes, and more new programs and programs and programs. Mentioning parents is insensitive and politically incorrect.

17   Over the years, I've talked to countless teachers about the problem of kids who don't learn. And just about all of them say the same thing: They are sick and tired of being blamed for the failings of parents.

18   Some of it comes down to arithmetic: A teacher spends only five hours a day with a room filled with kids. And the teacher is limited on how much time and attention can be given to any one child.

19   In contrast, a parent has the kids most of the rest of the day—about 18 or 19 hours. Plus the 48 hours of the weekend, the holidays, and the two and a half months of summer vacation.

20   But as a frazzled teacher once told me: "If a kid is having problems, and you try to talk to the parents about it, some of them say: 'It's your job to teach them, not ours. You're the teacher.' They think they can put a child in our care a few hours a day and that's it. They don't have to take an interest, show interest, apply discipline, or provide an environment that encourages study and attendance. Just turning off the TV set or stereo would be a major contribution, but many won't do even that. The TV is a pacifier and a sitter."

21   So why would any parents be that indifferent? Unless you've been hiding in a cave, you've heard about the splintered and dysfunctional black family—probably this country's biggest social problem.

22   Although much of Evanston looks like something out of an old Norman Rockwell cover for the Saturday Evening Post, that doesn't mean that many of its black families are immune to the social and financial problems found in the city.

23   The welfare dependency is there. So are homes without husbands, the drugs, higher crime rate and the tempting excitement of social life in a street gang.

24   It takes more than a teacher, no matter how dedicated, to make up for those gaps and blights on a childhood.

25   So what can be done? Well, step one is to stop pretending that you don't know what the problem is. The teachers know. Many of the students know. You don't have to be a social worker and hold an advanced degree in education to see the obvious.

26   And that not only applies to Evanston, but in Chicago and everywhere else that some groups of kids drift through schools without learning much and not caring.

27   Until the educators and politicians have the stomach to start demanding something from parents—and are given means to back up the demands with action—we're going to have generation after generation, slogging along in the same rut. We can't afford it. Today it is a problem. In a generation or two, it will be chaos.

READING RESPONSE JOURNAL

1. Write a summary of Royko's article.

2. Can you relate anything Royko says here about school and family problems to your own life? What, for example, was your high school like? Were the students from fairly stable families?

3. Does Royko's article spark any other idea in you?

4. Explain in your words why Evanston administrators don't want to point to black family life as the cause for lower scores of black students.

5. What "usual suspects" does Royko find not guilty of causing the gap in scores?

6. According to Royko, how would a racist explain the difference in scores; and why does Royko say the racist would be wrong?

7. Why does Royko claim that blaming parents for the poorer scores of black children "is insensitive and politically incorrect"?

8. How does "arithmetic" figure in Royko's pointing to parents' responsibility for their children's schooling?

9. According to teachers Royko consulted, how do some parents use the TV and stereo?

10. What problems does Royko suggest come from the "splintered and dysfunctional black family"?

11. What first solution does Royko suggest for the gap in student scores?

12. Once having acknowledged the problems in black family life, what further step must "educators and politicians" take to solve our education crisis?

13. What warning does Royko give?

WRITING FROM READING

The Thesis Statement and the Problem-Solution Essay

The controlling or main idea of a paragraph is a topic sentence. For a longer piece of writing such as an essay, the main idea is called a thesis statement or thesis sentence.

What is the thesis sentence of Royko's article? (See the title.) Try to write it in your own words.

The thesis statement for Royko's article is found in the title, a placement common to many newspaper articles: "Schools may have problems, but they often begin at home." Everything in the essay relates to this main idea, including Royko's solution at the end:

> Until the educators and politicians have the stomach to start demanding something from parents—and are given means to back up the demands with action—we're going to have generation after generation, slogging along in the same rut.

In a paper longer than a paragraph, you must have a clear thesis statement as a basis for your writing.

1. You have read Royko's article. Prewrite about the reason why white students do better in school than black students. After prewriting, do a longer writing on this question. Try to begin with a thesis sentence: Whites do better in school than blacks because . . .

2. Do you agree with Royko's assessment of the future if the problems of black families are not addressed? First, prewrite about your response. Do some thinking and then write a longer paper about the future of our society. Begin with a thesis statement: Our society must . . .

3. Like the sample student paper in an earlier section, the structure of Royko's article is problem-solution; that is, the problems are described first, followed by suggested solutions at the end. Royko

holds that "educators and politicians [must] start demanding something from the parents—and [must be] given means to back up the demands with action." Explain what you think is the "something" that must be demanded of parents and suggest some specific "means" to enforce this. After doing your prewriting, write a longer paper on this topic.

COLLABORATIVE LEARNING ACTIVITY

Taking the "I" out of Your Thesis

Before you listen to each other's prewriting and first draft, read your tentative thesis statement out loud to your group. The thesis should be clear and strong. Omit such phrases as "I think," "I feel," and "in my opinion" because they weaken or soften your thesis.

For example, "Schools must get parents involved in their child's education" is stronger than "*I think* schools must get parents involved in their child's education."

WRITING TIPS

The Writer's Tone

Tone is the writer's attitude toward his or her subject, whether straightforward, cynical, sarcastic, humorous, and so on. In the first part of his article, Royko explains that administrators in the Evanston school system claim they don't know why blacks don't score as well as whites on tests. What is the tone of the essay? Royko is pretending disbelief, that in truth the Evanston school administrators are "taking pains to be politically correct and trying to avoid some shin-kicking controversy."

For the reader, it's important to understand the tone of the piece, in this case Royko's sense of disbelief.

VOCABULARY DEVELOPMENT

Royko claims that Evanston school administrators who say they can't understand the difference in scores are being *politically correct*. What does that term, often abbreviated as *p.c.,* mean? The third edition of the *American Heritage College Dictionary* (1993) gives two long definitions of *politically correct*:

> 1. of, or relating to, or supporting a program of broad social, political, and educational change, esp. to redress historical injustices in matters such as race, class, gender, and sexual orientation. 2. Being

or perceived as being overly concerned with this program, often to the exclusion of other matters.

Both of these definitions help us. Define in your own words what Royko means by describing the Evanston school administrators as politically correct. Which part of the first definition is Royko referring to in this case? Who and what are the Evanston school administrators failing to blame?

REVIEW

Just as a topic sentence is a signpost for a paragraph, the thesis statement guides the reader and writer of an essay and shapes its structure. Every paragraph of the essay must relate to the thesis statement.

DROPPING BACK IN

Andrea J. Fine

This article describes a young woman's dramatic rise from dependence on welfare to economic independence.

VOCABULARY IN CONTEXT

"I was scared and *naive*"—unaware, not perceptive

"it was *exhilarating* to see"—thrilling, joyful

"*paralegal*"—lawyer's assistant

"*empowerment* zones"—inner-city areas targeted for development and economic upgrading

"*viable* college education"—useful, productive

PREREADING

1. Read the first paragraph, a flashback to a key event in this woman's life, and the last paragraph. Predict what the article will say.

Dropping Back In

Andrea J. Fine

1 "This lawyer sat back and asked me two questions no one had ever taken the time to ask: 'Hannah, why are you on public assistance when you are so articulate?' and, 'Why don't you go back to school?'"

2 Although this conversation occurred in 1982, Hannah Oakman recalled it as if it were yesterday. With characteristic defiance, Oakman thought, "As rotten as I was in high school . . . I don't think so. And who is this guy, anyway? This guy doesn't know me; he can't possibly know what he's talking about."

3 But before she could respond to the lawyer, he added, "Just think about it, please. You don't have to do anything about it today or tomorrow, just think about it."

4 Oakman grinned. "I thought about it. And then I thought, OK, I'll apply to college, but it will just be to see if I get in. That was my only goal, to see if I would get in, not to go. I didn't want to go; I hadn't really liked school. Since I had gone to a Catholic girls high school in Philadelphia, I thought I would apply to a Catholic university; I picked LaSalle. My mother

said, 'Girl, you have lost what's left of your mind. It's been almost 11 years since you were in high school. You were almost last in your class then.'"

5   When the acceptance letter arrived from LaSalle, no one was more surprised than Oakman.

6   "I'd been fired years before from the only job I ever had. At that point, an older woman I knew told me I'd better go on welfare, so I would be sure my children had medical coverage. I was scared and naive; no one else showed me other options.

7   "By the time I heard from LaSalle, I'd been on public assistance from 1976 to 1982, which gave me an income of less than $4,500 a year. I had four sons at the time, and the five of us were living in an apartment owned by a slumlord. This place had no heat, no hot water. There was raw sewage coming up out of the toilet into the bathtub and holes in the floor. When the bus went by on 15th Street, the windows would rattle. I was depressed. My self-esteem had dropped and my weight had increased.

8   "That's when I had the conversation with this lawyer I knew, the one who asked me to just consider the possibility of going back to school. He must have seen something inside me I wasn't aware of at the time. His challenge became my impetus to change.

9   "Being accepted to college was just amazing. That was my first thought: This is amazing! It boosted my self-esteem so much."

10   Enough so that Oakman felt confident declining LaSalle and applying to Philadelphia Community College.

11   "I had first applied to LaSalle because all my education up to that point had been in the Catholic school system. But by the time I started considering the reality of LaSalle, I had to face the fact that I'd become disillusioned with the Catholic Church. So I chose community college. Mind you, I had no idea how I was going to pay for this.

12   "I went to the college and told them I wanted to go to school in the fall of 1983. I said, 'I don't know what to do or how to do it. I need you to tell me.'

13   "The admissions counselor gave me all sorts of applications, including grant applications, and he told me to fill them out. Between federal grants and a student loan, it took care of my tuition and books, plus it gave me enough for child care."

14   While it was still a struggle financially, Oakman said, "we weren't starving. I would spend my money on my kids. It was hard to get things for me, but as long as my kids were OK, I was OK."

15   When it came to academics, Oakman, who had ranked 363rd out of 365 in her high school class, excelled in college.

16   "I actually made the dean's list in my second semester. I loved college! I was like a sponge, and everything they taught me, I was soaking up. It was exhilarating to see I could actually do college-level work. It was so wonderful to discover that I was a much better student at 25 than I was at 16 or 17.

17   "I had believed I was just like the welfare stereotype—lazy, shiftless and stupid—and I began to see that just wasn't true. I had never understood the options that existed for me. The welfare system just isn't designed to help people become self-sufficient. Case workers were definitely not dream-makers. They were not interested in assessing my skills or interests or my potential; all they cared about was getting food stamps and rent. I needed more, something that would carry me through my life. I needed a career."

18   In Oakman's first year, she did begin to feel overwhelmed and scared.

19   "Then one of my professors, a man who became my mentor, told me, 'Hannah, forget where you came from. Just focus on where you're going.' Those words motivated me to keep going; those words became my walking shoes.

20   "I tried to get involved in the school as much as I could. I was part of the honor society and vice president of the criminal justice club."

21   These activities were like therapy for Oakman when her mother was diagnosed with cancer and in failing health.

22   "I wanted to stay as busy as I possibly could. By then, my mom realized I had finally gotten to where I needed to be, and in January of my last year at Community, she died. That was the first semester I got anything below a B. After she passed, I made all the funeral arrangements and everything. Because I was the first one in my family who went to college, everyone turned to me. I was learning to be self-sufficient; I was learning I could do anything."

23   A week before she graduated with a degree in criminal justice, Oakman received the school's In Spite of the Odds Award, which included a $1,000 scholarship for paralegal training at Widener University.

24   "I also graduated from there with honors. I was moving so fast. From there, I got a job as a deputy clerk with the 3rd Circuit Court of Appeals. I was making $14,000, and even with all my children, that was a lot of money. I felt like I had made it. Ironically, I only stayed at the job six months because I decided it wasn't challenging enough for me."

25   A month later, Oakman had a job as a paralegal working with a Philadelphia Bar Association program to help get legal services to the poor.

26   "This was the beginning of my feeling totally empowered. I wrote a booklet for single mothers about my experiences of getting off welfare titled, 'How to Become Self-sufficient.' "

27   "I also started an organization to work with single mothers called Personal Empowerment Now. I developed the program in 1988 to help women get the mentoring people gave me. It's been pretty successful. Women have gone to college or remained in college because they had support. A lot of these women don't recognize the skills they already have."

28   Oakman said this reaching out to others was part of her growing faith.

29   "In 1988, after years of struggle with the Catholic Church, I got involved with the Baptist Church and really began to grow spiritually. Soon, I began to realize I was supposed to be doing things for God, not just

for myself. All these years, I had this hole inside. I kept trying to fill it with husbands or more children. I finally began to realize only God could fill that hole. I learned how to be humble; I learned how to submit my will.

30   "Now, when things go crazy, I don't immediately think, How is this going to affect me? I just pray, 'God, what is it you want me to learn? How can you use me?' "

31   Oakman's talents as a speaker and community organizer have not gone unnoticed. She received a Horn of Plenty grant from Moms Online, an Internet support community.

32   "And last February," Oakman said, "I went to the White House to speak with the president and vice president on my experiences doing community services. I was asked to speak at a conference on empower-ment zones. I prayed the words would flow. I knew God had chosen me for this because I'd had my trial by fire. I wanted to do a good job. I wanted to carry a message of compassion, hope and hard work. Going from welfare to the White House made my spirit say, 'Amen!' "

33   Oakman still works to get out her message both through her organi-zation, which she funds herself, and back at the community college, where this single mother of seven now works in the career planning center.

34   "What I want people to know is that a viable college education coupled with no-nonsense basic training will not only remove people from welfare but will help them sustain their new lives, so they don't return to the welfare rolls. The current quick and dirty programs that push people into any job no matter what education or skills they lack will only be detrimental to our neighborhoods and cities later. This is about economic empowerment for a lifetime, not temporary fixes."

READING RESPONSE JOURNAL

1. After you have finished the article, summarize it in one paragraph.

2. Does Hannah Oakman's story have any relevance to your life?

3. Is there anything else for you to write about here, perhaps about someone you know who has struggled with welfare?

4. Explain the turning point in Hannah's life.

5. What had been Hannah's attitude toward school?

6. What did Hannah's mother think of her applying to college?

7. What were Hannah's living conditions like when she was on welfare?

8. How did Hannah feel about her success in the community college?

9. What opinion did Hannah have of the welfare case workers who had helped her?

10. What did Hannah learn from making the arrangements for her mother's funeral?

11. How did Hannah help others who were on welfare?

12. What spiritual awakening did Hannah feel?

13. What's been the high point of Hannah's career?

14. Explain Hannah's recipe for success.

WRITING FROM READING

Developing a Thesis and Writing an Argumentative Essay

One of the important kinds of writing that you must do in college is argument writing. You will often be called upon to write argument essays for history, sociology, psychology, and other classes. These essays may range in length from five or six paragraphs to as many as ten pages. In this sense, *argument* doesn't mean "fighting" or "bickering," but "persuading" and "explaining." You take a position on a subject (your thesis) and then explain why you hold your view.

Let's turn to a question that arises from Hannah Oakman's thoughts on welfare from the reading in this chapter. She explains, "The welfare system just isn't designed to help people become self-sufficient." Think about Hannah Oakman's point here. Whether or not you agree with her, explore your own feelings about welfare.

Prewriting

For ten minutes, brainstorm, freewrite, or cluster *your* views on welfare.

Thesis

Once you've done this prewriting, look back at it to help you form a thesis, a one-sentence statement of your ideas on welfare. In one sentence, write your general opinion of welfare. Don't worry about being perfect. Just get something down. It's fine if you want to change your thesis later. In fact, that happens a lot.

There are two important requirements for your thesis:

1. It must be a complete sentence.
2. It must be strong enough for you to write more about and to explain yourself.

At this point, you may wish to do some more prewriting, to give your-self some more ammunition, in a sense, for your argument. You can, of course, use ideas from the article on Hannah Oakman. You might also wish to read some more about welfare, an almost daily topic in newspa-pers, magazines, and on the Internet. If you know somebody on welfare, you might even consider interviewing him or her for more information and a personal viewpoint.

Once you have enough information for an essay of five or six para-graphs, you can resume writing. Your thesis will guide you in using your ideas. Again, you may even wish to change or refine your thesis as you write.

Introductory Paragraph

To write even a short argument paper of five or six paragraphs, such as this one on welfare, you begin with an introductory paragraph, the last sentence of which will be your thesis. The structure of the paragraph might look like this:

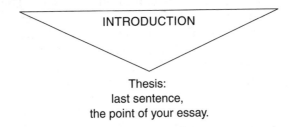

Using the structure of the inverted triangle, you begin with a generaliza-tion, a sentence about the topic, and you narrow down to your thesis or main point, the bottom of the triangle.

Your thesis doesn't necessarily have to go at the end of your intro-duction, but it is a good place for it.

Try writing an introductory paragraph ending with your thesis. You could begin with a story like Hannah Oakman's, a definition of welfare, or some facts about it.

Here is a sample thesis and introduction for you to look at.

Sample Thesis

Welfare must be changed so that it helps those who really need it, not those who abuse it.

Sample Introductory Paragraph

Even with our supposedly good economy in America, many people "fall through the cracks" and have a hard time surviving. Single moms, especially those who have dropped out of school, need

money and food for themselves and their children. At the same time, many people who could be working rely on welfare. They are living off the taxes the rest of us pay. *Welfare must be changed so that it helps those who really need it, not those who abuse it.*

Body of the Essay

Having completed your rough draft of an introduction, stop and look back at your prewriting and your thesis to help you develop the middle or body of your paper. Pick two or three points that you want to develop, writing a paragraph for each one.

Which of these is your strongest point? That one will go last, the strongest position in the body of an argument.

Here are some sample ideas for developing the thesis in the body of the paper.

> **Thesis:** *Welfare must be changed so that it helps those who really need it, not those who abuse it.*

> **Points to Develop Thesis**
>
> 1. **Some people live off welfare who are lazy and have no ambition.**
> 2. **Every year there are stories in the newspapers about welfare cheats who acquire phony social security numbers for more welfare.**
> 3. **There are people who legitimately need welfare like unwed mothers, the old, and the sick who lose out because of the cheaters who give welfare recipients a bad name.**

Each of your points can be the topic sentence, the first sentence, for a paragraph. Of these three points, the last one is the most forceful and will go in the final paragraph of the body of the paper.

Now write paragraphs for each of the points you chose earlier. Remember to keep your strongest one for last.

Sample Topic Sentences for the Body Paragraphs

The writer revised some of his points and decided on this structure (which follows the introductory paragraph):

> **Paragraph 2—Topic Sentence**
>
> 1. **The current welfare system allows many people to cheat.**

> **Paragraph 3—Topic Sentence**
>
> 2. **Welfare has allowed the lazy and unmotivated to rely too much on the system.**

Paragraph 4—Topic Sentence

3. **Because welfare is a necessity for the truly needy, like single mothers, the sick, and the aged, we must keep it—but correct the abuses.**

Again, these three points will be topic sentences, the first sentence for each of the three middle paragraphs in the sample essay.

Sample Body

Here are three paragraphs for the body of the sample paper. The student arranges the paragraphs in order of importance, the strongest argument last. Each of these middle paragraphs begins with one of the topic sentences shown previously.

First, the current welfare system allows many people to cheat. Some crooks obtain multiple social security numbers to collect extra welfare checks and food stamps, thus robbing the poor and stealing our tax dollars. Every year the government catches some of these cheats and punishes them with fines, probation, and jail time. However, in the meantime these cheaters have given truly deserving welfare recipients a bad name and brought criticism down on a system meant to give temporary, necessary relief to the poor.

Second, welfare has allowed the lazy and unmotivated to rely too much on the system. Such people seek no education, acquire no job skills, and perform no function in our society. Some families are in their third generation of welfare—from grandparents on down. What kind of lessons do the shiftless give their children, that the way to survive in our society is through government handouts? For their own sake as well as ours, people must be weaned off welfare and become productive members of our society.

Finally, because welfare is a necessity for the truly needy, such as single mothers, the sick, and the aged, we must keep it—but correct the abuses. Unfortunately, teenage unwed mothers are a reality in our world today, and they and their children must be provided for. At the same time, with the help of day care and education, these single parents must be encouraged to acquire an education and job skills—like Hannah Oakman in the reading—to carve out a life for themselves and their children. Also, the sick and disabled in our society, with those too old to work, deserve to be taken care of. With a country as large and prosperous as ours, it is our responsibility to take care of those who can't provide for themselves.

To visualize the structure of your argument essay up to this point, consider this diagram:

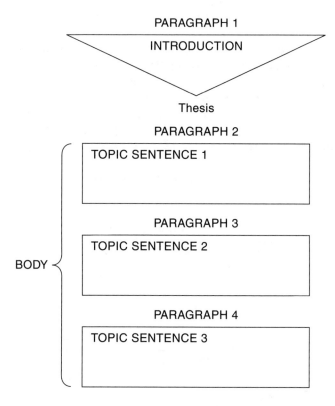

Conclusion

With all the work you've done so far, the conclusion—your last para-graph—will be easy. You may begin by restating your thesis, either word for word or by paraphrasing, changing the words a little for variety.

Then, summarize the three points you have developed in the body of your essay, in the same order you wrote them originally. That's it. Now you try it. Write your concluding paragraph, remembering to begin with your paraphrased thesis and to repeat your topic sentences in order.

Here is a sketch of the structure for your concluding paragraph:

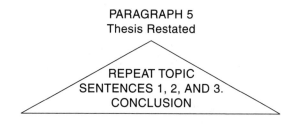

Sample Conclusion

In summary, welfare must be reformed and designed for the truly needy, eliminating its abuses. The cheaters who now defraud the system must be caught, and all loopholes closed. Welfare for the lazy and unmotivated has become a way of life; these people must learn to acquire the skills and jobs necessary for their own independence. Finally, welfare is necessary for some people in time of need, so we must keep it, but with the abuses corrected.

Here is a visual representation of the full, completed essay:

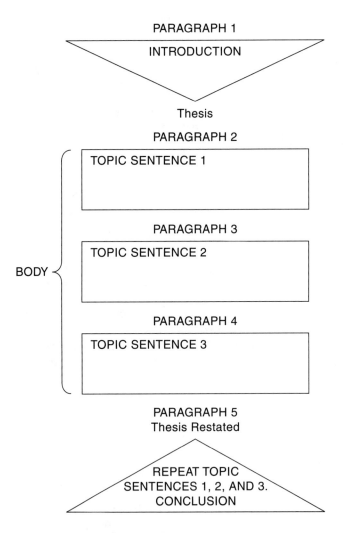

With your conclusion now completed, you may wish to rewrite your five-paragraph essay. Note that transitions like *First, Second,* and *Finally* or *Third* may begin each paragraph in the body.

Caution: Be aware that there are other ways to write an argument paper. But the method just described is simple and clear and can be used for papers of any length by writing the introduction and conclusion and by shortening or lengthening the body.

COLLABORATIVE LEARNING ACTIVITY

Listening for the Reporter's Questions

As your group members listen to your drafts, have them briefly write down how you answer the Reporter's Questions, the five W's.

WRITING TIPS

Think Structure

It may sound simple, but it is crucial for you to think about organizing your thoughts around the structure of beginning, middle, and end. The system used in the argument essay provides a frame for you to write in.

REVIEW

In this chapter we saw the importance of writing with a structure, a plan to develop your ideas. Because much of school writing, or what is called academic writing, calls for you to have a way to organize ideas, this system of argument essay can be very useful to you, no matter what class or field you are working in.

YES I CAN

Abbie Jones

The article in this section is about an African American woman's struggles to reach the top of the medical profession.

VOCABULARY IN CONTEXT

"*mentor* to medical students"—advisor

"I was always very quiet, shy, *introverted*"—turned inward

"*internship*"—training period

"*residency*"—advanced training period for a medical specialty

"white medical *establishment*"—those in leadership, control

"*disproportionately* high rates of *renal* disease"—high percentage compared to other groups; kidney

"*antigens*"—substances capable of stimulating an immune response

"*immunosuppression*"—suppression or inhibition of normal immune responses

"does not rest on the *laurels* of a . . . success story"—triumphs, achievements

PREREADING

1. Read the title and the first two and last two paragraphs. Predict what the rest of the article will say.

Yes I Can

Abbie Jones

1 Dr. Velma Scantlebury, one of only two African-American women transplant surgeons in the United States, knows what it's like to compete with men. Now, having earned her place next to the country's esteemed male transplant pioneers, she's not afraid to have a little fun at their expense.

2   Relaxing in her office at the University of Pittsburgh Medical Center, she pulls out a favorite birthday card, which reads: 'It's your birthday. Try to be the center of attention. Only do things that make you happy. Talk about yourself all day. You know—pretend you're a guy."

3   She has a right to laugh. After all, Scantlebury, 40, is not only an associate professor of surgery at the Thomas E. Starzl Transplant Institute, but she's also a campaigner for organ donation, mentor to medical students, community award winner, wife and mother of two.

4   Her rise from Barbados schoolgirl to colleague of the illustrious transplant pioneer Dr. Thomas E. Starzl is an against-the-odds story fought with dogged determination.

5   At age 13, the shy and bookish girl was brought to Brooklyn's tough Bedford-Stuyvesant neighborhood by her parents, who wanted to make a life for themselves in the United States.

6   In Barbados, she had been well-schooled in the classics, such as "Hamlet" and "Romeo and Juliet." When she went to check out a book at her new school, the librarian told her she was too young to be reading Shakespeare.

7   "I didn't fit in," Scantlebury says. "I wasn't born here, and I didn't have as many friends entering high school, and I was always in the library. I was a nerd, to say the least. I was always reading, and that worked against me."

8   The move to a big-city public girl's school, where violence and muggings were commonplace, was a shock.

9   Then, when she began to think about college, a guidance counselor suggested she get a job instead, Scantlebury was not to be led astray.

10   "I was always very quiet, shy, introverted. I was never one to really express my feelings in terms of what I wanted to do and what I saw myself becoming. I wasn't very verbal, and that might have played a negative role in what they saw as my abilities," she says.

11   Although she was accepted to some bigger-name colleges, she stayed close to home and chose Long Island University, which offered her a four-year scholarship. Next was medical school at Columbia University College of Physicians and Surgeons in New York, where there were only 10 blacks out of a class of 148.

12   There she hit another roadblock when her faculty adviser didn't think she could make it as a surgeon and recommended other areas of medicine.

13   "Medical school was tough," she says. "If you were female, it was OK to be a pediatrician, or a gynecologist, obstetrician or dermatologist. I definitely wanted to be a surgeon, but it was so male-dominated a field that most men felt women were too fragile to be able to cut it.

14   "For women to enter surgery, you really had to be sure of yourself and be in for a fight because there was a lot of competition. Even though I was shy and quiet, I was also very, very stubborn. I think my determination is what has helped me each step of the way."

15   The skeptics told her she was too small, that she would need a step stool to operate. There were times the snickers and the sexist jokes got so bad she would tape an inspiring message on her mirror that said, "Yes I can," just to help her get through the day.

16   After an internship and residency in general surgery at Harlem Hospital Center in New York City, Scantlebury came to the University of Pittsburgh in 1986. She worked under the direction of Starzl, who had received the attention of the world in the late 1980s with his innovative transplantation practices.

17   For Scantlebury, she was Dorothy in Oz. But working the liver circuit was erratic and required surgery on short notice. Although she conducted transplants while nine months' pregnant, she eventually switched to kidney transplantation, which allows a greater window between the time a donor is found and surgery begins. With a husband, professor Harvey White, and daughters Akela, 6, and Aisha, 4, it was a sensible move.

18   "Having a career and having a family are compatible, but you have to realize there are also some sacrifices you are going to have to make in order to create that balance," she says. "Sometimes I go home and say I wish I was a man. I wish I had it so easy. I could stay here in my office and do research and write until 9 o'clock, but I'm the mom, I'm the wife, it's my obligation."

19   Her role as a rarity among doctors, women and African-Americans has afforded Scantlebury the ideal platform as a campaigner for organ donation in the black community. African-Americans are traditionally wary of the white medical establishment, she says, and are reluctant to donate their organs for a variety of cultural and religious reasons.

20   "That's frustrating, particularly because blacks suffer disproportion-ately high rates of renal disease caused by hypertension and diabetes," she says. Although blacks make up 12 percent of the population, one-third of all patients on kidney dialysis are black. The Center for Organ Recovery and Education, a non-profit organ procurement organization says there are 33,571 people awaiting kidney transplants, 11,749 of whom are black. Only 9 percent of blacks donate their organs.

21   "African-Americans as a group are fearful of organ donation. The people I talk to still aren't willing to donate. It's because of those under-lying myths out there and distrust of the medical community," she says. We must reach "the leaders of the churches so they can tell the congre-gations that it's OK to donate. It's not going to [mean that] the pearly gates will be closed because you're missing a heart or two kidneys or your liver. That's not going to determine your spiritual hereafter."

22   She and other physicians such as Dr. Clive Callender, director of the transplant center at Howard University Hospital in Washington, have campaigned for a change in the national guidelines on organ sharing, which traditionally have been based on how well the antigens in the blood of the patient and the donor organ match. Blacks, who have a complex antigen setup, are not going to match at the same rate as Caucasians, for example, and their waits are longer. They have argued that with the advancement of immunosuppression, which can decrease the risk of rejec-tion, less emphasis should be placed on matching—a position that is slowly being accepted by the United Network for Organ Sharing, the body that establishes the guidelines, Callender says.

23   "If you want to avoid long waiting lists, find a living donor, find a spouse, a cousin—as long as it is somebody compatible who truly and honestly wants to donate a kidney to you—then you will do just as well," Scantlebury says.

24   Although Scantlebury works on adults and children, her office is filled with inspiring pictures of kids who have survived the grueling procedures.

25   "It's sad when you see little kids come in. They are only 7, 8 or 9, and they've already had three transplants. The ones who come in here [for their fourth transplant] always send my adrenalin going because you feel like you are really on the line. When you get to No. 4, you really want to be sure you're doing what's in the best interest of the patient."

26   Barbara Barlow, professor and chief of pediatric surgery at Harlem Hospital Center, says Scantlebury immediately caught her attention as an intern. Under the intense pressures of training and the emotional decisions involving children, she never lost her cool, never dissolved into tears and always remained in control.

27   This is an incredible accomplishment. To succeed as a woman in many fields of medicine, you have to work twice as hard as men and be really goal driven, really focused, Barlow says. There was no way anyone was going to stop her.

28   Callender says Scantlebury achieved legendary status at Howard University when she assisted in that hospital's first liver transplant. And although she has achieved so much with the odds against her, he would like to see her rise to the next level.

29   "If we were in a world that didn't have sex or race as a critical feature, she would probably be at the full professor level or maybe even chairing a department at this point. She's doing extremely well, but she could be further along," he says.

30   Scantlebury does not rest on the laurels of a double minority success story. She doesn't dwell on who did or did not come before her. In fact, she hopes her presence will make it easier for the next black transplant surgeons in the ranks. She is a mentor to students and this year was awarded the Woman of Spirit Award for her competent and compassionate service in personal and professional life by Carlow College, a private Catholic liberal arts college for women in Pittsburgh.

31   "One of the things I usually tell students," she says, "is to try to not let others' perceptions of your own abilities interfere with your perceptions of what you're able to achieve. If you let those intertwine, then you begin to believe what they say is true."

READING RESPONSE JOURNAL

1. Summarize Dr. Scantlebury's story.

2. Is there anything in this reading that you can relate to your own life—especially Dr. Scantlebury's advice to students:

   Try to not let others' perceptions of your own abilities interfere with your perceptions of what you're able to achieve. If you let those intertwine, then you begin to believe what they say is true.

   Have there been any bad times in your life or any people in your life who thought you couldn't or shouldn't go to college? Think about this question and your answer for a writing assignment.

3. Is there anything else in this reading for you to write about?

4. Mention some of the specific obstacles Dr. Scantlebury had to overcome to become a transplant surgeon.

5. Explain the humor in Dr. Scantlebury's birthday card:

   It's your birthday. Try to be the center of attention. Only do things that make you happy. Talk about yourself all day. You know—pretend you're a guy.

6. Give two examples of bad advice Dr. Scantlebury had to ignore so she could pursue her own goals.

7. What causes kidney problems for African Americans?

8. Explain two reasons why African Americans fear to donate organs for transplant.

9. Why is Dr. Scantlebury's "a *double minority* success story"?

10. Dr. Scantlebury explains the reasons for her success: "Even though I was shy and quiet, I was also very, very stubborn. I think my determination is what has helped me each step of the way." Can you apply these words to yourself?

11. In addition to her professional life as a transplant surgeon and her role as a wife and a mother, how does Dr. Scantlebury serve the community?

WRITING FROM READING

Using Chronological Order to Organize Your Essay

Begin a paper about the roadblocks you have had to go around to attend and achieve success in college. Explain specific problems that you had (and maybe still have) to overcome. To organize your paper, follow the pattern used by reporter Abbie Jones. The first four paragraphs of Jones's article introduce the reader to Dr. Scantlebury. In paragraph 4, Jones states her thesis: "Her rise from Barbados schoolgirl to colleague of the illustrious transplant pioneer Dr. Thomas E. Starzl is an against-the-odds story fought with dogged determination." This thesis—Dr. Scantlebury's "against-the-odds story"—will shape the rest of the essay.

After the introduction and thesis, reporter Jones presents a flashback in chronological order (according to time, from first to last) from Dr. Scantlebury's girlhood in Barbados to her present career as transplant surgeon.

In the conclusion of your paper, bring the reader up-to-date in your life—as Jones does for Dr. Scantlebury—by explaining your present role as a college student. You may even wish to draw a moral or make a point from your experience like Jones does from Dr. Scantlebury's story: "try to not let others' perceptions of your own abilities interfere with your perceptions of what you're able to achieve."

COLLABORATIVE LEARNING ACTIVITY

Working with Lists

1. Working in your group, talk about obstacles between you and the completion of your education. Make a master list for your group of all difficulties. Be specific.
2. Next, brainstorm and talk about ways to overcome the difficulties you wrote about. Dr. Scantlebury's determination and stubbornness drove her to succeed. She even taped a "Yes I Can" message on her mirror. What will get you through? Make a list of your plans for success.

WRITING TIPS

Using Specifics

In Abbie Jones's article about Velma Scantlebury, Jones mentions specific obstacles in the doctor's way: A librarian counseled "she was too young to be reading Shakespeare," a guidance counselor in high school told her to get a job and not attend college, a faculty advisor in medical school thought Dr. Scantlebury couldn't be a surgeon, and critics told her she was too small and "would need a step stool to operate."

REVIEW

Prewriting with lists and putting events in chronological order can help get specific details into your writing.

Abbie Jones explained definite, specific hurdles Dr. Scantlebury overcame—a demeaning librarian and discouraging advice from counselors in both high school and medical school. The writer must be specific.

WORDS, GOOD OR BAD, CAN ECHO THROUGH A LIFETIME

Bob Greene

This essay by Bob Greene tells how important—for good or bad—our words can be in the lives of others.

VOCABULARY IN CONTEXT

> *"chastised"*—scolded, reprimanded
>
> "high school *equivalency* diploma"—diploma awarded for passing adult education tests, equal to a high school diploma

PREREADING

1. Read the first two paragraphs and then the last five sentences to predict what the full essay will say.

Words, Good or Bad, Can Echo through a Lifetime

Bob Greene

1 "Are you too stupid to do anything right?"

2   The words—spoken by a woman to a little boy who evidently was her son—were spoken because he had walked away from her. Chastised—these words were said at a volume high enough that all the strangers in the vicinity could hear—the boy, his face blank, his eyes downcast, returned quietly to the woman's side.

3   Not a big moment, perhaps—not anything that could qualify as abuse or neglect or any of the other unhappy words that have become a part of our national lexicon. Yet small moments sometimes last for a very long time. Small moments sometimes last for eternity.

4   And a few words—words that mean little at the time to the people responsible for them—can have enormous power. "Are you too stupid to do anything right?" Words like that can echo.

5   So can words of the other kind.

6   What makes me think about this is a story I heard recently from a man named Malcolm Dalkoff. He's 48; for the last 24 years he has been a professional writer, most of these years spent in the advertising industry. Here is what he told me:

7   As a boy in Rock Island, Ill., he was terribly insecure and shy. He was quiet, he was scared, he mostly stayed to himself. He had few friends, and no sense of self-confidence.

8   In October of 1965, his English teacher at Rock Island High School— her name was Ruth Brauch—gave the class an assignment. The students had been reading "To Kill a Mockingbird," by Harper Lee. Mrs. Brauch assigned the class members to write a chapter that would follow the last chapter of the novel. Their own chapter.

9   Malcolm Dalkoff wrote his chapter and turned it in. Today, he cannot recall feeling anything special about the act of writing that chapter, or what grade Mrs. Brauch gave him.

10   What he does remember—what he will never forget—are the four words his teacher wrote in the margins of the paper:

11   "This is good writing."

12   Four words. And they changed his life.

13   "Up until I read those words, I had no idea of who I was or what I was going to be," he said. "After reading her note I went home and wrote a short story, something I had always dreamed of doing but never really believed I could do."

14   Over the rest of that year in school, he wrote many short stories, always bringing them to school for Mrs. Brauch to look at and evaluate. She was encouraging; she was tough; she was honest. "She was just what I needed," Dalkoff said.

15   He was named co-editor of his high school paper; his confidence grew, his horizons broadened, he started off on a successful and fulfilling life. He is convinced that none of this would have happened had that woman not written those four words in the margin of his paper.

16   At his 30th high school reunion in Rock Island, the teachers did not attend—just the returning students, now men and women in middle age. But Dalkoff, back home for reunion weekend, went to Mrs. Brauch's house. She was now retired.

17   And he told her. He told her what her four words had done for him. He told her that because she had given him the confidence to believe that he might be worth something, the confidence to try to be a writer, he had been able to pass that confidence on to the woman who would become his wife, who became a writer herself. He told Mrs. Brauch about a woman who worked in his office—a woman who was working in the evenings toward a high school equivalency diploma—who had come to him for help. She respected him because he was a writer, he said—that is why the woman trying to get her diploma at night turned to him for advice and assistance.

18   Mrs. Brauch was especially moved by that story—the story of helping the young woman. "I think we both realized at that moment that Mrs. Brauch cast an incredibly long shadow," he said.

19   When Dalkoff came to Mrs. Brauch's house, he brought as a gift some books he had especially enjoyed over the years.

20	She said to him, "You shouldn't have."
21	He thought to himself: She's right. It should have been castles.
22	"Are you too stupid to do anything right?"
23	"This is good writing."
24	So few words. And they can last forever. They can change everything.

READING RESPONSE JOURNAL

1. After reading the full essay, write a one-paragraph summary.

2. Make a list of some times in your life when words hurt or helped you. These occasions can be used as topics for assignment 1 in "Writing from Reading."

3. Now try to recall situations when *your* words may have been hurtful or helpful to somebody else.

4. Why does Bob Greene begin his essay with the mother's scolding words?

5. What kind of boyhood did Malcolm Dalkoff have?

6. How did Mrs. Brauch's words change Malcolm Dalkoff's life?

7. How did Mrs. Brauch "cast a long shadow"?

8. What did Dalkoff mean that instead of bringing Mrs. Brauch books, he should have brought her "castles"?

WRITING FROM READING

Repeating the Thesis in Your Conclusion

Look again at the ending of Greene's essay:

"Are you too stupid to do anything right?"
"This is good writing."
So few words. And they can last forever. They can change everything.

What is Greene's purpose here in repeating the two quotations? Even in this fairly short essay, he summarizes his main ideas, as we do when we repeat the thesis in the conclusion of an essay. Greene shows how important words are by saying them again. When you write about "words, good or bad" in the assignment that follows, look back to the beginning of your paper to see your main idea and then repeat it in your conclusion. If you don't want to use the exact same words, substitute synonyms for some of the words while keeping the idea. But remember, it's fine to repeat your thesis exactly—like Bob Greene does when he uses those two important quotations.

1. Think back to the most hurtful or praiseworthy words that ever affected you. Use the Reporter's Questions—who, what, when, where, why—as you do your freewriting or brainstorming. It's important to tell *why* these words had such a powerful effect on you.
2. At times, of course, we too can offend—or help—others with our speech. Try to recall an incident when *you* hurt someone by what *you* said, or conversely, when you helped someone with your words. Again, use the Reporter's Questions in your prewriting before writing a final paper about this topic, and repeat your main idea in the conclusion.

COLLABORATIVE LEARNING ACTIVITY

Capitalizing Titles

Notice that articles in newspapers and magazines often have titles capitalized in a journalistic style. The academic rules for capitalizing titles are different: capitalize the first word, the last word, and all other words except for articles (*a, an,* and *the*), coordinating conjunctions (*and, but, or, nor, yet, for,* and *so*), and prepositions.

In your group, pick some titles of current books and movies to practice the rules of capitalization. Check to make sure you follow the academic rules explained in the preceding paragraph.

WRITING TIPS

Journalistic Style vs. Academic Style

Green's essay was written for his newspaper column. Because of restricted space, the format for newspaper writing demands short, punchy sentences and paragraphs. This journalistic style allows for sentence structure that would be incorrect in the academic or school writing that you do in college—where you have to be sure of sentence boundaries. Notice that Greene uses what academic writing would consider sentence fragments, like these two examples in the middle of his article:

"Their own chapter."
and
"Four words."

What is the sentence fragment in the last paragraph?

REVIEW

In your conclusion, look for an opportunity to repeat your thesis, either word for word in a paper of many paragraphs or a paraphrased version for a shorter paper. Remember the rule of paraphrasing: the same idea expressed in different words. A thesaurus, a dictionary of synonyms, can help you find alternate word choices.

Word Demons

Some words are easily confused; and if you don't get a handle on them, they will continue to bother you.

IT'S, ITS

Two hard words are *it's* and *its*. The best way to tell them apart is that *it's* with the apostrophe means "it is." The apostrophe shows that the *i* is missing from *is*. *It's* is a contraction, two words joined together to make one. "*It's* cold today" means "*It is* cold today."

Its without the apostrophe is used far less often than *it's*. *Its* usually means ownership by something not human, as in "The college has changed *its* admissions policy.

When you meet these words, remember the one simple rule: *It's* means "it is."

Practice

Now make up a sentence of your own in which you use *it's* correctly. Remember with the apostrophe *it's* always means "it is."

Next, write a sentence in which you use *its* properly, remembering to show ownership by a nonhuman.

Complete the following sentences with either *it's* or *its*:

1. Today _____ humid out.
2. _____ one solution or the other.
3. The rose hardly ever loses _____ color.
4. In Ireland, _____ a long way to Tipperary.
5. Over the years, a car can lose _____ paint job.

THERE, THEIR, THEY'RE

Three words that are often misused are *there, their,* and *they're. There* most often means place or location, as in "His school is over *there.*"

   Their refers to ownership, as in "*their* home" or "*their* family." You can ask the question "whose home?" or "whose family?" If the answer is "*their* home or family," spell it *their.*

   They're, like *it's,* is a contraction and is formed from the words "they are," as in the sentence "*They're* home sick today." Try the full words *they are* to check if *they're* is the right word: "*They are* home sick today."

Practice

Now construct your own sentence using *there* to show location.

Next, write a sentence using *their* to show ownership.

Finally, make your own sentence with *they're* meaning "they are."

Complete the following sentences with *there, their,* or *they're:*

1. _____ will be no lottery winner today.
2. _____ constant criticism makes it hard for people to be around them.
3. _____ striving to be the best they can be.
4. _____ always battling for first place in _____ division.
5. The kids are playing over _____ near the school.

TOO, TO

The words *too* and *to* are often hard for students to tell apart. One reason is that *too* has two different meanings—"overly" as in "*too* late" and "also" as in "I, *too*, will go." Notice that when *too* means "also," there are usually commas around it.

To is usually a preposition meaning "toward"; for example, "Patrice is going *to* the deli."

Practice

Write your own sentence using *too* to mean "very."

Then make up your own sentence with *too* meaning "also." Remember to surround *too* with commas.

Finally, construct a sentence in which *to* means "toward."

Complete the following sentences with either *too* or *to*:

1. Pete works _____ hard for his grades.
2. Sherman marched _____ the sea in the Civil War.
3. Clinton, _____, wished to avoid legal troubles.
4. _____ the beginning golfer, the game seems overwhelming.
5. Our spring was _____ cold.

UNIT II

The Immigrant Experience in America

America is a nation of immigrants. Only Native Americans can claim to have been here first. In this unit of the book, you will encounter some readings with strong feelings about immigrants to America that may help you to think and write about your own place in our country today.

GERALDO NO LAST NAME

Sandra Cisneros

Sandra Cisneros's story "Geraldo No Last Name" describes the sudden death of an anonymous young Latino immigrant.

VOCABULARY IN CONTEXT

> "*brazer*"—from *bracero*, Spanish for "strong, physical," a slang term for illegal immigrant
>
> "*wetback*"—illegal immigrant who comes across a river to get into America
>
> "*cumbias, salsas, rancheros*"—Spanish dances

PREREADING

1. Read the title and first paragraph. Why doesn't Geraldo have a last name?
2. After reading the final paragraph, predict what the rest of the story will say.

Geraldo No Last Name

Sandra Cisneros

1   She met him at a dance. Pretty too, and young. Said he worked in a restaurant, but she can't remember which one. Geraldo. That's all. Green pants and Saturday shirt. Geraldo. That's what he told her.

2   And how was she to know she'd be the last one to see him alive. An accident, don't you know. Hit-and-run. Marin, she goes to all those dances. Uptown. Logan. Embassy. Palmer. Aragon. Fontana. The Manor. She likes to dance. She knows how to do cumbias and salsas and rancheras even. And he was just someone she danced with. Somebody she met that night. That's right.

3   That's the story. That's what she said again and again. Once to the hospital people and twice to the police. No address. No name. Nothing in his pockets. Ain't it a shame.

4   Only Marin can't explain why it mattered, the hours and hours, for somebody she didn't even know. The hospital emergency room. Nobody but an intern working all alone. And maybe if the surgeon would've come, maybe if he hadn't lost so much blood, if the surgeon had only come, they would know who to notify and where.

5   But what difference does it make? He wasn't anything to her. He wasn't her boyfriend or anything like that. Just another *brazer* who didn't speak English. Just another wetback. You know the kind. The ones who always look ashamed. And what was she doing out at three a.m. anyway? Marin who was sent home with her coat and some aspirin. How doe she explain?

6   She met him at a dance. Geraldo in his shiny shirt and green pants. Geraldo going to a dance.

7   What does it matter?

8   They never saw the kitchenettes. They never knew about the two-room flats and sleeping rooms he rented, the weekly money orders sent home, the currency exchange. How could they?

9   His name was Geraldo. And his home is in another country. The ones he left behind are far away, will wonder, shrug, remember. Geraldo—he went north . . . we never heard from him again.

READING RESPONSE JOURNAL

1. Summarize in one paragraph "Geraldo No Last Name."

2. Does this reading provide any writing topics for you?

3. Are there any other thoughts from the reading for you to write about?

4. What does the title of the story mean?

5. The narrator emphasizes that Marin thought of Geraldo only as "someone she danced with." But what doesn't that explain?

6. Why does Marin play down her relationship with Geraldo, that, "He wasn't anything to her." He wasn't her boyfriend or anything like that"?

7. Why does Marin describe Geraldo as if she were prejudiced: "Just another *brazer* who didn't speak English. Just another wetback. You know the kind. The ones who always look ashamed."

8. Who is *they* in the narrator's statement that "They never saw the kitchenettes. They never knew about the two-room flats and sleeping rooms he rented, the weekly money orders sent home, the currency exchange"?

9. Why does the story end with a reference to Geraldo's former country-men: "The ones he left behind are far away, will wonder, shrug, remember. Geraldo—he went north . . . we never heard from him again."

WRITING FROM READING

Repeating Key Ideas

Writers often repeat ideas in different words to stress their importance. For example, at least four times in the story, Cisneros tells us that "He [Geraldo] wasn't anything to her [Marin]"—while at the same time she was out with him at three in the morning and spent hours afterward at the hospital. By emphasizing how much she doesn't care about Geraldo, Marin really means she cares very much. Important ideas must be repeated in writing—with different words. Look back at the major idea from one of your papers in earlier assignments, and repeat it at the end—saying the same thing more than once means it's important.

1. What is the implication of Marin's description and complaint: "The hospital emergency room. Nobody but an intern working all alone"? Marin also says that things might have been different "if the surgeon would've come . . . if the surgeon had only come." What is the suggestion here? Sadly, in America we know that health care is different for the poor than for the rich. Have you ever received less than adequate health care or known somebody who has? Explain the circumstances and describe the lack of quality care. Give concrete examples, using the Reporter's Questions. At the end of your paper, repeat your main idea.
2. Cisneros makes clear in her story that Marin feels ambivalence, both affection and dislike, toward Geraldo: "Only Marin can't explain why it mattered, the hours and hours, for somebody she didn't even know." Is there somebody in your life for whom you have mixed feelings, like Marin in the story? Describe this person and, using contrast, tell why you both like and dislike him or her. (For more about the use of contrast as a method of development, see the section featuring "Momma Confronts the Dentist" by Maya Angelou, page 182.) At the end of your paper, summarize in one sentence your divided feelings for the person you describe.

COLLABORATIVE LEARNING ACTIVITY

Listing Specifics

Read your paper out loud to the others in your group. Ask them if your writing has enough specifics and examples to make it clear.

WRITING TIPS

Proper Structure

Even this short piece "Geraldo No Last Name" has a beginning, a middle, and an end. Yours should too.

REVIEW

Repeat your main idea in the conclusion. By doing this, you reinforce in the mind of your reader what is most important to you.

JIMMY AND DEATH,
from *BRONX PRIMITIVE*

Kate Simon

Bronx Primitive is an autobiography, Kate Simon's story of her upbringing as a Polish-Jewish immigrant girl in the Bronx, a section of New York City. She tells of the struggles of her father, a shoe salesman, and of her mother, who warns Kate of the dangers of women's submission to husbands and explains to her the possibilities that only an education can bring.

In her book, Simon describes her love-hate relationship with her brother and the responsibilities she bears in helping raise him and her little sister, themes that most students can relate to their own lives. Simon also tells of her first awakenings of interest in sex and of the abuse committed against her by her father's immigrant nephew brought over from the old country.

We are a nation of immigrants; and even if we are neither immigrants ourselves nor the children of immigrants, we can learn from this powerful and well-written autobiography.

In this selection, Kate Simon, an immigrant, describes the death and its aftermath of Jimmy Petrides, a neighbor and fellow immigrant.

VOCABULARY IN CONTEXT

"The first *intimations* of Jimmy's illness"—hints or signs

"*Ungarische dripke*"—Yiddish for Hungarian slob, slattern

"*behemoth*"—giant

"*funerary garland*"—funeral flower or decoration

"*Goyish*—Yiddish for non-Jewish

"combine *inextricably*"—"inseparably"

"mourning *cherubim*"—babies, angels

"*obliterated*"—destroyed

"*stoicisms*"—sufferings, acts of patience

PREREADING

1. Read the first and last paragraphs to predict what the full selection will say.

Jimmy and Death

Kate Simon

1 Jimmy Petrides, my brother's best friend from the time we moved to Lafontaine Avenue when both boys were about five, was lank and had a neat face, as if someone had made a careful drawing of it before he was born; the lines of his thin eyebrows and thin nose straight, the lower line of his eyes straight, and the arches above as complete and round as the pretty hollow at the back of his neck. Like all the other boys he leaped and bellowed in the street but he was quiet and shy when he came to our house on rainy or cold days to make trains of boxes or spools and to match baseball cards with my brother. Although they lived in our house, two stories below us, we knew very little of his family. His father was one of the many anonymous men in caps with paper bags under their arms who rushed to the El in the morning and came back more slowly at night. Jimmy had a younger sister whom he began to take to school when he was about eight, a dark-gold little girl who clutched his hand and wouldn't talk to anyone else. Once home from school, she stayed in her house; we rarely saw her on the street even as she grew older. Mrs. Petrides was also rarely visible and wonderful when she was, a silent solitary thing like a tree alone in a field. There may have been other Greek families on the block but not in our immediate houses, and she had very few English words to exchange with her neighbors. Nevertheless, families in immigrant neighborhoods being inevitably interdependent, for shopping advice, for medical information, for the care of each other's children and the exchange of kitchen delicacies, Mrs. Petrides was offered strudel by Mrs. Nagy, the *Ungarische dripke* who was the best baker on the block. Big, clumsy Mrs. Kaplan, the loudest behemoth of the house, took her a length of *kishka* (stuffed intestine), her specialty, which Jimmy told us they couldn't eat; all that rubbery stuff. My mother's contribution was to ask Jimmy if his mother would like to go to the English classes with her, explaining that they were held during afternoon school hours and she would be back before three o'clock. He said, "She won't, she's too ashamed," the word for embarrassed or shy. There must have been a number of women like Mrs. Petrides on the block, who had no one to speak with when the husband and children were away, no one to ask where she could buy feta cheese or Greek oil. Tall and slender, with Jimmy's long eyebrows and straight nose, her sandy hair in a long full knot at the back of her head, her high-arched eyes fixed straight ahead, she looked like a lady on the front of a storybook ship, as strong and as lonely.

2 My mother and the other women said that if Mrs. Petrides had taken them into her house to see Jimmy when he got sick—it didn't need words—or had asked the De Santis boys to take him to Fordham Hospital,

Jimmy might not have died. We never found out the cause of his death; children were told about the deaths of the old but never of children, a knowledge too dreadful to speak. The first intimations of Jimmy's illness came from my brother, who was hanging around one rainy October day being mean and restless. He got in my mother's way as she was trying to boil diapers in the steaming cauldron on the stove; he woke our little sister, who had been sick and was napping; he hid my brand-new pencil with the removable cap eraser. My mother suggested he go down to play in Jimmy's house or ask him to come up. He said Jimmy was sick, he hadn't gone to school that day. The next day and the next when he was asked if Jimmy had been in school he again answered, "No," and although the weather had cleared, he refused to go down into the street. He pushed spools and boxes around for a while, read for a while, colored a picture with the baby for a while, but mostly he hung around, like a tired little old man.

3   The whole house was quiet. The women didn't talk much; only Tobie Herman clattered noisily up and down the stairs. My mother must have known that Jimmy was dying, but I knew nothing until my brother burst into the house crying as neither my father with his beatings nor I with my fierce teasing could make him cry. His face was broken, tears pouring down his sweater, his fists clenched and shaking as if he were fighting, his feet stamping. When we calmed him a little, though he still shuddered and wept, he told us that Mr. Petrides, home from the factory that day, came over to him and said that Jimmy was dead, that we would never see him again. "What does he mean, *never*? That I won't ever see Jimmy again? What does he mean?" and his heels stamped the floor and his fist punched the air again and the terrible crying started again. I wanted to console him, not quite knowing what to say, saying something while my mother held him on her lap, a big boy of nine who allowed the indignity because he was in terrible trouble.

4   That evening when my father came home he was still shuddering, lying on our bed with the baby, who offered him her doll and conversation. He didn't respond, which made her cry. That night he didn't eat, and he slept deeply, shuddering every once in a while. Like the street, school was hushed the next morning. The news of Jimmy's death, carried in whispers through the auditorium, in the playground, on the stairs, in toilets, was a funerary garland that wrapped itself around the whole red brick building. Street life stopped: no ball, no marbles, no ropes lashing at the sidewalk, no stickball, no fights, no singing on the stoop. The day of the funeral must have been Saturday, there was no school. We returned books to the library and picked out others early and quickly, then went home to clean up and wait, not knowing quite what we were waiting for. We had seen funerals in the movies, in the news, but they were of grand and old people, not of a boy, not on our street. It was a cool sunny day, the big garbage cans and the metal roof of the De Santis garage shining

bright and hard. As we sat on the stoop we heard stirrings on the inside stairs. The inner door opened and two men came down into the small hall where the letter boxes were, carrying a long black box. My brother gasped and I dragged him down the block, looking back to see what was happening. After the box came Mr. Petrides in a black coat and Mrs. Petrides with a black veil over her head and falling down her black coat. Behind them a few more people in black, one of the women holding by the hand the little Petrides girl whose head, too, was covered with a black scarf. The box was carried slowly down the stoop stairs, into the gutter, and then, followed by the family, headed toward 180th Street. Telling my brother that funerals were quiet so he shouldn't make noise, I ran ahead to look at Mrs. Petrides from the sidewalk. She wasn't crying; she had died, too, with only the clear drawing of her features left on dull white paper.

5   As the family walked slowly, following the black box, held high by the four black arms like burned tree branches, the children began to trail after, led off by the two youngest De Santis boys, both in their early teens, and then the other Italian children, who seemed to know about funerals: Maria Silvestri and her brother Louis, Caroline and Petey Santini, the Bianchi kids. My brother ran into the gutter to join Petey, and I followed him, hesitating for a moment, to walk with Caroline. Awkwardly, hesitantly, the Jewish kids watching from the sidewalk began to walk with us, some of them kids who might later be hit for joining a *goyish* funeral. The two Ruthies came and Helen, Rachel, and Hannah, Sidney and Milton, the Sammies, the Izzys. My brother began to cry, quietly, and I went to him while Caroline took Petey, whose face had begun to quiver. More crying around me, behind me, growing louder and louder, coming out of twisted eyes, leaking into open mouths. (Those weeping faces combine inextricably in my memory with the image of the mourning cherubim of Giotto, wailing as they hover over the body of Christ.)

6   I couldn't understand why they were all crying. My brother, yes, Jimmy had always been his very best friend and he liked him more than anyone else in the world, more than our mother. The other boys had liked him too, an easy, gentle boy who yielded to them rather than fight. But why were the girls crying over a Greek boy they had hardly ever played with? What did they know about death that I didn't? What were they seeing? What were they feeling? Like them, I knew dead people were put in a hole in the ground and covered with earth. Were they crying because the earth might choke him, because he might open his eyes in the dark, alone, screaming, and no one to hear him? Maybe then he would really, truly die. Was that what they meant by "frightened to death"? As a Christian boy he should become an angel. Was there a saw in the coffin to cut through the black wood and a shovel to dig away the dirt? And once out, how long would he have to stand in the dark alone before God sent the blond lady with the naked baby down through the windy night clouds to carry him back up with her?

7   Seeing sick Jimmy standing alone, waiting—for how long?—to be rescued from the dark made me cry as fully, with my whole body, as I couldn't on Third Avenue in the dark, when I was five. Maybe my brother was crying the same memory: in a dark, unknown place, lost, unprotected. We were crying for the same reason that we hid our heads in the movies when a child wandered alone, that we quickly skipped pages when a book threatened to tell about an abandoned child. (Maybe we were also crying, like the women who went to the movies "to enjoy a good cry," for the relief not too often permitted us.)

8   By the time we reached 180th Street, my mother had caught up with us. Taking us each by the hand, she said she didn't think they would let us into the Greek church and certainly not into the cemetery; come home, stop crying. We ate, we slept, we went to school, we asked no questions. One of the block chroniclers said the Petrides family had gone back to Greece, another said they moved downtown near cousins who had a stable. We were no longer interested in the family—the godlike child's gesture of quickly dissolving away anything that wasn't immediately attached to our ears, our eyes, our greeds, our envies. Our fears hung on for a while. No one mentioned Jimmy. His name was a black omen, a sign that children could die, and as fast as we could, we obliterated his name, too.

9   The Halloween after Jimmy's death was a brutal time. When the slashing dark rains of late fall came on Halloween, I was glad to stay at home. On clear nights I was impelled to go, curious, defying my reluctance and fear. The only children in costume—no witches, no gypsies, no pumpkin heads, no pirates—were small wandering foreign bands stumbling in their fathers' old pants, tottering on the crooked high heels of mothers' shoes. They did not invade houses to ask for "trick or treat," expecting apples or candy. Their collections were made on the street, accosting adults with "Got a penny, mister?" The pickings on Lafontaine were poor; this was begging, and begging was the ultimate disgrace, contemptible even for kids. Furthermore, there weren't too many spare pennies around, and those had to be saved for a stick of gum, a string of licorice for one's own kids. We were impressed and wary of their boldness, these invaders from Washington, Bathgate, and Third Avenue with their threatening, demanding hands, and when we saw them coming, moved step by step backward to the top of our stoops, ready to disappear into the inner halls.

10   It was an evening of mayhem for the bigger boys on our street, joined by a couple of their heroes from Arthur Avenue. They wheedled long black stockings, a color and shape of magic and malevolence, from mothers who were ignorant of their use that night and were too careless or busy to ask. The stockings were filled with flour or chalk carefully collected from schoolroom discards and pounded into white powder. They became whip sausages to beat legs, leaving white clouds on stockings and flesh. Nothing serious, a mark of being with the daring on this night, a good time for

displaying agility in jumping, turning, running, avoiding the whips. A more viscious invention, automatically blamed on the Italian and Irish boys, was to fill the stocking with unbroken pieces of chalk or, lacking enough of those, ash, coal, and small rocks. To the game of hunter and prey was added the exciting element of real injury, a young perverse version of Russian roulette: which whip would only mark, which whip would bruise or crack a bone?

11   That especially violent night, the big bellowing boys twirling the black whips over their heads like cowboys' lariats, like frenzied dervishes, I decided to get out of the fun that was not fun and turned my back to run up the stoop stairs and home. A sharp blow hit my calf, throwing me on the top step. I looked at my leg. Something completely impossible was happening to it: a thin spurt of blood was coming through my stocking, straight as an arrow. I knew blood dripping from a scraped knee, a cut finger, a bleeding nose, but never in a thin fast burst like this, straight out into the air. When it slowed, after moments when I saw my life leaving me very quickly, to a dripping trickle, I went upstairs and into the bathroom. My mother was reading yesterday's English paper in the kitchen, and my father was busy with the piecework he had set up in the dining-living room. No one asked any questions. I washed the bloody stocking and my leg, given plenty of time for a careful examination of my calf, which showed only a puncture like a mosquito bite, by my brother's arrival. He was covered from head to foot, a ghost boy, in layers of chalk and soot, ordered into the hall to slap it off before he came into the house again. Then take a bath. It wasn't bath time, he protested, it wasn't Saturday; he wasn't dirty; he hated baths; it wasn't fair. My mother was implacable and called to me to start running water into the tub, and then to get ready for bed.

12   Alone in bed, I examined my calf again. There was only that tiny hole, hardly visible, but because my blood had jumped out of it in such a weird way, I knew I had a terrible blood disease. And would soon die, like the children with rare diseases reported by the Sunday *American*. My left calf became the focus of my life, never forgotten for a moment. The bruise turned strange colors, purplish streaked with a sick yellow like pus. It didn't hurt much, but my leg felt heavy, draggy, beginning to reveal diagnostic signs of the disease that would kill me. Some weeks before I had seen, in the Sunday *American* magazine section that Mr. Haskell left with the jokes, a drawing that filled most of a page: a woman carrying a little nude girl past a piece of sharp-edged furniture whose corner sent a chip of the child's buttock flying into the room. I read the article, mesmerized, memorizing each detail. First one affected area turned white and hard and then another. The child gradually turned to stone, as immobile as a statue: an actual statue, dead, when her lungs and heart became marble. That was my disease. I poked my arms and legs; they felt cold and stiff and the white mark made by my finger took an interminable time to turn pink

again. My legs moved sluggishly, as if I were dragging stone shoes. My eyesight was becoming misty and I had to bend deeper into my book to see. I wasn't hearing too well, either. My mother said I wasn't listening, not paying attention, and I wasn't. It took great concentration to avoid the sharp corner of the piano, not to bump against a dresser or a classroom desk, not to cause a chip to fly off my arm, my back, a sign of the end. Death was surely coming, but I was not yet ready for conclusive signs.

13   At night, lying next to my brother, who thrashed around in fight dreams muttering the dirty words he was not allowed to say during the day, listening to the gurgles of my sister wrapped in her baby cocoon of sleep, I pushed and felt my heavy cold body and tested my eyes by trying to pierce the dark. Was I seeing the hook on the door and the knob on the closet, or only remembering, as people going blind must? Would I hear the clatter of the milkman's bottles or imagine them? What would my brother do when he found me motionless with white stony eyes one morning soon? What would my mother say? What would she do? Would everyone follow my box, crying, as when Jimmy died? Since I couldn't become an angel like Christian children, I would lie in the box, smelling myself rot, hearing the flesh fall off my bones, feeling my eyes roll out of my head and my hair creep down to my shoulder bones. At one moment during one of those dying nights the stoicisms I had been practicing, maybe to this end of suffering and dying without a murmur and alone, left me. I found myself running down the hall to my parents' bedroom. Their door was half open. I slipped through it and stood for a long time looking at them and listening to their breathing. They usually snored—a duet my brother and I imitated masterfully—but now there was no sound. I bent lower to listen to my mother's breathing, to watch her chest rise and fall. Nothing. My father's chest wasn't moving either, and there was not the faintest sound of breath. They had caught my disease and turned to stone. They were dead. I had given them my death.

14   I shrieked and both my parents sat up, sleepy-eyed and bewildered, as if they had come a long way and didn't know where they were. They asked me what had happened—was I sick? Was the baby all right? And my brother? I said nothing, not knowing how to think, what to say. On their repeated questioning I said I had a terrible bellyache. My mother got out of bed and took me to the bathroom for a large dose of the milk of magnesia that was always in the medicine cabinet. I took it eagerly and stayed home from school the next morning because I had to go to the bathroom a lot. By lunchtime I was hungry and ate a large bowl of rice boiled in milk, which was good for bellyaches, and went off to school, hoping I hadn't missed yet another complication of percentages, an impenetrable subject. By what means I made a miraculous recovery, escaping imminent death, transferring my death to my parents and their rejection of that death, the whole terrible matter capable of being dispelled in a fake bellyache and milk of magnesia, is difficult to explain. It was proba-

bly a swing in the vagrant, impassioned imaginings of childhood that plummet into black pits and fly into blossoming trees in dizzy alternations. At any rate my flesh bounced back pinkly when I poked it, my fingers became dexterous enough to weave a long string rope on a spool with four nails hammered into it, and I outran Miltie, something of a champ runner, in a race around the block.

READING RESPONSE JOURNAL

1. Summarize the selection.

2. Think of some death that affected you greatly when you were a child, perhaps the death of a friend or relative. Write about how this death strongly influenced you.

3. Is there anything else in this selection to write about, perhaps the isolation that immigrants may feel in a new country?

4. What were the first hints in Kate Simon's house of Jimmy Petrides's serious illness?

5. Why weren't the children told the details of the death of Jimmy Petrides?

6. What were the immediate effects of Jimmy's death on Kate's brother?

7. What were the effects of Jimmy's death on the neighborhood children?

8. During the funeral procession for Jimmy, why did kids who barely knew him cry along with his friends?

9. What connections did Kate Simon make between her injury, Jimmy's death, and Halloween?

10. How did Kate know she was fully recovered from her "death" and leg injury?

WRITING FROM READING

Using Specific Examples

Read again this section of a paragraph from Simon:

> The first intimations of Jimmy's illness came from my brother, who was hanging around one rainy October day being mean and restless. He got in my mother's way as she was trying to boil diapers in the steaming cauldron on the stove; he woke our little sister, who had been sick and was napping; he hid my brand-new pencil with the removable cap eraser.

What examples does Simon give to show us that her brother was "mean and restless"? In your writing, too, give specific, detailed examples.

1. Think of a death that affected you strongly as a child. Write about the details of the death, using the Reporter's Questions of who, what, when, where, and why. This is a hard, unpleasant topic to write about, but it often produces good writing. Think back and write about your feelings at the time of the death and now looking back on it.

2. Kate's leg injury coming at Halloween so soon after Jimmy's death led her to scary thoughts that she was dying. Was there ever a time

in your life when you thought you might die, whether from a serious illness or from the delusions of a hyperactive imagination like Kate's? Try to recall the details of your suffering, real or imagined, and again use the Reporter's Questions to describe it fully. Also, include the feelings you have now looking back at that time.

3. Kate's mother tells her and her brother that if Jimmy's mother had brought one of the neighbors in to see Jimmy when he was sick, he might have been brought to the hospital and saved. Speaking only Greek, Jimmy's mother was isolated from any help from her non-Greek neighbors. What problems have you seen, perhaps even in your own family or in society generally, from people not being able to speak English? Try to think of specific instances when lack of fluency in English was a serious problem. Write about such incidents, explaining the difficulties immigrants encounter when they can speak little or no English.

COLLABORATIVE LEARNING ACTIVITY

Providing Complete Information

Share your prewriting with your other group members. As they read, listen for the five W's in their work and write them down. This is a good way of checking for completeness in each paper.

WRITING TIPS

Keeping Audience in Mind

As a writer, you must always think of what your audience needs to be told. You know all the details of your story; your audience doesn't. In recounting the story of the death of Jimmy Petrides, Kate Simon describes the language problems, the loneliness, and the isolation of the Greek family—all of which may have prevented the Petrides family from seeking help during Jimmy's illness. For the readers as audience, this background information helps in understanding the shock of Jimmy's death.

In your paper, think of your readers. Ask your classmates what more they need to know to understand your paper. Let your audience help shape your writing.

REVIEW

As a writer, you must provide specifics, like names, details, and examples that root your writing to reality and to life. Readers relate to writing that speaks of the world they know through its facts and realities.

A SONG UNSUNG
The History of a Student Essay

Violet A. Mieliulis

This paper by student Violet Mieliulis is in response to an assignment: Describe a family member important to your development. Look at the family photograph that may have inspired her to write about this relative. We'll trace Violet's thinking from prewriting to final draft, so that you can learn more about the writing process from her example.

Later, you'll study the final draft as a prompt, or stimulus, for a paper of your own.

Prewriting

Violet Mieliulis's essay about her Aunt Terry evolved over two weeks from prewriting to final draft. What follows is her brainstorming list and page of freewriting.

Look at the phrases from the brainstorming list and check to see how many of them made it into her final draft. Some of the sentences from her freewriting also appear in her final draft. Look for these also.

Brainstorming List

Violet A. Mieliulis

Lithuania	America — opportunity
fight for freedom	many deaths
oppressors	left behind
Russian troops	no escape
Partisans	under constant watch
Aunt Terry	in secret
photographs	hiding
stories	happy, determined
mine fields	screaming
food	running
killings	
stake burning	
people fleeing	
open fields	

Freewriting

If you continue on beyond a certain point, you reach the mine fields, fields which used to be fenced in until the Russians took the fence down, and left the mines in the ground.

Aunt Terry's story goes back to when World War II was ending. After the war ended for America, Lithuania began its own — fighting for their country's freedom, and that of every individual that lived there.

Many left to come to America, which is what my aunt's family did.

But it's not just events of the past; it's also the people that can dramatically contribute, in some way, to the life of another individual.

At the time when her family was leaving, Aunt Terry was at the home of a close friend.

Every one arrested was taken to a special site where they had to live, almost like a camp, but larger to accommodate all of the people.

If the women would ever get caught, they'd be tortured, then killed — tortured to find out the location of the men, and killed whether they told them or not.

First Draft

Violet's first draft has a strong introduction and many thoughts that make up her final draft. Notice again how much of this draft makes up the final draft.

1st draft

Violet A. Mieliulis

1   I've always had a strong conviction that the past
either influences, or has some type of effect on,
one's future. For a long time, I couldn't put reasons
behind why I felt this way. But it's not just events
of the past, but also it's people that can
dramatically contribute, in some way, to the life of
another individual.

2   In my life, I carry with me a very special part
of the past. The memory of my Aunt Therese, or Terry
as she was called. Maybe it's not fair of me to say
memory, because I did not know her personally. She was
dead five years before my birth.

3   The only reminders we have are old photographs
taken in Lithuania. The only proof we have that she
actually existed.

4   The only reminders we have are old photographs
taken in Lithuania. That, and her birth certificate.
The photographs, her birth certificate, and the
stories from surviving relatives are the only proof
that she existed.

5   But we don't need physical proof. Inside
every heart of her surviving family members, her
memory lives on. Their word is the only proof we
need.

6   Over the years, I've grown very attached to my
aunt. For she was a hero in every sense of the word.
I learned about her from the stories I heard, and kept
her picture in a very special place. She is my role
model, and the pillar of strength I lean on when times
get tough.

7   Many of my relatives say that I remind them of
her. Terry was stubborn and determined. Terry was
strong-willed.

8   Even after the end of World War II, Lithuania was
still fighting. Fighting for their country's freedom,
and that of every individual that lived there. But
when Russia's troops became larger, stronger, and
armed with more weapons, it left Lithuania's people
with three choices: fight and die, flee and take a
chance, or surrender and live oppressively.

9   Many left to come to America. Which is what my
mother's family did. Every member except Terry. With
the uncertainty of where the Russian troops would show
up next, people did not have time to plan their
departure. At the time when my mother's family was
leaving, Terry was at the house of a close friend.
Within a matter of minutes the troops seized the house
and its occupants. Terry was one of the ones that were
captured.

10   Every one arrested was taken to a special site
where they had to live. Almost like a camp, but larger
to accommodate all the people. If you looked, you
would have found that the majority of if not all of
the people were women and children. Few men were
there. The reason? Many men were part of the group
called Partisans. They would rather die than live a
life under Russian rule. They made up the small army
that Lithuania depended on. But they had to remain in
hiding. If found, they would be shot immediately.
Rebels were only trouble for the Russians, and not
worthy to be kept alive.

11   From time to time, some of the women would go to
bring food to these men. My aunt was one of them. She
volunteered. It was not an easy job to do. It was a
long travel, and death was certain if you were caught.
Plus, if anyone found out, it meant death for the
Partisans.

12   If a woman were caught and would not disclose the
whereabouts of the men, her death would not be an easy
one. They would tie her to a tree, put twigs and
brush underneath her feet, and burn her alive. Just
like witches.

13   One day, the women were making their usual trip to
take the men their food. My aunt had gone ahead of
them. Not really sure of where she was going she
continued on. At a certain point she was supposed to
turn to her right, and not go straight. The others

behind her noticed where she was going, and tried to call out to her. But in a field, your voice is carried off by the wind and not always heard. One of them tried to run and stop her (screaming while doing that). The last thing they saw was her turn her head to try to hear what they were trying to tell her. He right foot, at that moment, landed on a mine, and killed her. FENCE TAKEN DOWN.

Discovery Draft

"A Priceless Sacrifice" is the discovery draft of the paper for class. There are many fine things in it: a strong sense of the writer's voice, loving attention to family history, and a conclusion that draws personal inspiration from the life of Aunt Terry.

The problems with sentence structure in this draft are distracting, but they can be revised and edited.

A Priceless Sacrifice

Violet A. Mieliulis

1   I've always had a strong conviction that the past either influences, or has some type of effect on one's future. For a long time, I couldn't put reasons behind why I felt this way. But it's not just events of the past, it's also the people that can dramatically contribute, in some way, to the life of another individual.

2   In my life, I carry with me a very special part of the past. The memory of my aunt Therese, or Terry as she was called. Maybe it's not fair of me to say memory, because I did not know her personally. She was dead ten years before my birth.

3   The only reminders we have of her, are old photographs taken in Lithuania. The photographs and her birth certificate are our only proof that she existed. But we don't need physical proof. Inside the heart of every one of her surviving family members, her memory lives on. Their word is the only proof we need.

4   Over the years, I've grown very attached to my aunt. To me, she was a hero in every sense of the word. I learned a lot about her from the stories I

heard, and keep her picture in a very special place. She is my role model, and the pillar of strength I lean on, when things get rough.

5   Aunt Terry's story goes back to when World War II was ending. After that war ended for America, Lithuania began its own. Fighting for their country's freedom, and that of every individual that lived there. And they had to fight one of history's most hated enemy—the Russians. Lithuania would not give up their land and their individuality to become part of something they despised. But when Russia's troops became larger, stronger, and armed with more weapons, it left Lithuania's people with three choices: fight and die, flee and take a chance with your life, or surrender and live oppressively.

6   Many left to come to America. Which is what my aunt's family did. Every member except Terry. With the uncertainty of where the Russian troops would show up next, people did not have time to plan their departure. At the time when her family was leaving, Aunt Terry was at the home of a close friend. Within a matter of minutes, the troops seized the house and its occupants. Terry was captured. Every one arrested was taken to a special site where they had to live. Almost like a camp, but larger to accommodate all of the people. If you had looked, you would have found that the majority, if not all, of the people were women and children. Few men were there. The reason? Many men were Partisans. They were part of the small army that Lithuania depended on to fight and regain their freedom. In order to continue doing so, they had to remain in hiding to prevent being killed without being engaged in battle. Russian troops were searching everywhere for these men, and their orders were to "shoot at first sight."

7   Only certain women from the camp knew the whereabouts of these men. And from time to time, they would set out to bring them food. Timing and secrecy were important. If the women would ever get caught, they'd be tortured then killed. Tortured to find out the location of the men, and killed whether they told them or not. The women would be killed like witches were . . . tied to a tree with twigs under their feet, and set on fire.

8   My aunt was one of those women that took food to the men. But the risk that she kept taking finally took her life.

9   On one of her usual trips, my aunt was walking ahead of the other women. She's familiar with the route, but not certain with the turns that have to be made. And the turns are very important. If you continue on beyond a certain point, you reach the mine fields. Fields which used to be fenced in until the Russians took the fence down, and left the mines in the ground.

10   My aunt missed the turn, and kept going straight. One of the women started to yell to tell her to stop, but the wind in a field carries it off, and it's never heard. When she wasn't slowing down, another woman tried running to catch up to her. She also yelled out. It seems that my aunt heard her, because she did turn her head to try to hear what they were trying to tell her. Unfortunately, at the same time, her right foot landed on top of a hidden mine, and she was killed instantly.

11   My aunt was a simple person, but she took risks for what she thought was right. She made a choice to help her people. She could have been one of the women who stayed at the camp, but she wanted to help. My admiration for her never ceases. If things were different, she'd be alive today and telling the story of the Partisans herself. I would have known the woman who gave up her life for the fight for freedom.

12   If there's one thing she taught me, it was to fight for what you believe in. True, she may have been an unknown hero to others with an unsung song, but she stood firm and with a purpose in life. I may never surpass her, but I won't give up trying.

Final Draft

With advice from peers and her teacher, Violet composed the final draft. This draft corrects the fragments and run-on sentences of the discovery draft.

In addition to the sentence editing and some word changes, the final draft has a change in title to "A Song Unsung," which the student relates to her conclusion, that in her paper the student is "singing her [Aunt Terry's] song." The student's paper is her song for her aunt.

A Song Unsung

Violet A. Mieliulis

1   I've always believed that the past influences the future. For a long time, I couldn't explain why I felt this way. But it's not just events of the past; it's also the people who can contribute dramatically in some way, to the life of another individual.

2   In my life, I carry with me a very special part of the past: the memory of my aunt, Therese Maila, or "Terry" as she was called. Perhaps I shouldn't say "memory," because I did not know her personally. She was already dead ten years before my birth.

3   The only relics we have of her are old photographs taken in Lithuania. These photographs and her birth certificate are our only proof that she existed. But we don't need physical proof. Inside the heart of every one of her surviving family members, her memory lives on. Their word is the only proof we younger generation need.

4   Over the years, I've grown very attached to my Aunt Terry. To me, she was an unsung hero. I have learned a lot about her from family stories, and keep her picture in a very special place. She is my role model and the pillar of strength I lean on when my own life gets rough.

5   As much as I know about her, she was always responsible. She understood that because her family had so little, each member would have to pitch in to see that ends meet. Even in her early years, she was a hard worker, full of restless energy. She never married or had the "house full of children" she had so often talked about when she was in her teens. Because she was a middle child in a family of eight children, you wouldn't expect her to really stand out. But she managed to carve for herself a reserved place in our personal family history.

6   Aunt Terry's story goes back to 1949 when she was twenty years old, living in the town called Sausininkai. At that time, America's World War II had ended and Lithuania was beginning its own personal war—fighting for their country's freedom, and that of every individual who lived there. And they had to fight one of history's most cruel enemies—the

Russians. Lithuania would not give up their land and their identity to join a system they despised. But when Russia's army troops became larger and stronger, Lithuania's people were faced with three choices: fight and die, flee and risk your life, or surrender and live under harsh oppressors.

7   Many Lithuanians fled to Germany. My aunt's family, because of their eviction by Russian troops, also headed for Germany all except for Terry, who was accidentally and tragically left behind. With the uncertainty of where the Russian troops would show up next, people did not have time to plan their departure. At the very time her family was forced to leave, Aunt Terry was away visiting at the home of a close friend. Within a matter of minutes, the troops seized the house and its occupants. Terry was captured. Every one arrested was taken to a special site where they had to live, almost like a camp, but larger, to accommodate all of the people. The majority, if not all, of the prisoners were women and children. Few men were there because they were Partisans, part of the small army of guerrillas that Lithuania depended on to fight and regain their freedom. To continue doing so, they had to remain in hiding to avoid being killed. Russian troops were searching everywhere for these men with orders to "shoot at first sight."

8   Only a few women from the camp knew the hiding places of the Partisans. And from time to time, these women would set out to smuggle food to their men. Timing and secrecy were important. If the women would ever get caught, they'd be tortured, then killed— tortured to find out the location of the men, and killed whether they told them or not. The women would be killed like witches, tied to a tree with twigs under their feet, and set on fire.

9   My Aunt Terry was one of those unsung heroes who took food to the men. But the risk that she kept taking finally claimed her own life. On one of her missions of mercy, Terry was walking ahead of the other women. She was familiar with the route, but not sure of the turns that had to be made. And the turns were very important. If you continued on beyond a certain point, you reached the mine fields, which had been fenced in until the Russians took the fence down,

and left the mines in the ground to scare people away from helping the Partisans.

10   Terry missed the turn, and kept going straight. One of the women yelled to tell her to stop, but the wind carried the words off, and her warning was never heard. When Terry didn't slow down, another woman tried running to catch up to her. She also yelled out. My Aunt Terry heard her, because she did turn her head to try to hear. Unfortunately, at the same time, her right foot landed on top of a hidden mine, and she was killed instantly.

11   My aunt was a simple person who took risks for what she thought was right to help her people. She could have been one of the women who remained at the camp, but she wanted to help. My admiration for her never ceases. If things were different, she'd be alive today and telling the story of the Partisans herself. I would have personally known the woman who gave up her life for the fight for freedom.

12   If there's one thing she taught me, it was to fight for what you believe in. She may have been an unknown hero with an unsung song, but she stood firm with a purpose in her life. In some small way, I am "singing her song" writing this paper, telling the world about the courage of my Aunt Terry, one of thousands of Lithuania's "unknown heroes."

ANOTHER LOOK AT "A SONG UNSUNG"

Read over Violet's essay again to do the journal writing that follows.

VOCABULARY IN CONTEXT

"*Lithuania*"—North-central European nation bordering on the Baltic Sea

READING RESPONSE JOURNAL

1. Does this story strike a chord in you about *your* family history, perhaps about a relative who served in the armed forces?

2. Is there anything else from this essay for you to write on?

3. How do we know that Aunt Terry held a special place in Violet's heart?

4. Why didn't Terry escape with her family?

5. Who were the "Partisans"?

6. How was Aunt Terry killed?

WRITING FROM READING

The Importance of Self-investment in Writing

Self-investment means putting yourself on the line in writing a paper, taking a risk that something you care about can be shared with your readers. In her essay, Violet tries to reconstruct a person and a time that is far removed from the experiences of most of her classmates. But because the memory of her aunt is so important to her, she wishes to share it with us (her readers), and she tries to make her aunt more real to us by including a precious family photograph.

1. Is there an "unsung hero" in your family you would like to write about? If you have such a story, write it, using the Reporter's Questions, the five W's, to make sure it's complete. Like Violet in her essay, put yourself into your paper, even if it means taking a chance by revealing family history.

2. Look up the history of Lithuania in the library, on the Internet, or on CD-ROMs. Find out what happened after World War II, what happened with the breakup of the Soviet Union, and what the coun-

try is like today. Write a paper telling what you have learned from your research.

3. Violet's aunt died for her country even though she never wore a uniform or fired a bullet. Write about what values or people *you* would sacrifice your life for if you were pushed to do so.

4. Family photographs and birth certificates are the only tangible records the family has of Aunt Terry. Is there anyone, perhaps a grandparent, great-grandparent, aunt, uncle, or family friend, who still lives in your family history? If there is, write about him or her after consulting with other family members to learn more about that person. Again, show your interest in your subject by sharing family details.

COLLABORATIVE LEARNING ACTIVITY

Using Questions for the Reader

Share your prewriting and final draft with the members of your group. As you listen to each reader, write down questions that might help to reveal more about the favorite relative. Share your questions with the reader to help him or her learn what more the audience needs to know.

WRITING TIPS

Using Oral Family History

In doing the writing assignments for this chapter, you may wish to interview another family member for more information. Usually older family members are flattered by your interest and attention. You might want to use a tape recorder and/or take notes while they speak. It may also help you to have questions prepared beforehand—for example, the Reporter's Questions.

A LESSON IN EDITING

Sentence Fragments

Before you do this section, your instructor may wish you to study the punctuation rules in the Mini-Handbook at the back of this book. Knowing punctuation basics and being able to use them in your own writing will help you edit better.

We're going to look back at the discovery draft of Violet's paper ("A Priceless Sacrifice"), and we'll focus only on one aspect: sentence structure. As you read this draft out loud, underline those places where you sense that something is wrong with the sentences, that they just don't sound right. Then go over your underlined sentences; read them out loud again, looking for any fragments or incomplete sentences.

Write down the sentence before the fragment and then the fragment itself. We'll do the first one for you as an example. In the second paragraph of her essay, Violet writes, "In my life, I carry with me a very special part of the past. *The memory of my Aunt Therese, or Terry as she was called.*" The first sentence here is fine, but the second is not. "The memory of my Aunt Therese, or Terry as she was called" is incomplete, a sentence fragment. There is no verb for *memory*, a possible subject.

When the first sentence and the fragment are read together, however, the whole sentence works:

In my life, I carry with me a very special part of the past: the memory of my Aunt Therese, or Terry as she was called.

A colon (:) is used here for emphasis: the "special part of the past" is the "memory of my Aunt Therese." A comma or a dash (—) could also be used here because either punctuation mark would join the fragment to make a longer, correct sentence.

Now it's your turn. Use the sentences you've underlined in Violet's draft. Go ahead and try to correct them, and don't worry about making mistakes.

First, write the sentence before the fragment and then the fragment itself. Second, revise the sentence and fragment into a correct sentence by combining the two parts or by any other method you can think of. Almost always the fragment has been split from the preceding sentence and can be corrected by being joined to it.

1. Original Sentence and Fragment:

   Revised Sentence:

2. Original Sentence and Fragment:

Revised Sentence:

3. Original Sentence and Fragment:

Revised Sentence:

4. Original Sentence and Fragment:

Revised Sentence:

5. Original Sentence and Fragment:

Revised Sentence:

What follows are the original sentences with their fragments and then the correctly revised sentences. Remember again that there are several ways to correct fragments, but always look first to join the fragment to the preceding sentence. The fragments are underlined.

ORIGINAL (from par. 5): "After that war ended for America, Lithuania began its own. Fighting for their country's freedom, and that of every individual that lived there."

REVISED "After that war ended for America, Lithuania began its own, fighting for their country's freedom, and that of every individual that lived there." Note here that a dash (—) could be used here as well as the comma.

Comment: -*ing* fragments are common. Usually they are participles; that is, they have characteristics of both verbs and adjectives. In this sentence, *fighting* modifies or describes *Lithuania*—Lithuania fighting for its freedom.

With these -*ing* words, always look for some way to attach them to the previous sentence before looking for other ways to correct the fragment.

ORIGINAL (par. 6): "Many left to come to America. Which is what my aunt's family did. Every member except Terry."

REVISED: "Many left to come to America, which is what my aunt's family did, every member except Terry."

Comment: The word *which* very often begins a subordinate clause (which is a fragment).

ORIGINAL (par. 6): "Every one arrested was taken to a special site where they had to live. Almost like a camp, but larger to accommodate all of the people."

REVISED: "Every one arrested was taken to a special site where they had to live, almost like a camp, but larger to accommodate all of the people."

Comment: There is no main verb or subject here. This fragment clearly modifies *site.*

ORIGINAL (par. 7): "If the women would ever get caught, they'd be tortured then killed. Tortured to find out the location of the men, and killed whether they told them or not."

REVISED: "If the women would ever get caught, they'd be tortured then killed, tortured to find out the location of the men, and killed whether they told them or not."

Comment: There is no subject for *tortured* and *killed.* These two words are participles that modify *they* in the previous sentence. Again, note that a dash here would be as effective as the comma.

ORIGINAL (par. 9): "If you continue on beyond a certain point, you reach the mine fields. <u>Fields which used to be fenced in until the Russians took the fence down, and left the mines in the ground."</u>

REVISED: "If you continue on beyond a certain point, you reach the mine fields, <u>which</u> used to be fenced in until the Russians took the fence down, and left the mines in the ground."

Comment: The repetition of *Fields* in the original sentence helped to cause the fragment. The subordinate clause beginning with *which* modifies *fields* in the original correct sentence.

Each fragment we've studied in this draft can be corrected by the student's attaching it to the sentence before. The student cut off the correct sentence too soon, leaving a dangling fragment that should have been part of the preceding sentence.

To help you edit for sentence fragments, always read each sentence out loud to yourself and/or another student. Stop *completely* after each period (which will make fragments obvious). Reading sentences out loud will help you "hear" those that don't sound correct.

REVIEW

Computer spellcheck or grammarcheck programs won't catch these sentence-fragment problems, so always have a friend or fellow student be another pair of eyes and ears for you. You, in turn, can do the same editing for a fellow student. It's easier to work on somebody else's paper rather than our own, because we get so used to our own writing. Also, as writers, we are reluctant to find errors in our own work.

SHOULD IMMIGRANTS BE WELCOMED OR REPUDIATED?

Elvia Martinez

A student, Elvia Martinez gives her strong personal views on America's debate about immigration in a paper written for a class assignment on this question. She had to read several articles about immigration to help her form her views. At the end of her paper is the "Works Cited" section, the list of authors and articles she used.

VOCABULARY IN CONTEXT

"*repudiate*"—to refuse to accept

PREREADING

1. After reading the title and the first and last paragraphs of this essay, predict what the rest of it will say.

Should Immigrants Be Welcomed or Repudiated?

Elvia Martinez

1 Immigrants from all over the world have been coming to America for many years. Americans will either welcome them or repudiate them. Many citizens feel that it is time to cross the line and start getting tough with illegal immigrants. Should illegal immigrants stay in their country, or do they have the right to come into America? *Many are the conflicts of whether to accept immigrants or deny them any rights.*

2 As a natural born citizen of the United States, I feel very proud to be in a free country with all the opportunities of a better education, and a bright future. "Illegal immigration is not the American way," asserts Pete Wilson (182), former governor of California. So what is the American way? Many countries don't have these opportunities to offer. I myself am very proud of my father who came as an illegal immigrant twenty-eight years ago. People who

are against immigrants coming would say something like "Send back your poor, huddled masses yearning to breathe free, we've got troubles of our own" (Gallagher 182), as if sending them back would terminate all troubles. This country and every country will always have some kind of problem. Fear of immigrants has been going on ever since America was born; though years may pass by, this situation is not out of style (Chapman 29).

3   I love hearing my father tell the story of how he came to America. He was only seventeen when he and five friends decided to come to Chicago and seek a better future. My dad's main priority was to support his twelve brothers and sisters. He of course was the oldest of the boys. He and his friends walked for days without water or food. When they were about to cross the border of Tijuana, the patrol officers caught them and sent them back to Mexico. After this occurred, three of his friends backed out and decided not to go back a second time. But not my father. He and his other friends decided to try one more time. They waited five days and started their journey once more. This time my father was successful in crossing to the American side. He got on a bus from California heading to Chicago. One thing my father says he will never forget is that while on the bus, they were stopped by patrol officers who wanted to check if there were any illegal immigrants aboard. My father thought that for sure he was in big trouble. Suddenly, a Caucasian woman next to him handed him a pair of sun glasses, a cap, and a book to read. When the officers got on the bus, they did not notice anything out of the ordinary, so they left. My father says he will never forget this woman for saving his life. Thanks to her goodness and his courage, he was able to get a job and help his family. He got a job as a dishwasher at the Drake Hotel at a rate of 3.00/hr. He now is the head captain of all the banquets and parties that are held there. My father's story reminds me of Reese's comment that many immigrants "have come to this country with nothing, not even knowledge of English, who never took a penny of public money" and built their own success (Reese 187).

4   I have always been proud of my father. He went through so much to be where he is today. Many people

insulted him for not speaking English, but he made
sure that it didn't get to him. He is a citizen of
the United States now and pays taxes just like
everyone else. Because of his struggle and sacrifice,
his family has a nice home and owns farm land. His
English is not as perfect as a person who is born
here, but you can sure understand every word he says.
We can learn so much from immigrants. Many of us tend
to criticize immigrants because we have not suffered
the way they have. Many of us were born in America,
in a free country, and many immigrants were born
in a foreign country where jobs and hunger have
increased so badly that they are forced to leave
their country.

5   Chapman cites Topel: "Immigrants are taking jobs
from natives, particularly unskilled blacks" (29).
Maybe if the natives were not so lazy, it would not
happen. A lot of these immigrants are getting
paid minimum if lucky. I am happy to know that
illegal aliens have been given the right of provided
benefits, such as welfare and education. Now don't
misunderstand me; I'm not saying they should be
supported by welfare forever it should only be used
to give them a push so they get their butts to work.
And also so they can understand that in order to
live one has to work very hard. Now as far as
education is concerned, I agree 100% that illegal
children and adults should have the right to an
education and a better future. It is very true that
we have an economic problem, but it is not based so
much on the immigrants but on other situations
such as lending money, owing money, and poor job
salaries, etc. Immigrants to America are like a
flower needing water to grow; this is the reason
America is free and a very outstanding country
(Chapman 29).

6   I hope someday we can all accept immigrants and
try to understand that they had to go through hunger,
pain, and humiliation just to seek a better life. We
natural born citizens have not been through all that,
we need to be thankful that we were born in a free
country. There are so many opportunities given to us.
Unfortunately, we citizens take these chances for
granted.

Works Cited

Chapman, Stephen. "Debunking Unfounded Worries About U.S. Immigration." *Chicago Tribune.* 8 June 1995, sec. 1:29.

Gallagher, Maggie. "Bad Rap on Immigrants." *Reading and Writing Short Arguments.* Ed. William Vesterman. 2nd edition. Mountain View, California: Mayfield Press, 1994. 184–86.

Reese, Charley. "A Problem of Numbers" *Reading and Writing Short Arguments.* Ed. William Vesterman. 2nd edition. Mountain View, California: Mayfield Press, 1994. 186–88.

READING RESPONSE JOURNAL

1. Read the full essay and make a summary of it.

2. Does anything strike you from this essay that you can write about?

3. Do any other ideas for your own writing spring from this essay?

4. What is Elvia's thesis as stated in her introduction?

5. What are some of the details about Elvia's father's struggle that impress you?

6. What hope does Elvia express in her conclusion?

WRITING FROM READING

Using a Story as an Extended Example

In Elvia's story of her father, she tells of his persistence in crossing the border, the kindness of his anonymous helper, and his eventual success in America—all to illustrate her own views on immigration. Her account of her father brings us up-to-date in his life as an example of an immigrant's hard work and success in America. If you choose to write an "immigrant" story as one of your writing assignments, try to do as this writer did— bring the reader to a sense of update or conclusion. Tell the beginning, middle, and end of your story, making an extended example of it.

1. Perhaps you, too, have strong opinions on the immigration question (remember that your thoughts are your own; you don't necessarily have to agree with Elvia's opinions here). Explain your viewpoint on immigration; and if you have an "immigrant" story as an example, try to make it as complete as the one in this essay.
2. If you have an anti-immigrant stance, write an essay explaining your thoughts. Do you have any example of interaction with immigrants that illustrates your view, possibly an incident that contributed to your feeling? If this is the case, make an extended example of the incident or incidents, explaining the beginning, middle, and end. Be sure to tell why the event(s) affected you so much.

COLLABORATIVE LEARNING ACTIVITY

Correcting Run-on Sentences

Before working to correct run-on sentences, your instructor may ask you to study the punctuation rules in the Mini-Handbook at the end of this text.

Run-on sentences are incorrectly punctuated compound sentences (a sentence of two or more ideas). Run-ons can be fused sentences (no punctuation between them) or comma splices (only a comma between two ideas.)

Sample Fused Sentence

Writing two sentences together without punctuation is a fused sentence the writer fails to end the first idea before beginning the second.

Sample Comma Splice

A comma by itself cannot join two ideas, the writer must use a comma and a conjunction.

The run-on sentence is the most common writing problem and can be resistant to correction, but here are some ways to combat it:

1. Use a comma and a coordinating conjunction (*and, or, nor, for, so, but, yet*) to join two ideas in one sentence:

Immigration is a hotly contested issue in America today, <u>and</u> no easy answers present themselves.

2. Use a semicolon (;) by itself to join two ideas in one sentence:

Immigration is a hotly contested issue in America today; no easy answers present themselves.

Another way to avoid run-ons is to read each sentence aloud in your group, emphasizing a pause after each period. Reading out loud helps you to "hear" when one sentence ends and a new one begins.

The student essay "Should Immigrants Be Welcomed or Repudiated?" has much good writing, but it has some run-on sentences that need to be corrected. Let's study one:

Now don't misunderstand me, I'm not saying they should be supported by welfare forever it should only be used to give them a push so they get their butts to work.

Read this sentence out loud, and try to "hear" where each sentence ends.

Where is the first place that calls for a period?

Now don't misunderstand me.

Where does the next sentence end?

I'm not saying they should be supported by welfare forever.

Note that a semicolon could also go here. A semicolon is used to join two related ideas:

I'm not saying they should be supported by welfare forever; it should only be used to give them a push, so they get their butts to work.

The last part of the sentence is correctly punctuated with the addition of a comma before the conjunction:

It should only be used to give them a push, <u>so</u> they get their butts to work.

There is one run-on sentence in the last paragraph of the essay. See if your group can pick it out and rewrite it. There are three correct options, including putting a period after the first sentence. See if you can figure them out.

WRITING TIPS

Time Transitions

Look back over Elvia's description of her father and notice how she uses transitions: "After this occurred," "This time," and "He is a citizen of the United States *now*." Do the same in your writing—use transitions to tie the story together for your reader.

REVIEW

Stories make up our lives and make for powerful examples in writing.

DO IMMIGRANTS RUIN AMERICA?

(student name withheld)

This is an essay by an Eastern European immigrant telling her own thoughts and experiences in America. Because the world of an immigrant can be small, the student wishes to guard her privacy by remaining anonymous. Her essay uses articles in addition to her personal experience. The "Works Cited" section lists those articles.

VOCABULARY IN CONTEXT

"*green card*"—passport allowing entry to the United States

PREREADING

1. Read the title and the first and last paragraphs of the essay. Predict what the complete essay will say.

Do Immigrants Ruin America?

(student name withheld)

1   The American mass media is filled with debates and comments about the declining economy of America. One of the possible causes for that situation might be a large number of new immigrants. Charley Reese points out that "with the present state of our economy, we [America] cannot continue to absorb nearly a million legal—and goodness knows how many illegal—immigrants year after year" (186). Many Americans believe that it is time to completely close the door because immigration is the reason for the ailing economy of U.S.

2   In the summer of 1995, I received a letter that said that I have an invitation to live and work in the United States of America. It meant that I became the lucky one who won a "green card." The letter stated that I have a right to take with me a spouse and children (if we would have any). It also had a list of restrictions that would not give us a right to become "legal aliens" of U.S. First of all, there was a requirement of at least a high school education,

second—the absence of criminal entries, then—good health and proof that we have enough savings or already have jobs in U.S. and were not going to become a burden to American society.

3   The government of the USA has developed a pretty good system to control the number and attributes of new immigrants. It is so simple: if you win the lottery, America will check who are you before inviting you over. If you did not win, sorry, the number of seats is limited. Yet, many Americans believe that it is time to completely close the door because immigration is the reason for the ailing economy of the U.S.

4   Some politicians are propagating anti-immigrant ideas that contradict reality. Stephen Chapman argues one of them in his article, "Recent immigrants are prone to go on welfare and commit crimes" (29). How big are chances that a person who did not commit a crime in his native country is going to become a criminal in America? As a policy of "green card" lottery says, a person with a criminal background will not be able to get permission to live in the U.S. As for welfare, many immigrants left their countries because they were not paid enough to survive. Here they have chance to work and be fairly paid for a job. They are happy with that opportunity, and do not look for financial aid from American society.

5   After a year of procedures, my husband and I left Eastern Europe and landed in the O'Hare airport of Chicago as "legal aliens," fulfilled with hopes and dreams of a better life. Actually, our situation was miserable. We had little savings, almost no knowledge of English, no ideas what kind of jobs we could find. The first job we found was work in a car wash, together with other "fresh" (mostly illegal) immigrants. To get this job, we paid the manager of the car wash four hundred dollars for both of us. The owner of the place had no idea about the secret income of manager, who was the only one there speaking both languages. If the weather was nice, we worked ten hours a day, six days a week. Besides, we were not paid more for overtime. When it was raining, or snowing, or fewer customers, we were laid off, and not paid at all. Anyway, we were happy to have some source of money to pay rent and buy food. Please, do not tell me, that this is an example when immigrants took

the job from unskilled natives (Chapman 29) An
American would never take this job; only immigrants
who do not know the language and legal system are
working in places like this.

6   Another issue that Chapman argues is that "the
skills and education of immigrants is declining" (29).
The research says that the number of immigrants with
four-year college degrees has risen (29). Most of my
friends, immigrants from Europe, have some or a
complete college education. Unfortunately, our
education is not always valid here, so we go back to
class again. Here I would like to mention about our
friends who immigrated a year earlier than we did.
Larry received his Medical Doctor's degree in Europe,
and Rita interrupted her Master's studies because of
the emigration. They decided that Larry would spend a
first year to increase his knowledge of the language,
and second one to pass an examination required for
foreign doctors, while Rita would work to support both
and buy expensive books for Larry's studies. Today,
after almost three years of gigantic effort, Larry is
working in one of Cleveland's hospitals as an intern,
and Rita is looking forward to complete her education.
They are "the people who came to this country with
nothing, [. . .] who never took a penny of public money
and, with plain hard, smart work [will] build
successful lives and give much back to their adopted
country" (Reese 187).

7   I think, that illegal immigration might be the
factor which drives America down. Many of these people
come like guests, but forget to leave when their visa
has expired. Their target is a possibility to make
money. So they stay for a couple of years, work hard,
rent basements, and pay no income taxes. Imagine how
much they can save that way, and this money usually
has a much bigger value in their native countries.
Naturally, Uncle Sam is getting robbed here. It seems
like some institutions are not doing their jobs well.
Paul C. Roberts also thinks that "the Immigration and
Naturalization Service has not developed the
aggressiveness of other federal agencies in exploiting
its charter" (185).

8   As a history of America says, it is a country
which is built from immigrants. The difference is only
in time. We all appreciate this country equally, no
matter when we came, two or two hundred years ago.

Works Cited

Chapman, Stephen. "Debunking Unfounded Worries About U.S. Immigration." *Chicago Tribune*. 8 June 1995, sec. 1:29.

Reese, Charley. "A Problem of Numbers." *Reading and Writing Short Arguments*. Ed. William Vesterman. 2nd edition. Mountain View, California: 1997. 186–88.

Roberts, Paul Craig. "Courts Give Illegals Too Many Rights." *Reading and Writing Short Arguments*. Ed. William Vesterman. 2nd edition. Mountain View, California: 1997. 184–85.

READING RESPONSE JOURNAL

1. Once you've read the entire essay, summarize it.

2. What thoughts does the essay spark in you that you could write more about?

3. Does any other aspect of the essay strike you, perhaps the exploitation of the writer and her husband by a fellow countryman?

4. What is the thesis of the essay?

5. How does the writer begin her own personal story?

6. How did the manager of the car wash exploit the student and her husband?

7. How does the student use the example of Larry and Rita in her essay?

8. How does the writer conclude her essay?

WRITING FROM READING

Refuting an Opposing Opinion

In her essay, the student makes her point by contradicting another opinion. She begins her fourth paragraph by asserting, "Some politicians are propagating anti-immigrant ideas that contradict reality." She then quotes a source: "Stephen Chapman argues one of them in his article, 'Recent immigrants are prone to go on welfare and commit crimes'" (29). She follows this quote with a rhetorical question that stops us and forces us to think of an answer: "How big are the chances that a person who did not commit a crime in his native country is going to become a criminal in America?" She then mentions the background check required of a legal alien: "A policy of the 'green card' lottery says a person with a criminal background will not be able to get permission to live in the U.S."

What the student does here is to refute her opponent by making her own point—that legal aliens have no criminal past and are unlikely to become criminals in their new country. This is an effective method that you can use in arguing a thesis. Begin with the contradictory point and then argue against it.

1. Write a paper pro or con (for or against) immigration. To get started, look for an article with which you disagree and then respond to that argument with your own. Remember to do as the writer does here; that is, quote your source accurately and then frame your response to it.
2. Take any other controversial question, find a view opposed to your own, and then write your opinion. As in the previous assignment, make sure to get a good source to use and then build your argument against it. Notice how in the student essay, the writer *begins* with the argument she wishes to refute.

COLLABORATIVE LEARNING ASSIGNMENT

Shaping the Thesis

As you do your group reading, pay attention to determine if each writer refutes an opposing claim to shape his or her thesis. Is the thesis clear? Write the thesis of each student's paper, and read it back to be sure the writer agrees.

WRITING TIPS

Making a Topic Personal

This essay is powerful because of the student's interest and involvement. Any time you can make a topic personal to you, it increases the reader's interest—just what the writer hopes to do.

REVIEW

In explaining your side of an argument, it is often helpful to show why the opposing viewpoint is wrong.

Word Demons

EXCEPT, ACCEPT

These words are pronounced very much alike and can easily be confused. One help in seeing how they are different is thinking of the *ex-* in *except*, which has the root meaning of "exit," or "to leave out," as in "All the stars *except* Leo DiCaprio attended the Oscars." *Except* is a preposition or a verb meaning "to exclude or leave out," as in the previous sentence. Think of the word *exception*—"left out."

Accept is a verb meaning "to receive," as in "James Cameron did *accept* many awards on Oscar night" or "I *accept* your offer of help."

Practice

Create a sentence of your own for *except* and then one for *accept.*

Complete the following sentences with *except* or *accept:*

1. Please _____ my invitation to study; I need your help.
2. Every star of the movie *Titanic* _____ the heroine, Kate Winslet, joined Leo in the Oscar celebration.
3. Many Hollywood greats do not _____ criticism easily; in fact, they resent it.
4. _____ for patience, she has all the requisites to be a fine teacher.
5. Every human being must _____ his limitations and learn to live with them.

AFFECT, EFFECT

Affect is a verb meaning "to influence or change," as in "Bad grades may *affect* her morale" or "The death of a loved one can *affect* a student's performance dramatically."

As a noun, *effect* means "result or outcome": "The *effect* of a teacher's praise can last a lifetime." Less often, "effect" can be a verb meaning "to cause or bring about": "Lincoln tried to *effect* a compromise between the North and the South."

Practice

Write a sentence for *affect* and one for *effect*.

Complete the following sentences with either *affect* or *effect*:

1. President Lincoln knew that the Civil War would _____ the United States profoundly.
2. One _____ of the Civil War was the ability of former slaves to own property.
3. The most devastating _____ of the Battle of Gettysburg was the death of 50,000 men, almost as many as died in the Vietnam War, a century later.
4. Lincoln's choice of General Meade to head the Union Army a week before Gettysburg would _____ the outcome of that battle in a major way because Meade was cautious and would make no crucial mistakes.
5. Even today, it is difficult to assess the _____ on our nation of the Civil War.

A LOT

Spellcheck can sometimes confuse students by suggesting the verb *allot*—meaning "to give or apportion"—when students have typed *alot*. The phrase that students really want to use is *a lot,* meaning "many," as in "*a lot* of problems" or "*a lot* of money." Remember that *a lot* is two words.

Practice

Create a sentence in which you use the phrase *a lot,* meaning "many."

A, AN

The article *a*, meaning "one" or "any" is used before words beginning with a consonant (nonvowel) or a consonant sound including those spelled with a pronounced *h* like "hatchet": "*a* dog," "*a* war," "*a* hatchet," "*a* union." Note that the *u* in *union* has the consonant sound of *y*.

An means the same as *a*, but is used before words beginning with vowels or vowel sounds including the silent "h": "*an* eye," "*an* idiot," "*an* hour," "*an* opinion."

Practice

Make up a sentence in which you use both *a* and *an* properly.

Complete the following sentences with either *a* or *an*:

1. _____ guard who was supposed to be on duty to protect President Lincoln left his post.
2. _____ assassin, John Wilkes Booth, crept next to the unguarded Lincoln and shot him from a few feet away with _____ derringer.
3. In making his escape from the Ford's Theatre, Booth broke _____ leg.
4. Eventually, Booth was tracked down and shot to death by _____ eagle-eyed trooper.
5. _____ mass hanging was held in public to execute those men and women even remotely involved in the assassination.

AN, AND

An is the word referred to earlier. It is sometimes used incorrectly in place of the conjunction (joining word) *and*. Think of *and* as a joining word: "peanut butter *and* jelly."

Practice

Write a sentence of your own using *an* and *and* correctly.

Complete the following sentences with either *an* or *and*:

1. After Lincoln was shot, he was carried to a house across the street _____ watched over by doctors, family, _____ friends.

2. While keeping _____ all-night vigil over his body, the other leaders of the government worried _____ prayed about our nation's future.

3. Lincoln's body was carried by train from Washington to Springfield, Illinois, _____ mourners along the route stood by in silence to honor the dead President.

4. Lincoln's service to the nation is commemorated by _____ image of him, the Lincoln Memorial.

5. In Springfield, to this day, Lincoln's tomb is honored _____ cherished.

UNIT III

Living with Disabilities

Alcoholism, learning disabilities, and physical challenges caused by accident or disease form the focus of this unit. You will learn about people who triumph daily over their disabilities, perhaps inspiring you to face *your* challenges with greater courage.

ON BEING 17, BRIGHT, AND UNABLE TO READ

David Raymond

This is a young boy's account of the problems of living with dyslexia, a learning disability. His story has a happy ending because he later goes on to receive his college degree.

VOCABULARY IN CONTEXT

"*dyslexia*"—learning disability in reading sometimes causing the student to see letters in a reversed order

PREREADING

1. Read the first and last paragraphs and predict what the essay will say.

On Being 17, Bright, and Unable to Read

David Raymond

1   One day a substitute teacher picked me to read aloud from the textbook. When I told her "No, thank you," she came unhinged. She thought I was acting smart, and told me so. I kept calm, and that got her madder and madder. We must have spent 10 minutes trying to solve the problem, and finally she got so red in the face I thought she'd blow up. She told me she'd see me after class.

2   Maybe someone like me was a new thing for that teacher. But she wasn't new to me. I've been through scenes like that all my life. You see, even though I'm 17 and a junior in high school, I can't read because I have dyslexia. I'm told I read "at a fourth-grade level," but from where I sit, that's not reading. You can't know what that means unless you've been there. It's not easy to tell how it feels when you can't read your homework assignments or the newspaper or a menu in a restaurant or even notes from your own friends.

3   My family began to suspect I was having problems almost from the first day I started school. My father says my early years in school were the worst years of his life. They weren't so good for me, either. As I look back on it now, I can't find the words to express how bad it really was. I wanted to die. I'd come home from school screaming, "I'm dumb. I'm dumb—I wish I were dead!"

4   I guess I couldn't read anything at all then—not even my own name— and they tell me I didn't talk as good as other kids. But what I remember about those days is that I couldn't throw a ball where it was supposed to go, I couldn't learn to swim, and I wouldn't learn to ride a bike, because no matter what anyone told me, I knew I'd fail.

5   Sometimes my teachers would try to be encouraging. When I couldn't read the words on the board they'd say, "Come on, David, you know that word." Only I didn't. And it was embarrassing. I just felt dumb. And dumb was how the kids treated me. They'd make fun of me every chance they got, asking me to spell "cat" or something like that. Even if I knew how to spell it, I wouldn't; they'd only give me another word. Anyway, it was awful, because more than anything I wanted friends. On my birthday when I blew out the candles I didn't wish I could learn to read; what I wished for was that the kids would like me.

6   With the bad reports coming from school, and with me moaning about wanting to die and how everybody hated me, my parents began looking for help. That's when the testing started. The school tested me, the child-guidance center tested me, private psychiatrists tested me. Everybody knew something was wrong—especially me.

7   It didn't help much when they stuck a fancy name onto it. I couldn't pronounce it then—I was only in second grade—and I was ashamed to

talk about it. Now it rolls off my tongue, because I've been living with it for a lot of years—dyslexia.

8   All through elementary school it wasn't easy. I was always having to do things that were "different," things the other kids didn't have to do. I had to go to a child psychiatrist, for instance.

9   One summer my family forced me to go to a camp for children with reading problems. I hated the idea, but the camp turned out pretty good, and I had a good time. I met a lot of kids who couldn't read and somehow that helped. The director of the camp said I had a higher I.Q. than 90 percent of the population. I didn't believe him.

10   About the worst thing I had to do in fifth and sixth grade was go to a special education class in another school in our town. A bus picked me up, and I didn't like that at all. The bus also picked up emotionally disturbed kids and retarded kids. It was like going to a school for the retarded. I always worried that someone I knew would see me on that bus. It was a relief to go to the regular junior high school.

11   Life began to change a little for me then, because I began to feel better about myself. I found the teachers cared; they had meetings about me and I worked harder for them for a while. I began to work on the potter's wheel, making vases and pots that the teachers said were pretty good. Also, I got a letter for being on the track team. I could always run pretty fast.

12   At high school the teachers are good and everyone is trying to help me. I've gotten honors some marking periods and I've won a letter on the cross-country team. Next quarter I think the school might hold a show of my pottery. I've got some friends. But there are still some embarrassing times. For instance, every time there is writing in the class, I get up and go to the special education room. Kids ask me where I go all the time. Sometimes I say, "to Mars."

13   Homework is a real problem. During free periods in school I go into the special ed room and staff members read assignments to me. When I get home my mother reads to me. Sometimes she reads an assignment into a tape recorder, and then I go into my room and listen to it. If we have a novel or something like that to read, she reads it out loud to me. Then I sit down with her and we do the assignment. She'll write, while I talk my answers to her. Lately I've taken to dictating into a tape recorder, and then someone—my father, a private tutor or my mother—types up what I've dictated. Whatever homework I do takes someone else's time, too. That makes me feel bad.

14   We had a big meeting in school the other day—eight of us, four from the guidance department, my private tutor, my parents and me. The subject was me. I said I wanted to go to college, and they told me about colleges that have facilities and staff to handle people like me. That's nice to hear.

15   As for what happens after college, I don't know and I'm worried about that. How can I make a living if I can't read? Who will hire me? How will

I fill out the application form? The only thing that gives me any courage is the fact that I've learned about well-known people who couldn't read or had other problems and still made it. Like Albert Einstein, who didn't talk until he was 4 and flunked math. Like Leonardo da Vinci, who everyone seems to think had dyslexia.

16   I've told this story because maybe some teacher will read it and go easy on a kid in the classroom who has what I've got. Or, maybe some parent will stop nagging his kid, and stop calling him lazy. Maybe he's not lazy or dumb. Maybe he just can't read and doesn't know what's wrong. Maybe he's scared, like I was.

READING RESPONSE JOURNAL

1. After reading the full essay, write a one-paragraph summary.

2. Do you know anyone who has a learning disability? If you do, write about that person, explaining the difficulties he or she has in school.

3. Can you think of anything else from this reading to write about, for example, any problems that you may have had in school? Write about these difficulties and tell how they affected you personally.

4. Why do you think David Raymond begins his account with the story of the substitute teacher?

5. What specific things couldn't Raymond read?

6. How did Raymond's disability affect other parts of his life, like playing sports?

7. How was Raymond's self-esteem affected by his dyslexia, especially in dealing with other kids?

8. What "different" things did Raymond have to do in school because of his disability?

9. What successes did Raymond begin to have in high school?

10. Explain one of the worst experiences Raymond had.

11. How did Raymond deal with homework and reading books?

12. What gives Raymond courage?

13. At the end of his essay, what does Raymond say about why he wrote it?

WRITING FROM READING

The "Sign of the Cross" Structure

Raymond's essay is written in a method described irreverently as "sign of the cross" by author Donald Murray, Pulitzer Prize winner and professor of English at the University of New Hampshire. This is a basic form of the magazine article that begins with a specific anecdote (a short story or incident) followed by a delayed lead, or thesis, explaining the context and then a series of anecdotes developing the point of view of the piece.

In Raymond's essay, the anecdote about the substitute teacher begins the piece (the top of the cross). Paragraph 2 is the horizontal part of the cross, the thesis or delayed lead: "Maybe someone like me was a new thing for that teacher. But she wasn't new to me." The rest of the essay (the longer vertical portion of the cross) is made up of more anecdotes and comments about them, describing the life of a dyslexic student.

1. Students with learning disabilities, like Raymond's, have difficulties in school with other students. Have you ever been in a class or a school where kids were picked on for their learning problems? If you have seen such a situation, write about it in the structure of "sign of the cross." Begin your paper with an incident, like that of Raymond with the substitute teacher. Follow the incident with a thesis or "lead." Then use more anecdotes to explain how the problems affected the student's life.

2. Use an encyclopedia or medical dictionary to learn more about dyslexia. Write about what you discover, telling the causes of dyslexia, its treatment, and perhaps some famous people who have survived it.

3. Pretend that you are an elementary school teacher. Do you have any ideas about how you would work with a student like Raymond? Write your thoughts about this, being as definite and as practical as you can.

COLLABORATIVE LEARNING ACTIVITY

Tone

David Raymond's story of his battle with dyslexia is told with a tone that is hopeful and inspirational—despite the horrors it describes.

As you listen to the writing of your classmates, try to discern the writer's *tone*, his or her attitude toward the subject.

WRITING TIPS

Purpose in Writing

A very important consideration for a writer is *why* he or she writes. For example, what purpose did Raymond have in describing the pain of his dyslexia?

In your writing for composition class, you are writing to fulfill an assignment, but you're also writing for another reason: to explain or persuade or argue or inform. The purpose of your writing guides how you do it; in Raymond's case he writes for teachers and students, so that he can help somebody else with a problem like his. Thinking about your purpose in writing will make you a better writer.

REVIEW

Think about your purpose for writing; then use a structure and tone that convey your purpose.

THE THIRSTY ANIMAL

Brian Manning

This is the story of a young man's deadly battle with alcohol, from its beginning to where he is today.

VOCABULARY IN CONTEXT

"we laughed too *raucously*"—roughly, wildly
"cases of *Bordeaux*"—a kind of French wine
"bottle of *vintage port*"—well-aged; type of wine
"*lolling* in my chair"—relaxing

PREREADING

1. Read the first and last paragraphs of the essay and write a prediction of what the full work will say.

The Thirsty Animal

Brian Manning

1 I was very young, but I still vividly remember how my father fascinated my brothers and me at the dinner table by running his finger around the rim of his wineglass. He sent a wonderful, crystal tone wafting through the room, and we loved it. When we laughed too raucously, he would stop, swirl the red liquid in his glass and take a sip.

2   There was a wine cellar in the basement of the house we moved into when I was eleven. My father put a few cases of Bordeaux down there in the dark. We played there with other boys in the neighborhood, hid there, made a secret place. It was musty and cool and private. We wrote things and stuck them in among the bottles and imagined someone way in the future baffled by our messages from the past.

3   Many years later, the very first time I drank, I had far too much. But I found I was suddenly able to tell a girl at my high school that I was mad about her.

4   When I drank in college with the men in my class, I was trying to define a self-image I could feel comfortable with. I wanted to be "an Irishman," I decided, a man who could drink a lot of liquor and hold it. My favorite play was Eugene O'Neill's *Long Day's Journey into Night*, my model the drunken Jamie Tyrone.

5   I got out of college, into the real world, and the drunk on weekends started to skip into the weekdays. Often I didn't know when one drunk ended and another began. The years were measured in hangovers. It took a long time to accept, and then to let the idea sink in, that I was an alcoholic.

6   It took even longer to do anything about it. I didn't want to believe it, and I didn't want to deny myself the exciting, brotherly feeling I had whenever I went boozing with my friends. For a long time, in my relationships with women, I could only feel comfortable with a woman who drank as much as I did. So I didn't meet many women and spent my time with men in dark barrooms, trying to be like them and hoping I'd be accepted.

7   It is now two years since I quit drinking, and that, as all alcoholics know who have come to grips with their problem, is not long ago at all. The urge to have "just one" includes a genuine longing for all the accouterments of drink: the popping of a cork, the color of Scotch through a glass, the warmth creeping over my shoulders with the third glass of stout. Those were joys. Ever since I gave them up I remember them as delicious.

8   I go to parties now and start off fine, but I have difficulty dealing with the changing rhythms as the night wears on. Everyone around me seems to be having a better time the more they drink, and I, not they, become awkward. I feel like a kid with a broken chain when everyone else has bicycled around the corner out of sight. I fight against feeling sorry for myself.

9   What were the things I was looking for and needed when I drank? I often find that what I am looking for when I want a drink is not really the alcohol, but the memories and laughter that seemed possible only with a glass in my hand. In a restaurant, I see the bottle of vintage port on the shelf, and imagine lolling in my chair, swirling the liquid around in the glass, inhaling those marvelous fumes. I think of my neighbor, Eileen, the funniest woman I ever got smashed with, and I want to get up on a bar stool next to her to hear again the wonderful stories she told. She could drink any man under the table, she claimed, and I wanted to be one of those men who tried. She always won, but it made me feel I belonged when I staggered out of the bar, her delighted laughter following me.

10   I had found a world to cling to, a way of belonging, and it still attracts me. I pass by the gin mills and pubs now and glance in at the men lined up inside, and I don't see them as suckers or fools. I remember how I felt sitting there after work, or watching a Sunday afternoon ball game, and I long for the smell of the barroom and that ease—toasts and songs, jokes and quality. I have to keep reminding myself of the wasting hangovers, the lost money, the days down the drain.

11   I imagine my problem as an animal living inside me, demanding a drink before it dies of thirst. That's what it says, but it will never die of thirst. The fact an alcoholic faces is that this animal breathes and waits. It is incapable of death and will spring back to lustful, consuming life with even one drop of sustenance.

12   When I was eighteen and my drinking began in earnest, I didn't play in the wine cellar at home anymore; I stole there. I sneaked bottles to my room, sat in the window and drank alone while my parents were away. I hated the taste of it, but I kept drinking it, without the kids from the neighborhood, without any thought that I was feeding the animal. And one day, I found one of those old notes we had hidden down there years before. It fell to the ground when I pulled a bottle from its cubbyhole. I read it with bleary eyes, then put the paper back into the rack. "Beware," it said, above a childish skull and crossbones, "all ye who enter here." A child, wiser than I was that day, had written that note.

13   I did a lot of stupid, disastrous, sometimes mean things in the years that followed, and remembering them is enough to snap me out of the memories and back to the reality that I quit just in time. I've done something I had to do, something difficult and necessary, and that gives me satisfaction and the strength to stay on the wagon. I'm very lucky so far. I don't get mad that I can't drink anymore; I can handle the self-pity that overwhelmed me in my early days of sobriety. From time to time, I daydream about summer afternoons and cold beer. I know such dreams will never go away. The thirsty animal is there, getting a little fainter every day. It will never die. A lot of my life now is all about keeping it in a very lonely cage.

READING RESPONSE JOURNAL

1. After reading the essay, summarize it in a paragraph.

2. What ideas does Manning arouse in you that you can write more about, perhaps your own personal struggles with alcohol and/or drugs?

3. What other thoughts from the essay give you material to write about, for example, the sufferings of your family or friends from alcohol or drugs?

4. How did drinking as a young man affect the writer socially?

5. What does the writer mean when he says he wanted to be "a man who could drink a lot of liquor and hold it"?

6. How did the writer's drinking deteriorate?

7. Name some specifics the writer misses about drinking.

8. What does the writer do to help imagine his drinking?

9. Explain the cause of Manning's problems and then their effects on him.

WRITING FROM READING

Development by Cause and Effect

Earlier in this book, we studied readings developed by problem-solution, for example, Mike Royko's "Schools May Have Problems, but They Begin at Home." Manning's essay uses another method of development: cause and effect. In this essay, the effect (Manning's sobriety) is caused by his reflection on his problems and desire to change. Using cause and effect to develop your ideas can be a powerful way to trace the causes of an event or condition.

1. Write about how alcohol and drugs (the cause) may have affected you or someone you love (the effect). This may be a painful topic for you to write about, but often from contemplating personal suffering comes release and understanding.

2. Brian Manning admits that he misses many of the things that are connected to drinking like the brotherly feeling and ease in talking with women. What are the attractions of drinking and/or drugs for

you or for someone you care deeply about? In your writing, try to name specific, real things.

3. Take some other problem in society besides drug and alcohol abuse and analyze it from the logic of cause and effect. In your paper on this subject, name specific causes and specific effects.

COLLABORATIVE LEARNING ACTIVITY

Listing Causes and Effects

You might wish to analyze your writing task in this chapter by listing causes on one side of a page and effects on the other.

As you listen to members of your group read their papers, write down the causes and effects they describe.

WRITING TIPS

Figures of Speech

To picture his drinking, Manning used a figure of speech called a simile, a direct comparison using *like* or *as* between two unrelated things: "I imagine my problem as an animal living inside me, demanding a drink before it dies of thirst." Try to compare some human failing you may have with something unrelated. We say, for example, "I was as mad as a hornet," or "He is as cold as a fish." Manning's "thirsty animal" relates, of course, to his thirst for alcohol, so it's a powerful image.

VOCABULARY DEVELOPMENT

Let's examine one difficult word in context to see if we can decipher its meaning. Explaining his desire for alcohol, Manning says, "The urge to have 'just one' includes a genuine longing for all the *accouterments* [sometimes spelled *accoutrements*] of drink: the popping of a cork, the color of Scotch through a glass, the warmth creeping over my shoulders with the third glass of stout. Those were joys." What does *accouterments* mean? The colon in the sentence gives us examples of accouterments, such as the cork popping, the color of Scotch, and the warmth. If these are accouterments, what does the word mean?

REVIEW

Thinking about cause and effect relationships can provide you with a natural method of organization.

MONIKA TEACHES ME TO WALK

Elia Herrera

This article from the Daley College student newspaper, *The Daley Express*, is one student's tribute to the courage and kindness of a classmate.

VOCABULARY IN CONTEXT

"*Daley College*"—one of the City Colleges of Chicago, a community college on Chicago's South Side.

PREREADING

1. Read the title and the first and last paragraphs, and write a prediction about what the article will say.

Monika Teaches Me to Walk

Elia Herrera

1 When I began the 1997 Fall semester English class, I saw this lady for the first time; she was walking down the hall into the English classroom. For some reason I could not stop looking at her. She was walking with two canes, and I got the impression that without those canes her legs would bend down and she would not be able to stand up again. Her personality impressed me. She always knew what to ask and when to ask questions in class. She seemed to me to be a very intelligent person.

2 Little by little we started talking and she told me she was taking six classes at the time. Her name is Monika; Monika began helping me with my class (English) because I was confused and I could not understand what was going on. She noticed that I was getting behind in my writing assignments and asked me to go to her house so she could explain to me how we were to do the writing for the mid-term grade.

3 One Sunday I went to her house and between work and a cup of coffee I asked her what happened to her legs. She answered me as normally as if I had asked her any other question even though I knew I was getting too personal. She told me that one time she was swimming and she fractured her spine; the doctors told her that she would not walk again. Her problem got her in many years of depression. She was not interested in doing anything for herself.

4 But one day about three years ago, she said, "I got tired of feeling sorry for myself and I decided to do something to change my life." She

133

began therapy for her legs although the doctor told her that she was not going to walk again, but with her power and her determination she walked again with the canes after two years of everyday therapy. She now can do everything for herself including going up and down the stairs in her second floor apartment. That was her new life.

5   She decided to go to school and make a career; that's when she enrolled at Richard J. Daley College. Last semester (Spring 97) she took six classes and her goal was to get an "A" in every class. At the end of the semester she got an "A" in every class. At the beginning of the Fall 1997 semester she signed up for six more classes and for her midterm grade she had an "A" in every class again. Her grades amazed me but what really amazed me the most was the courage she had to meet her goals. Courage was in her words when she was telling me about the desire she has for a career. I could feel those words in my skin. She has made me realize how many things that I have and do not appreciate; for example, my legs, the opportunity to get things easier than some other people, the power that my desire can reach, etc.

6   She helped me very much with my English class; she gave her essays to me to proofread so that I could fix my own essays. I think Monika has a very good spirit. She is always trying to help me. If I ask her for her notes, she has never had a problem for me to get them. Or if I ask a question, she has the patience to explain until I understand her. I really think that my grade for the midterm was thanks to her, to her help and to her words. I was about to drop the class but thanks to her I am still in class; she gave me some of her courage to continue on and not to give up, not only in the English class but throughout college. I feel that I have the power to do it. By knowing Monika I know I can go on.

7   I am very glad to have met somebody with so much strength, with so much power in what she does. Thanks to Monika I am in class, and I think differently about life. Life might be tough but if I try hard I can do anything, even finish college and go into nursing; I know I can do it.

8   Monika, thank you for not giving up, thank you for being so strong.

9   And thank you for not letting me give up, and for giving me some of your strength.

10   Thank you, Monika.

READING RESPONSE JOURNAL

1. After reading the article, write a one-paragraph summary of it.

2. Is there anything in this article that you can relate to your life and write about?

3. Is there anything else about Monika or the author for you to write about?

4. How did Elia Herrera first meet Monika?

5. What kind acts did Monika do for Elia?

6. What most impressed Elia about Monika?

7. What personal question did Elia ask Monika?

8. What lessons did Elia learn from Monika to apply to her own life?

9. What goals does the student writer, Elia, have in her own life?

WRITING FROM READING

Complementary Introduction and Conclusion

Notice how Elia's paper has a beginning, a middle, and an end—starting when Elia first met Monika in class, then details of their relationship, and her thanks to Monika in her conclusion. In your papers, you also want to have a beginning, a middle, and an end—an introduction, development, and conclusion.

1. Elia Herrera thanks Monika for "giving me [Elia] some of your strength." Is there anybody in your life who has given you strength to go on and do well in school? If there is such a person, write about him or her. Tell, like Elia, how you met this great influence on you and give *specific* examples of how the person helped you. In her essay, Elia provides us with some examples: She tells us how Monika had her come to her house on Sunday for a study session, how Monika helped her proofread her essays, and how Monika loaned her class notes for study. Remember, also, to have a strong conclusion in your paper, perhaps summarizing what your chosen person means to you.
2. Monika is a person who triumphs over her disability daily. Can you write about someone in your life who overcomes a handicap, whether physical or otherwise? Write about that person, giving examples of his or her struggles. Again, try to write a conclusion emphasizing your subject's daily courage.

COLLABORATIVE LEARNING ACTIVITY

Brainstorming for Ideas

In your group, brainstorm about people you know who have overcome handicaps—whether celebrities or people from your own personal life. Do some prewriting about this and save it for a later paper.

WRITING TIPS

Transitions

In addition to the good general structure of the paper, Elia also uses transitions well. Look back at Elia Herrera's paper and see how she uses transitions, connecting words and phrases, particularly at the beginning of most of her paragraphs: "When I began the 1997 Fall semester English class" (par. 1) and "Little by little we started talking" (par. 2).

Pick out the transitions at the beginning of paragraphs 3 and 4 and write them down.

The transition at the beginning of paragraph 3 is about *time*: "One Sunday I went to her house." The transition at the beginning of paragraph 4 is different; it's not merely about time: "*But* one day about three years ago, she said, 'I got tired of feeling sorry for myself, and I decided to do something to change my life.'" What does the word *but* signal here to the reader? Look at the last sentence of paragraph 3. The word *but* shows *contrast*, a change from Monika's depressed attitude to a more positive outlook. What other words show contrast that could also fit here?

In your writing, when you wish to show contrast, difference, or change, you can use these words:

> *but*
> *yet*
> *however*
> *nevertheless*

There are other ways for a writer to signal contrast, for example, with phrases like "on the other hand" and "on the contrary."

The important point to remember is that transitions function as signposts for the reader. If your purpose is to show chronological order, order according to time, use words and phrases like Elia does: "When I began the 1997 Fall semester" and "Little by little." Elia's transition "But one day about three years ago" not only signals time, but also contrast, the important change in Monika's attitude.

REVIEW

In all writing, structure is important. Always think of your writing as needing an introduction, a middle section for developing ideas, and a conclusion that relates to your beginning.

TWO WORDS—"I DO"—SPEAK VOLUMES ABOUT BOB LOVE

Bob Greene

This article is about the struggles and eventual triumph of former NBA and Bulls star Bob Love who conquered a lifelong affliction of stuttering.

VOCABULARY IN CONTEXT

"his face would *contort*"—twist, seize up

"it was the *equivalent*"—equal, similar to

PREREADING

1. Read the first and last paragraphs to predict more of what the article will say.

Two Words—"I Do"—Speak Volumes about Bob Love

Bob Greene

1   The wedding of Bob Love and Rachel Dixon—perhaps you saw it on television—brought smiles to a lot of faces. Chances are, some of the smiles may have been there for the wrong reasons.

2   Love—who, before the arrival of Michael Jordan, was the highest scorer in the history of the Chicago Bulls—got married last weekend during halftime of a game between the Bulls and the San Antonio Spurs. The ceremony, performed on the basketball court and presided over by sportswriter Lacy J. Banks, who is also a Baptist minister, was, on the surface, the ultimate National Basketball Association promotion. A wedding at the United Center? With more than 20,000 "guests" in the seats? That's what most of the smiles were for—for the offbeat feeling of the idea.

3   Yet, for those people who have known Bob Love over the years, the smiles were mixed with genuine tears of emotion. Because as Love stood on the court and repeated the wedding vows—and then said "I do"—he was achieving a victory that, for so long, seemed beyond the realm of possibility. Love could always do remarkable things on a basketball court. Saying a few simple words was not one of them.

4   It is no secret that Love's horrendous speech impediments—"stutter-ing" and "stammering" do not do justice to the severity of what went wrong with his voice early in his life—were a problem for him during his basket-ball career. People have read about it and heard about it. But unless you knew Love during his days in the NBA, you can't really understand the depth of his torment. It broke your heart to sit with him and try to converse—and it came very close to breaking his heart, and his spirit.

5   He was an NBA all-star on three separate occasions; thousands of people shouted appreciation for his athletic skills every game night. But then he would leave the arena, and he would be locked in this terrible, solitary world he could not find his way out of. He just couldn't talk—he couldn't get the words out.

6   He would sit for a minute, two minutes, trying to form a single word. Nothing would happen. His mouth would move, his face would contort—he tried so hard. Nothing. Finally the word would come from his throat—and then the struggle would start all over again. This man who moved up and down the basketball court with such grace could not master the skill of speaking a sentence.

7   I remember once, 20 years ago, sitting with Love in the house in which he was living at the time. This was in Palatine, on the day of a game. He was attempting so fiercely to have a conversation; he would manage to get a word out, and then everything would shut down. He would work on the next word he wanted to say, and the tears would well up in his eyes, the tears of frustration and shame. He was a big, proud man who, every day of his life, was made to feel small and insignificant.

8   After his basketball career was over, Love ended up working as a busboy in a restaurant. It was the equivalent of one of today's NBA all-stars—a Scottie Pippen or a John Stockton or a Patrick Ewing—clearing tables and washing dishes for some of the same customers who, only a few years before, had applauded their every basket.

9   Love was saved because some kind and caring people noticed what had happened to him, and arranged for him to at last receive the kind of expert speech therapy that eventually unlocked his private prison. He worked extraordinarily hard, and the people who were assisting him worked extraordinarily hard; first he was able to speak in one-on-one situ-ations, and then he was able to speak with several people in a room, and finally he was able to speak before groups.

10   Which he does all the time now. He works as a community relations official for the Bulls, and on a regular basis speaks at schools and at neighborhood gatherings. Many people who hear him have a difficult time believing that this was a man who, not so long ago, could barely talk.

11   Which is why—with 20,000 people in attendance—it was such an extraordinary moment in Bob Love's life last weekend when he took his wedding vows. All of those eyes on him, all of those people watching. "I do," he said. Made you want to stand up and cheer. "I do."

READING RESPONSE JOURNAL

1. After reading the full article, write your summary of it.

2. Does this article remind you of someone in your life—a loved one or close friend—who, like Bob Love, won a battle with some personal problem? If so, describe briefly the connection you see.

3. Does this article suggest any other things for you to write about?

4. Why does Greene think some of the fans at the United Center may have been smiling "for the wrong reasons" at the wedding?

5. Explain the contrast Greene describes between Love's athletic skills and his inability to speak.

6. What personal example does Greene give of Love's stuttering?

7. What low point did Love have when his NBA career was over?

8. How was Love finally freed from his "prison" of stuttering?

9. What is Love's present job?

10. When Love recited his wedding vows in front of 20,000 people, what did Greene feel?

WRITING FROM READING

Having Empathy for Your Subject

Empathy is a strong feeling of identification with another person. In this essay, Bob Greene was moved by Bob Love's plight, identifying with his problems and rejoicing in his triumph over them. Writing and caring about your own personal hero is also important to you. When you empathize with the person you are writing about, this kinship comes through to your readers.

1. One of the most moving parts of Greene's description of Bob Love's problem with speaking is his paragraph about interviewing Love during his playing days:

   He would sit for a minute, two minutes, trying to form a single word. Nothing would happen. His mouth would move, his face would contort—he tried so hard. Nothing. Finally the word would come from his throat—and then the struggle would start all over again. This man who moved up and down the basketball court with such grace could not master the skill of speaking a sentence.

   Using as a basis your answer to Reading Response Journal question 2, write a paper describing the illness or handicap that *your* personal acquaintance has conquered, perhaps the daily struggle of an alcoholic, or a patient recovering from a disease. Let your empathy for the person come through.

2. In his article Greene tells us that Bob Love was saved because "some kind and caring people" helped him get speech therapy. Is there any example of "kind and caring people" you have witnessed in your life or in the lives of those around you? Tell who these people are and exactly what they did that showed their kindness.

COLLABORATIVE LEARNING ACTIVITY

Listening for Sentence Fragments

As you listen to the other writers in your group, write down what you think may be incomplete sentences, fragments.

The writing problem that most bothers writing teachers is the sentence fragment, a partial or incomplete sentence, because it reveals confusion about what a sentence is. This topic was discussed in the section on "A Song Unsung." Fixing sentence fragments is so important, however, that we'll work on it here too.

To be a sentence, a group of words must have a subject and a predicate (verb) and express a complete idea. Here is a sample sentence:

> Snow   is   on the way.
> ↓   ↓
> Subject   Verb   Complete idea

As in the case with run-on sentences (sentences not properly separated), fragments are fairly easy to pick out in an exercise for practice but much more difficult to spot in your own writing. What follows are some sentences from student papers containing fragments. First, see if you can pick out the fragment and then rewrite it correctly (often fragments can be attached to the preceding sentence).

Here is a student sentence:

> Students who have to take on being classified as remedial have been burdened with yet another problem affecting their lives. The pondering of their aimless pursuit of an education that they're told they can't reach.

The fragment here is the second word group—"The pondering . . . reach." This phrase explains the "problem" mentioned in the first sentence and should be attached to it by a colon (:).

Here is the corrected sentence:

> Students who have to take on being classified as remedial have been burdened with yet another problem affecting their lives: the pondering of their aimless pursuit of an education that they're told they can't reach.

Here is another student sentence:

> Only if the system would show patience in understanding the problems of our young people. Then maybe we would be able to open their minds.

The fragment here is the first group of words, and the clue is *if,* which begins a subordinate—not a main—clause. The *if* clause should be attached by a comma to the main clause following it.]

Here is the corrected sentence:

Only if the system shows patience in understanding the problems of our young people, then maybe we would be able to open their minds.

Here is another student sentence:

As my aunt ended her statement, others started joining in the gossip. Giving their testimony of some of the strange actions of my cousin Seal.

When you read this out loud, you notice that the last section, "Giving . . . Seal," cannot stand alone, but if you attach it to the previous sentence, you solve the problem.

Here is the corrected sentence:

As my aunt ended her statement, others started joining in the gossip, giving their testimony of some of the strange actions of my cousin Seal.

Notice that *-ing* phrases must always be attached to a full sentence. Here is a student sentence:

From my own experiences aboard an aircraft carrier for six months seeing friends' and shipmates' lives come and go like fireflies in the night. I have a deep respect for veterans of any war.

Reading this out loud reveals that the last part "I . . . war" is a sentence and that the first part needs to be attached to it.

Here is the corrected sentence:

From my own experience aboard an aircraft carrier for six months seeing friends' and shipmates' lives come and go like fireflies in the night, I have a deep respect for veterans of any war.

Here is one more student sentence:

Although she's only seven, my daughter has three trophies, a few certificates, a first-place bronze medal, and has been an honor-roll student since she was five. Also, has been elected the student of the month.

In this case the first part is a fine sentence. The last part needs a subject.

Here is the corrected sentence:

Also, she has been elected the student of the month.

In all of these examples, the writers might have been afraid to write longer sentences, causing them to leave the fragments unattached. Remember that -*ing* phrases, called participial phrases, must always be attached to a complete sentence; participial phrases cannot stand alone.

The same is true of subordinate clauses. These begin with the words *if, since, because, when, until, after,* and *although.* Subordinate clauses must always be attached to sentences. If they come first, they are followed by a comma.

Example of correctly punctuated subordinate clauses follow:

Since she first came to school, she has been an excellent student.
Because Brian was sick often, school was hard for him.
She has been an excellent student since she first came to school.
School was hard for Brian because he was sick often.

More Work on Sentence Fragments

The following are selections from student papers. Read them out loud, find the fragments, and rewrite them into complete sentences.

1. Once you give up on anything such as school, work, or life. It is hard to turn back because you can't find where you left off.
2. So if I want to become that success I hope for. I must always work hard and try hard.

In both of these sentences, the problem is the same: the writer has written introductory subordinate clauses as full sentences. The solution is to put a comma, not a period, after each subordinate clause and join it to the main clause, for example:

So if I want to become that success I hope for, I must always work hard and try hard.

WRITING TIPS

Using Comparisons

How does Greene explain to today's NBA fan how low Bob Love had sunk in his job as busboy? Greene imagines today's stars Scottie Pippen, John Stockton, and Patrick Ewing as having jobs "clearing tables and washing dishes"—this would be similar to Bob Love's case. By comparing Love with current NBA stars, Greene explains more about Love's status in his NBA days as three-time all-star.

Good writers think in comparisons as ways of explaining. In addition to comparing Bob Love to current NBA stars, Greene describes Love's stuttering as "his private prison." Perhaps in your paper about a personal hero of yours, you can compare his or her disability to something else, like when Greene compares Bob Love's stuttering to a prison. For example, some people triumph over the "barrier" of racism or the "poison" of alcoholism or drugs.

Just give this a try; thinking in comparisons, or analogies, will help you in your writing.

REVIEW

What you care about you will do well. Empathy for your writing subject makes for better writing.

AGAINST THE ODDS

John Boslough

This reading is a selection from a book by John Boslough about Stephen Hawking, the English physicist whose life is a daily triumph over ALS, Lou Gehrig's disease (amyotrophic lateral sclerosis).

VOCABULARY IN CONTEXT

"Gothic"—ornate architectural style from the Middle Ages
"façades"—the fronts of buildings, often decorative
"spires"—the upper tapering parts of structures; steeples
"garish tie"—strong, loud color
"ultimate *accolades"*—highest *praise*

PREREADING

1. Read the first and last paragraphs and predict what the reading will say.

Against the Odds

John Boslough

1 The dirty brick structure housing the Department of Applied Mathematics and Theoretical Physics, where Hawking works, looks like an abandoned nineteenth-century factory lost among the Gothic façades and spires of Cambridge. Its main door faces onto an alleyway off Silver Street. Toward the rear of the building, in another alley, is a twenty-five-foot ramp Hawking uses to enter the building through a swinging door. He commutes each day by motorized wheelchair from his home on the ground floor of a Victorian house in West Road about a half mile away.

2 The office facing into a gray and uninviting lounge is scientific gothic. It contains racks of physics texts, a computer terminal, pictures of three handsome children, and a special page turner Hawking fought the bureaucracy to obtain. There is also a specially fitted telephone that now sits idle. Lists of scientific papers are suspended by transparent tape on the walls so he can view them easily.

3 It is almost impossible to understand Hawking upon first meeting him. After a few hours of listening closely to his thin monotone—trans-

lated by Judy Fella, the young woman who was then his secretary—I found I could understand about half of what he was saying. Some words were incomprehensible even to Fella, who had worked with him for years, and Hawking was forced to spell them out. I told him, to his amusement, that part of the problem for an American in understanding him was his British accent.

4   As he works, his body occasionally droops down into his wheelchair, his head sometimes collapsing onto his chest. He has almost no head or facial control, and a smile sometimes turns into a grimace. Nonetheless, when I first appeared in his office, Hawking greeted me with an impish grin, his blue eyes twinkling behind heavy glasses.

5   His brown hair, flecked with gray, is early Beatles, and he normally dresses in standard scientist garb: baggy trousers, garish tie often mismatched with a broad-striped shirt, plaid or tweed sport coat, academic soft soles or boots with bottoms noticeably unused.

6   Hawking thinks things through carefully before speaking so that he will not have to repeat himself. He does not waste words. Sometimes after he stops working for a few minutes—for a bit of secretarial business or tea—he resumes talking in midsentence exactly where he left off. He so completely ignores his physical limitations that, after a while, I found myself doing the same.

7   One day, as I spoke with him, I had become so fully oblivious to his condition that I carelessly began talking about a problem I was having with my elbow as the result of a squash match in London the day before. Hawking made no comment. He simply steered his wheelchair out of the room and waited in the hall for me to return to the subject at hand, theoretical physics.

8   Most days at work Hawking just thinks. He spends much of his time developing new approaches to problems in theoretical physics. One of his colleagues, Ian Moss, told me one morning, "Stephen comes up with all the ideas. The rest of us only test them out to see if they work."

9   Hawking is blessed with a prodigious memory. He is able to work out and retain page after page of complex equations, weaving the mathematical hieroglyphs together as an ordinary person might arrange the words in a sentence. The University of Alberta's Werner Israel, a theoretical physicist and Hawking's co-author on the book *General Relativity,* has said that his feats of memory are akin to Mozart's composing an entire symphony in his head.

10   His colleagues are constantly stunned by what Hawking has remembered. A secretary who worked for him while he was visiting the California Institute of Technology said he once recalled twenty-four hours later a tiny mistake he had made while dictating—from memory—forty pages of equations.

11   One of Hawking's students told me that, while driving him to London for a physics conference once, Hawking remembered the page number of

a minute mistake he had read in a book years before. Other physicists have said that the complex equations that pour forth finished from his mind are both elegant and inspired—the ultimate accolades for a theoretical physicist.

12   Hawking's work has drawn an outstanding group of theoretical physicists to Cambridge from both sides of the Atlantic. Most days at lunch and again at teatime they assemble to share their wit and wisdom with Hawking. The setting is nineteenth-century institutional. But the discussion is twenty-first-century science fiction, jumping from red shifts and quantum effects to black holes and singularities at the beginning of time, light-years beyond the surroundings.

13   The talk is fast, punctuated with put-downs and one-liners. "Hey, Stephen's showing his age," one graduate student says when Hawking makes a minor mathematical error. Hawking lights up at such lines, and the sessions can be the high point of the day. One of his students once told me that teatime with Stephen can be more enlightening than a semester with somebody else.

14   It is remarkable that Hawking has been able to achieve what he has. Doctors, in fact, believe it is a miracle he is alive. An American doctor familiar with Hawking's disease told me that each day he lives he sets a new medical record.

15   Hawking's colleagues shake their heads at such dramatic pronouncements. "Stephen's just Stephen," a former graduate student of his, Malcolm Perry, now a physicist at Princeton University, said. "He doesn't take it very seriously, so we don't either."

16   Gerald Wasserburg, a geologist and physicist at the California Institute of Technology, who has met Hawking at a number of conferences, says of him, "He is one of the most striking examples in the history of science of the power of the human intellect."

17   However, Hawking is not without his critics in the tightly knit physics community. One top theoretician at Princeton told me once, "He's working on the same things everybody else is. He just receives a lot of attention because of his condition." Other physicists have accused him of being overly dramatic and argumentative at science conferences.

18   Despite these bouts with temperamental and jealous colleagues, Hawking's work has been widely honored. In 1978 he received the Albert Einstein Award, considered by some the highest honor in theoretical physics.

19   In 1982 alone he received honorary degrees from Notre Dame, the University of Chicago, Princeton, and New York University. Queen Elizabeth has named him a Commander of the British Empire. The media have frequently labeled Hawking this half century's answer to Einstein. Hawking himself disputes such notions with one of his standard remarks: "You shouldn't believe everything you read."

READING RESPONSE JOURNAL

1. Having read the full selection, write a one-paragraph summary.

2. Does the reading have any connections with your life or the lives of those you know? If so, write about any such connections.

3. Does the article suggest anything else for you to write about?

4. What difficulty did the writer have when talking with Hawking?

5. What special skill does Hawking often display in his work?

6. What does one American medical doctor say about Hawking's work?

7. Why is Hawking so deliberate in his speech?

8. Despite all his great work, what do some people criticize Hawking for?

9. What did Hawking do when the interviewer Boslough talked about something other than physics?

WRITING FROM READING

The Argument Essay Again

There is a movement in America to make life easier for physically challenged people, to give them better access to public buildings and to public transportation. Many of these adaptations are very expensive. Do you think our society needs to make such changes? Prewrite about this issue to form a thesis for an argumentative essay. (See page 51 for a review of the structure for the argument.)

Prewrite also about the pros and cons of adapting our environment to serve the physically challenged better. Making a list of the points for and against can help you find your thesis.

The next step is to prioritize your points for your argument, saving the strongest one for last. Your reasons—your pro points—form the body of your essay.

Remember to end your first paragraph (your introduction) with your thesis.

In your conclusion, repeat your thesis and summarize the points you made in the body of your essay.

As you write your argument, think of someone you know who is physically challenged and what this person needs to survive in our world and what he or she can achieve with proper access to our society.

COLLABORATIVE LEARNING ACTIVITY

Listening for the Pro Points

As your group members read their papers, listen for and write down the points they make for their view. Read them back to the student.

WRITING TIPS

Balance and Fairness

One quality readers respect is fairness. On the whole, this reading praises Hawking's life and work, but the writer includes a negative opinion, too, that of the unnamed Princeton physicist who is quoted: "He's [Hawking] working on the same things everybody else is. He just receives a lot of attention because of his condition." Boslough also mentions that others believe Hawking is "overly dramatic and argumentative" at science conferences.

So, Boslough balances his mostly praiseworthy description of Hawking with some criticism. In your papers, too, always try to give a balanced, fair picture, including both positive and negative aspects.

REVIEW

Note again how important the structure of the argument essay can be for you, giving you a ready-made outline for the development of your thesis.

Word Demons

CONSCIOUS, CONSCIENCE

Because these two words are so often pronounced alike and have related meanings, students often mix them up. *Conscious* is an adjective, meaning "awake or aware," as in "a *conscious* state," "a *conscious* condition." Think of Freud's theory of psychology with its emphasis on the *sub*conscious, that is, "*beneath* or *below* consciousness or awareness."

Conscience is a noun with the meaning "the facility or ability to judge right from wrong," as in "a guilty *conscience*." *Conscience* has the prefix *con* (meaning "with") and the root *science* (meaning "knowledge"), that is "with knowledge."

Practice

Write a sentence using *conscious* correctly—remember that it will usually precede and describe a noun, like "a *conscious* decision."

Now write a sentence for *conscience*, as in "Let your *conscience* be your guide."

Complete the following sentences with either *conscious* or *conscience*:

1. One of the worst atrocities of World War II was the murder of at least 4,000 Polish officers at Katyn Forest, when the Russians showed no _____.

2. The Russians made a _____ decision to cover up their crime by plowing tons of sand over the bodies of their victims.

3. When the Germans, their former allies, drove the Russians away from the Katyn Forest later in the war, they accidentally discovered the murders that would shock the _____ of the world.

4. The Russians, _____ of the world's reaction, denied that they had murdered the Polish officers.

5. Only since the Gorbachev years in a more open government has Russia cleared its _____ by admitting the murders in Katyn Forest.

NEW, KNEW

New is an adjective meaning "fresh," as in "a *new* tactic." *Knew* is a verb, the past tense of "to know," as in "He *knew* the answer."

Practice

Write a sentence in which you use *new* and *knew* correctly, as in "He *knew* he had learned a *new* tactic."

Complete the following sentences with either *new* or *knew*:

1. For many years after World War II, only the Russians truly _____ the real history of the Katyn Forest.

2. A _____ regime under President Gorbachev finally let the world see secret World War II documents about the murder.

3. Still embarrassed about their _____ admission of guilt, Russian dignitaries failed to attend the unveiling of a Polish memorial to the victims because they _____ the service would focus on the Russian role in the atrocity.

4. To the Poles, the memorial marks a _____ beginning.

5. The fact that they wouldn't attend the memorial service may mean that the Russians, who _____ about their complicity on the slaughter at Katyn Forest, haven't yet fully accepted their role in one of history's worst atrocities.

NO, KNOW

No means "negative" or "not any" as in "*No* Smoking." *Know* refers to "*know*ledge" as in "I *know* he's correct."

Practice

Write a sentence of your own in which you use *no* and *know* correctly; for example, "*No* student can *know* every possible answer."

Complete the following sentences with either *no* or *know:*

1. _____ history of Ireland can be complete without a description of the Irish Potato Famine.
2. History will never _____ the full extent of the famine's effects from its beginning in the 1840s.
3. The Irish feel there can be _____ forgiveness for the English, then rulers of Ireland, for shipping tons of food home to their mother country while the Irish starved.
4. Irish farmers did not _____ how to combat the blight, which killed most of the potato crop, the staple of Irish nutrition.
5. Hundreds of thousands of Irish people fled their native country during the famine because there simply was _____ food.

LOOSE, LOSE

Loose is an adjective that means "too big," as in "a *loose* jacket." *Lose* with one "o" is a verb meaning "to miss from one's possession," as in "He often will *lose* his keys."

Practice

Write a correct sentence for *loose* and then one for *lose*.

Complete the following sentences with either *loose* or *lose:*

1. Early America was a _____ confederation of states.
2. No state wanted to _____ its own autonomy.
3. The first great test of the unity of the United States grew over slavery because the South didn't want to _____ what it considered a vital part of its economy.

4. Because the North had more of a manufacturing than an agricultural economy, it thought of slavery as an issue of human rights; the _____ group of slave states considered slavery an integral part of their economic life.
5. Though Lincoln opposed slavery, he did not want to _____ the South as part of the United States.

MINE, MIND

These two words sound similar, but that is their only connection. *Mine* is a possessive pronoun showing ownership: "That book on the Civil War is *mine*," and "The red convertible is *mine*."

As a noun, *mind* means "intelligence" or "brain": "a bright *mind*." We often hear the saying, "A *mind* is a terrible thing to waste."

Practice

Write a sentence each for *mine* and *mind*.

Complete the following sentences with either *mine* or *mind:*

1. According to psychologists, the _____ grows in power during the ages of birth to five years more than at any other time.
2. The power to control my life is _____ and _____ alone.
3. Researchers believe that the key to understanding violence in children lies in the _____.
4. In the final analysis, each person must say, "The power to change my life is _____."
5. Some believe that pain control is simply "_____ over matter."

UNIT IV

Laugh So You Don't Cry

This brief section is a change of pace from more serious topics. Gary Soto writes a fond reminiscence of his sister's melding into adolescence in "The Locket." In "Getting Pucked," Michelle Genz describes the humor/horror of a friend's dating adventures. Dave Barry makes fun of men's activities in "Are Guys Smart, or What?"

THE LOCKET

Gary Soto

This reading is from an autobiography by Gary Soto. Tinged with humor and lighthearted memories, "The Locket" is a pleasant look at adolescence.

VOCABULARY IN CONTEXT

> *"bargaining chip"*—item used for trade in a transaction or barter
> *"canopy* bed"—bed with a covering overhead

PREREADING

1. Read the introductory and the concluding paragraphs to predict what the rest of the selection will be about.

The Locket

Gary Soto

1   I never liked jewelry. My sister Debra did. Twenty Bazooka comic strips and a dollar—after a three-week binge of reading teenage romances while waiting for the mailman—brought her a gold-plated locket, studded with plastic pearls and a fake diamond. I wanted her to choose the miniature binoculars because I helped her chew at least seven pieces of pink bubble gum and gave her a clean dime in exchange for our once-a-week pudding dessert. We were always selling desserts to each other. We were always short a dime or a quarter, and our only bargaining chip was dessert, especially the pudding Mother served in gold-rimmed goblets, the kind kings and queens used in Robin Hood movies.

2   I wanted Debra to choose the binoculars. My head was large, but my eyes were small as a cat's, maybe even smaller. I could look through both lenses with one eye, and what I wanted was a better look at our neighbor, a junior college student who swam in an aluminum-sided doughboy pool. She used a ladder to get in, and often just stood on the ladder fiddling with her top and snapping her bikini bottom back into place. I could spy on her from behind our fence, the binoculars to my right eye because that one seemed to work better.

3   But Debra chose the locket. When it arrived in a business-size envelope, I waved it at her and said, "It's here." Angrily, she snatched it from me and took it to her room. I ate an afternoon bowl of Cocoa Puffs and watched a movie about giant ants no flame thrower could stop. I looked at her bedroom door now and then, wondering what was going on. Later, just before the ants got fried with a laser, she came out stinking of perfume, the locket around her brown neck. She didn't look at me as she went out the front door and crossed the street to see her friend, Jill.

4   My sister was eleven. She still clacked the plastic faces of Barbie and Ken together, made them hug, made them cry and run back to each other, stiff arms extended, faces wet with pretend tears from the bathroom sink. But she and Jill played with them less and less. Now they were going for the real thing: boys with washed faces.

5   In spite of the plastic pearls and the chip of glass centered in the middle, the locket made her look grown-up. I didn't tease her, and she didn't tease me about wearing rummage-sale baseball cleats.

6   All summer Debra wore the locket, and Jill wore one, too, an expensive one her mother had bought at Penney's. But Debra didn't care. She loved the locket whose metal chain left her neck green. Mother admired the locket, said it made her look elegant. That summer, Debra began to complain less and less about doing the dishes.

7   When a pearl fell out, she glued it back in. Another lost its grip and rolled into the floor furnace. She vacuumed the furnace of its ghostly lint,

and shook out the bag and ran her fingers through the stinking hair, lint, broken potato chips, Cocoa Puffs, Cheerios, staples, bits of Kleenex, dead ants, and blue, flowery marble. She searched through the debris until, miraculously, she found the tiny pearl. She glued it back into place and gave her locket a rest.

8   One day, while Debra was at the playground swimming, I snuck into her bedroom to peek in the locket because I knew she kept something in the frame. She was always snapping it open and closed, always feeling pretty happy when she looked down at her breasts, twin mounds that had begun to cast small shadows. When I opened it, slowly because the clasp looked fragile, I saw a face that was mostly an eyeball looking at me. I stared back at the eyeball, and after a moment realized that it was Paul of the Beatles. It was Paul's eyeball, a bit droopy, a bit sad like his songs. Paul was favored by the girls who rode their bikes up and down the block singing "Michelle, ma belle."

9   A few days later I checked the locket again. Paul's eyeball was gone, and now I was staring at a smiling Herman and the Hermits. Herman looked happy. His hair was long and soft, and his teeth were large and charmingly crooked. I smiled wide and thought for a moment that I looked like Herman. A few days later it was back to Paul in a new picture that she had cut out of a magazine. I thumbed through the magazine, emptied of all the famous pop stars, and looked around the room. Almost everything was pink. The furry rug, the canopy bed, the bottles of perfume and nail polish, the much-hugged pillow, everything except the chest of drawers which she intended to paint by fall. I left in a hurry when I heard Debra's bike skid to a halt in the driveway.

10   All summer it was Paul's eyeball, Herman's teeth, and one time Paul Revere with his colonial hat. Debra began to polish her nails and walk more slowly, erect as a ladder. By fall, the chest of drawers was pink and Mother was no longer worried about the green around her neck where the chain rested—an allergic reaction to cheap metal. Debra no longer wore the locket. She was saving Bazooka comics for a camera that came with a free roll of film. She had her first boyfriend and wanted to take his picture on the sly, wanted more than a droopy eyeball or toothy smile. She wanted the entire face, and some of the neck.

READING RESPONSE JOURNAL

1. Summarize "The Locket."

2. Does "The Locket" stir any childhood memories of you and/or your siblings?

3. Does the reading suggest any other topics for you to write about?

4. What are some of the points of contrast between Debra and her brother?

5. Why does the narrator, the brother, want binoculars?

6. The brother does a good bit of snooping and spying on his sister. Why does he do this? What is *he* learning?

7. The brother and sister seem to have a truce on teasing each other about things that each thinks important. For the sister, it is the locket; for her brother, the secondhand baseball cleats. Why do they refrain from teasing each other about these things?

8. The contents of the locket progress from rock star's eyeball to face and neck of the sister's first boyfriend. What does this tell us about her development?

9. What are some examples of humor that Soto uses in his reminiscence?

WRITING FROM READING

Comparison and Contrast

Much of what we learn about Soto's sister comes from the contrasts between them: their different interests, activities, and attitudes. Comparison and contrast, the description of similarities and differences, is a method of development of ideas that we have studied before in "Do Immigrants Ruin America?" (page 111). Look at that reading for examples of this method of writing.

1. Write about how you differ from one of your siblings. Using the method of comparison and contrast, explain specific similarities and differences between the two of you.
2. Much of Soto's piece is about gender roles in early adolescence. Compare and contrast the expectations and demands on each gender in adolescence. What significant differences exist between adolescent boys and girls? Using comparison and contrast, write a paper about life for teen boys and for teen girls.

COLLABORATIVE LEARNING ACTIVITY

List Points of Comparison and Contrast

For each paper read in your group, list the points of comparison and contrast used. In your own prewriting, you may wish to make such a list to guide you—an outline of sorts.

WRITING TIPS

A Strong Beginning

Gary Soto presents the contrast between his sister and himself immediately: "I never liked jewelry. My sister Debra did." Be strong and clear when you announce your writing topic too.

REVIEW

If you are describing two persons, two places, or two ideas, think about comparison and contrast as a way to develop your writing.

Student Writing Bloopers

Over the years, a writing teacher sees a lot of bloopers, a bit like *America's Funniest Home Videos*. Most of the following bloopers are caused by confusion of similar sounds, words that sound alike but have different meanings. For each example, pick out the blooper and write a corrected version:

1. Parents often give kids too much leave way.
   Blooper:

   Correction:

2. The movie industry runs add champagnes to promote Oscar Night.
   Blooper:

   Correction:

3. College campuses dread the discovery of a cereal rapist.
   Blooper:

   Correction:

4. My grandmother paid taxes on her lakefront poverty.
   Blooper:

   Correction:

5. It takes two to tangle and have an unwanted child.
   Blooper:

   Correction:

6. We have the ability to have babies as soon as we begin ministration.
   Blooper:

   Correction:

7. During high school he dropped out and became a drug attic.
   Blooper:

   Correction:

GETTING PUCKED

Michelle Genz

This selection is a lighthearted account contrasting men's and women's attitudes toward dating. Because "Getting Pucked" was written as a magazine article, its paragraphs are short and its sentences succinct to fit narrow columns of space.

VOCABULARY IN CONTEXT

> "*couscous*"—grain of North African origin, similar to cracked wheat
> "*triage* nurse"—emergency nurse who determines severity of injuries and order of treatment

PREREADING

1. Read the title and first paragraph to predict what this piece will say.

Getting Pucked

Michelle Genz

1 What Allison Ward doesn't like about dating is the drill, she says, the whole routine: meeting the guy, then getting asked out, like, Good, you've measured up. Then the whole exercise of dressing up, waiting, making conversation. Besides, for her efforts, she has never had great results.

2 Fact is, at 37, she finds that whatever heartache might come from the occasional Saturday night alone is mild compared to the headache of dating.

3 And this headache topped them all.

4 They'd met at a party, he called her up, they went out once. The drill. And now, the second date. She made him dinner; the grilled dolphin was fine. But he didn't like asparagus. "Less than 4 percent of the world's population likes asparagus," he told her.

5 The couscous, he called "air-rice."

6 Allison kept an open mind. There are probably men who make excellent husbands, after all, who don't like asparagus. "Like George Bush and broccoli," Allison says. Then imagines a second date with George Bush.

7 "Anyway." The game would be fun. Her date, a college coach, was taking her to see the Panthers. She likes hockey. But an hour into the game, the success of the evening is still up in the air. And then something strikes her. At 75 miles per hour.

8   It is a two-inch-wide freezing-cold wad of hard rubber, a hockey puck, launched from the end of a player's stick directly into her forehead. It leaves a bloody dent midway between her hairline and her brow.

9   "We're talking gusher here," says Allison.

10   "Wow," says Allison's date flatly. "We have a problem here."

11   Allison is "stupefied." Someone from the crowd passes her a napkin to sop up the mess. She thinks later she should have checked it for mustard.

12   An usher escorts her out. Quickly. Allison, a publicist, understands: The smack of the puck has transformed her from a cheering fan to a big PR problem.

13   "I was *not* a good visual," says Allison.

14   Her date follows her up the stairs. Someone she knew in the stands later told her he was rolling his eyes as he walked: "Here we go, a girlie thing," is the way Allison interpreted that.

15   At the arena's first-aid station, a guy hands her his card. He is the insurance adjuster for the Florida Panthers, here every night, says Allison, just for this. It was a bad night for getting pucked. After Allison, two other people were hit.

16   "Why didn't you duck?" her date asks her as he drives her to the hospital.

17   "Why weren't you sitting in my seat?" she asked him.

18   He delivers her to the automatic doors of Mount Sinai [Hospital] and waits in the lobby. Small comfort that there is a basketball game airing on the wall TV; the hockey game is going on without him. Clearly he expects things to roll along now. He is wrong. He will spend the next three hours waiting for a woman he hardly knows to be tended to. Nurses report to Allison that he is pacing the floor, flagging down staff, demanding to know what's taking so long. "I'm on the date from hell," she tells Jody, the triage nurse, as she finally starts to sob. He had told her at the outset: he doesn't like high-maintenance women. "I'm a successful business-woman," insists Allison. "Normally, I don't *need* maintenance."

19   "We better call plastics," nurse Jody announces in a somber tone, washing off blood that has dripped down Allison's arms, splattered her Anne Klein pale blue knit top, soaked her expensive pants and permanently stained her Cole-Haan loafers. There is blood in her hair, and under her fingernails. She is minus an earring. Jody wipes the mascara off Allison's cheeks, all that is left of the pre-date optimism in the mirror.

20   It is nearly midnight by the time they stitch her up and turn her back over to her date.

21   "Can I have a drink when I get home?" she asks Jody. Jody recommends it highly.

22   Her date drives her to her Brickell Avenue townhouse, walks her in, decides to stay. He wants to make sure she's OK.

23   "On a scale of one to 10, you were an eight," he tells her proudly. As if she wanted someone keeping score. She pours a double Scotch, puts in a movie, Kevin Costner's *No Way Out*. He stays until 2 in the morning. It doesn't cross her mind that on any other date this might give a guy something to talk about.

24   But then, he had enough already. "Great bar talk," he told her later.

25   Allison got her own trophy. Three weeks later, a Fed Ex box arrived from the Florida Panthers. A wooden plaque, with a puck attached. "I was caught cat-napping by the Florida Panthers, 1995," it says.

26   "I don't want the goddamned puck," she says.

27   Meanwhile the "incident" didn't completely ice the potential romance. Since the hockey game, they've spoken several times on the phone and gone to a party on a boat. When he saw her scar he said, "Wow, it's really pink."

28   OK, so maybe this isn't the one who's going to make all the bells ring. Still, if he calls her again she's inclined to go out with him. What the heck. Beats getting hit in the head with a puck.

READING RESPONSE JOURNAL

1. Write a one-paragraph summary of the whole piece.

2. Does "Getting Pucked" remind you of any "dates from hell" you have endured?

3. Do any other writing topics from the reading come to mind?

4. In what ways does the reading emphasize that Allison's date is a jerk?

5. What does the last paragraph reveal?

WRITING FROM READING

Using Contrast for Humor

"Getting Pucked" employs contrast to draw a humorous picture of Allison's date. After she is hit by the puck, consider Allison's reaction and that of her date:

> "We're talking gusher here," says Allison.
> "Wow," says Allison's date flatly. "We have a problem here."

Later, they have this exchange:

> "Why didn't you duck?" her date asks her as he drives her to the hospital.
> "Why weren't you sitting in my seat?" she asked him.

1. Did you ever go on a "date from hell"? Using the Reporter's Questions, sketch a description of your terrible date.
2. For the dating situation in assignment 1, try to use humor in contrasting your partner with yourself. Did your date say anything stupid like Allison's date who complained that "Less than four percent of the world's population likes asparagus"—after she had made him dinner?

COLLABORATIVE LEARNING ACTIVITY

Sentence Structure in Magazine Writing

The standards of sentence correctness are relaxed for magazine writing. Fragments and run-on sentences are sometimes acceptable in a magazine or newspaper format. In academic (school) writing, standards are stricter.

In your group, search for the sentence fragments in "Getting Pucked." Make a list of them.

WRITING TIPS

Strong "Leads"

In paragraph 3, the writer of "Getting Pucked" has her *lead*, the term for *thesis statement* in magazine articles: "And this headache topped them all." This sentence announces what is to follow. Use strong leads in your papers too.

REVIEW

Use contrast by juxtaposing (placing side by side) dialogue that is humorous.

More Writing Bloopers

1. The young offender needs a row model.
   Blooper:

   Correction:

2. Juan is learning the era of his ways.
   Blooper:

   Correction:

3. Immigrants are coming in groves for free medical benefits.
   Blooper:

   Correction:

4. Shouting "wet bags," the red necks screamed at us along the walk to school.
   Blooper:

   Correction:

5. The pin is mightier than the sword.
   Blooper:

   Correction:

6. It was rumored that incense may have occurred in that family.
   Blooper:

   Correction:

7. Owning a baseball team must have been some type of eagle trip for him.
   Blooper:

   Correction:

ARE GUYS SMART, OR WHAT?

Dave Barry

Barry's article is a tongue-in-cheek satire on men's intelligence.

VOCABULARY IN CONTEXT

> "international *sanctioning* body"—rule-making organization
>
> "*Allied* or *Axis* side"—World War II terms for the opposing sides. Allied side: America, England, and other countries; Axis side: Germany, Japan, and Italy

PREREADING

1. Read the title and predict what the article will say.

Are Guys Smart, or What?

Dave Barry

1   Last July, when a group of Danish researchers announced that men have an average of four billion more brain cells apiece than women, a lot of us guys decided to celebrate this affirmation of our superior intelligence by spending a couple of months drinking beer and throwing furniture off the tops of buildings to see what happened to it.

2   But now we return to find that many women have been ridiculing the Danish discovery. These women have been saying that, OK, maybe males have more brain cells, but it doesn't matter, because males never use their brains to think about anything besides sex.

3   This is not true! Males are perfectly capable of thinking about other topics, as is shown by the following conversation, which was recorded on a cockpit voice recorder just before a recent airplane crash:

4   PILOT: I'll tell you what, that flight attendant has a major pair of . . . Whoa! Looks like engine No. 1 has stopped working!

5   CO-PILOT: Whoa! So have engines No. 2, 3 and 4!

6   PILOT: Whoa! (Pause.) So, how about those 49ers?

7   Another thing I wish to point out is that when men appear to not be thinking, they often *are* thinking, but it's about some issue that women would not understand. For example, back in July there was a widely publicized incident in which an elderly couple set out from their home in Kenilworth, N.J., to drive to a doctor's office 2.8 miles away, with the man,

of course, at the wheel. They were located more than 24 hours later; after having driven an estimated 800 miles through an estimated three states. We all know why this happened. According to the Associated Press story, the man "refused to ask directions during the entire trip."

8   Of course, you women are laughing about this. For years you have made fun of us men for refusing to ask directions. But did it ever occur to you that we have a *reason?* Did it ever occur to you that, with our 4 billion extra brain cells, we might be thinking about something that *you don't know??* That something is this: Under the Rules of Guy Conduct, if you're a guy driving a car, and you don't know how to get where you're going, and you pull over to ask another guy, and he *does* know, then he is legally entitled to *take your woman!* Yes! He can just lean through the window and grab her! That's what the elderly Kenilworth, N.J., guy was trying to prevent, and *you women laughed at him!* I bet you feel silly now!

9   And here's something else to consider: When guys are not using their extra brain cells to protect their loved ones by refusing to ask directions, they are thinking up important new ways to advance human society, such as Big Gun Radio-Controlled Warship Combat.

10   I am not making Big Gun Radio-Controlled Warship Combat up. This is a hobby wherein guys build large, elaborate models of World War II–era fighting ships—some of them 6 feet long—equipped with radio-controlled motors and CO_2-powered cannons that shoot ball bearings. The guys then go out to a pond somewhere to maneuver their ships around and try to sink their opponents' ships by shooting them; when ships are sunk, they're retrieved from the water, repaired and put back into action.

11   We are not talking about a casual pastime here. We are talking about an all-out, totally obsessive guy effort involving clubs, bylaws, an international sanctioning body and many pages of detailed rules and specifications. We are talking about model ships that can cost over $1,000. We are talking about guys spending entire weekends engaging in serious pond action, repeatedly sinking and re-floating their ships.

12   I'm sure many of you women out there are snickering at this. You're saying: "Why go to all that trouble? Why not just stay home and whack your model ship with a hammer?"

13   This is the problem with being a few billion brain cells short: You cannot gasp the essential significance of an activity such as Big Gun Radio-Controlled Warship Combat. I believe this significance was best expressed by Al Boyer, the alert reader who told me about this activity, and who was able, thanks to his large, highly analytical male brain, to pinpoint precisely the quality that defines it: "C-O-O-O-L."

14   I spoke with Phil Sensibaugh, who belongs to the largest warship combat club in the world, which is located, as you might expect, in Albion, Ind., where Phil has a private pond. Phil told me that when you build a ship, you have to decide whether you want to be on the Allied side or the Axis side. He also said that, during battles, there's a lot of trash-talking

between the two sides on the pond banks. For example, according to Phil, if a guy takes a shot at your ship, you might say, "Nice talking, you Axis dog!" Phil also said that he's had guys bring ships from as far away as California to fight on his pond.

15   "A lot of people think this is totally insane," he noted.

16   Not me. I think high heels are insane; I think Big Gun Radio-Controlled Warship Combat is one of the most important advances in guy thinking since the potato gun. To find out more about it, you can check the Internet site at: http://www.pacificnet.net/kehr/big-gunl.htm. If you don't know how to get on the Internet, my advice is: Whatever you do, don't ask directions.

READING RESPONSE JOURNAL

1. Summarize the essay.

2. What do you think you can write about from the article?

3. Do any other ideas from the article interest you for writing?

4. Explain a funny reference in the story.

5. According to Barry, how did men respond to the announcement by Danish researchers that men have more brain cells than women?

6. How does Barry answer women's ridicule of men for failing to ask directions?

7. What is Big Gun Radio-Controlled Warship Combat?

8. What is humorous in Barry's last paragraph?

WRITING FROM READING

The Reporter's Questions

As a writer telling a story, you must always think about what the *reader* does not know. Using the Reporter's Questions—who, what, when, where, and why—will flesh the story out with details for your reader.

1. Have you (as a man) ever refused to ask for directions, or have you (as a woman) been with a man who refused to ask for directions? If so, write a short account of what happened. Remember to use the Reporter's Questions in telling your story.
2. Barry pokes fun at games for men. Can you describe some other "dumb" male activities? Explain the activities step-by-step, what happens first, second, and so on.
3. If you are a male, turn the tables and point out some "dumb" female hobbies. Use the step-by-step method with transitions for each stage of the process you describe.

COLLABORATIVE LEARNING ACTIVITY

Sharing Stories

Get together in groups and tell your favorite "Man refuses to ask for directions" story. Tell what happened because you didn't get directions. Or you might wish to use your description of dumb activities from either assignment 2 or assignment 3 in Writing from Reading to share with your readers.

WRITING TIPS

Repetition

Barry's conclusion "Whatever you do, don't ask directions" echoes his humor from earlier in his piece. In your writing, too, try in your conclusion to remind the reader of something you said earlier in your writing.

REVIEW

The Reporter's Questions always provide you with an outline of what to tell your reader.

More Writing Bloopers

1. To avoid AIDS, absentee is the best way, but not the only way.
   Blooper:

   Correction:

2. Women should reframe from those situations.
   Blooper:

   Correction:

3. According to the Constitution, the judicial branch is not supposed to make the laws. They are to interrupt the law.
   Blooper:

   Correction:

4. My usage of paraphrases has improved from the mistakes of perjury
   of the past.
   Blooper:

   Correction:

5. A person's sexual prevalence is his or her own business.
   Blooper:

   Correction:

6. Learning English will take a person time to get it down path.
   Blooper:

   Correction:

Overcoming Racism

> This section explores powerful readings about racism
> against Hispanics, blacks, Native Americans, and others.
> The readings will lead you to think and to write about
> your attitudes about race in America today.

RACISM AS AN ADULT, from *YELLOW WOMAN AND A BEAUTY OF THE SPIRIT: ESSAYS ON NATIVE AMERICAN LIFE TODAY*

Leslie Marmon Silko

We have read earlier of the embarrassment as a schoolgirl Leslie Marmon
Silko's mixed ancestry caused her with white tourists. What follows is a
description of racism at a much later stage in her life.

VOCABULARY IN CONTEXT

> *"contraband"*—illegal materials, like certain drugs
> *"innate* dignity"—natural, inborn

PREREADING

1. Read the first sentence of paragraph 1 and the last sentence of paragraph 3. Write your guess of what the paragraphs will be about.

Racism as an Adult, from *Yellow Woman and a Beauty of the Spirit: Essays on Native American Life Today*

Leslie Marmo Silko

1 Scarcely a year later, my friend and I were driving south from Albuquerque, returning to Tucson after a paperback book promotion. There are no Border Patrol detention areas on the southbound lanes of I-25, so I settled back and went to sleep while Gus drove. I awakened when I felt the car slowing to a stop. It was nearly midnight on New Mexico State Road 26, a dark lonely stretch of two-lane highway between Hatch and Deming. When I sat up, I saw the headlights and emergency flashers of six vehicles— Border Patrol cars and a Border Patrol van blocked both lanes of the road. Gus stopped the car and rolled down his window to ask what was wrong. But the Border Patrolman and his companion did not reply; instead the first officer ordered us to "step out of the car." Gus asked why we had to get out of the car. His question seemed to set them off—two more Border Patrolmen immediately approached the car and one of them asked, "Are you looking for trouble?" as if he would relish the opportunity.

2   I will never forget that night beside the highway. There was an awful feeling of menace and of violence straining to break loose. It was clear that they would be happy to drag us out of the car if we did not comply. So we both got out of the car and they motioned for us to stand on the shoulder of the road. The night was very dark, and no other traffic had come down the road since they had stopped us. I thought how easy it would be for the Border Patrolmen to shoot us and leave our bodies and car beside the road. There were two other Border Patrolmen by the van. The man who had asked if we were looking for trouble told his partner to "get the dog," and from the back of the white van another Border Patrolman brought a small female German shepherd on a leash. The dog did not heel well enough to suit him, and I saw the dog's handler jerk the leash. They opened the doors of our car and pulled the dog's head into the car, but I saw immediately from the expression in her eyes that the dog hated them, and she would not serve them. When she showed no interest in the inside of the car, they brought her around back to the trunk, near where we were standing. They half-dragged her up into the trunk, but still she did not indicate stowed-away humans or illegal drugs.

3   Their mood got uglier; they seemed outraged that the dog could not find any contraband, and they dragged her over to us and commanded her to sniff our legs and feet. To my relief, the strange anger the INS agents had focused at us now had shifted to the dog. I no longer felt so strongly that we would be murdered. We exchanged looks—the dog and I. She was afraid of what they might do, just as I was. The handler jerked the leash violently as she sniffed us, as if to make her perform better, but the dog

refused to accuse us. The dog had an innate dignity, an integrity that did not permit her to serve those men. I can't forget the expression in her eyes; it was as if she was embarrassed to be associated with them. I had a small amount of medicinal marijuana in my purse that night, but the dog refused to expose me. I am not partial to dogs, but I can't forget the small German shepherd. She saved us from the strange murderous mood of the Border Patrolmen that night.

READING RESPONSE JOURNAL

1. Now read the full selection to summarize the three paragraphs.

2. Is there anything in these paragraphs that you can relate to your own life or the lives of those close to you?

3. Can you find any more to write about in this selection?

4. Why did the Border Patrol stop Silko and Gus's car?

5. What attitude did the Border Patrol officers have toward Silko and Gus?

6. What did Gus do to irritate the border guards?

7. How did the German shepherd help Silko and Gus?

8. What was the Border Patrol searching for?

9. What feeling did Silko have about this incident?

WRITING FROM READING

The Writer's Voice

As humans, we use our experiences to interpret the world, to figure out how we stand in relation to those around us. The writer, in this case Silko, provides us readers not only with facts and information, but also with her interpretation of them, what's called the writer's voice. From the way the border guards treated Gus and her, Silko describes their attitude: "There was an awful feeling of menace and of violence straining to break loose." Contemplating the lonely situation they were in, Silko imagines what could happen to Gus and her: "I thought how easy it would be for the Border Patrolmen to shoot us and leave our bodies and car beside the road." At the end of the last paragraph, Silko reminds us once again of the fear this encounter caused: "She [the German shepherd] saved us from the strange murderous mood of the Border Patrolmen that night." Silko's voice comes through to us here loud and clear.

Write about some situation in which you may have felt menaced or threatened or were made to feel very uncomfortable. Brainstorm about the facts of the experience first and then comment later on what happened, as Silko does. Notice that Silko intertwines, ties together, the facts with her commentary on them. So, relate the facts first and add your interpretation of them right after.

COLLABORATIVE LEARNING ACTIVITY

Listening for Voice

Listen to the other student papers for the voice of the student—his or her attitude and interpretation of the story he or she tells. As audience for other writers, you can help them by listening for a clear, strong voice.

WRITING TIPS

Using Quotes for Vividness

Note that Silko quotes the Border Patrol officers to give her writing more vividness: "One of them [the Border Patrol] asked, 'Are you looking for trouble?' " In your description of menace or danger, try to use people's exact words—quotes—to give your writing more force. Even if you can't remember the exact words used, re-create them (make them up) as closely as you can. This is permissible to do in a narrative like Silko's. If you were writing an argument paper or research paper, you would have to quote your sources verbatim (word for word).

REVIEW

The writer sometimes gives not only facts, but also interpretation or comments on the facts. As you write, occasionally comment on your experience.

MOMMA CONFRONTS THE DENTIST, from *I KNOW WHY THE CAGED BIRD SINGS*

Maya Angelou

This selection is an excerpt from a full-length book, an autobiography by Maya Angelou telling of her life as a young girl growing up in the South. The title of the book, *I Know Why the Caged Bird Sings,* is a line from the poem "We Wear the Mask" by Paul Lawrence Dunbar. Both the poem and the book describe the struggle of African Americans living with the effects and legacy of slavery. Despite the hardships and one terrible trauma in her youth, Angelou writes with liveliness and tenderness—full of humor and compassion. Hers is a fine memoir to read because the writing catches you up and involves you in the daily human struggle to survive— and to overcome.

In addition to her memoirs, Angelou has written poetry and many essays. She read one of her poems at President Clinton's inauguration in 1993.

This excerpt from *I Know Why the Caged Bird Sings* depicts crushing racism overcome by an older African American woman's strength of will.

VOCABULARY IN CONTEXT

"couldn't *aptly* remember"—clearly, plainly

"the pain was my world, an *aura* that haloed me for three feet around"—an air or radiance

"pass the *calaboose*"—slang for jail

"you *contemptuous* scoundrel"—deserving of blame, evil

"to slip into the *vernacular*"—informal speech

"a *crocus sack* of chicken feed"—a gunnysack or burlap sack

"*flounced* into the store"—paraded, promenaded

"her *retributive* sin"—for revenge, payback

PREREADING

1. Read the first two paragraphs and the last two paragraphs, the beginning and end of this story. What will the full story say? Write your prediction.

Momma Confronts the Dentist, from *I Know Why the Caged Bird Sings*

Maya Angelou

1   The Angel of the candy counter had found me out at last, and was exacting excruciating penance for all the stolen Milky Ways, Mounds, Mr. Goodbars and Hersheys with Almonds. I had two cavities that were rotten to the gums. The pain was beyond the bailiwick of crushed aspirins or oil of cloves. Only one thing could help me, so I prayed earnestly that I'd be allowed to sit under the house and have the building collapse on my left jaw. Since there was no Negro dentist in Stamps, nor doctor either, for that matter, Momma had dealt with previous toothaches by pulling them out (a string tied to the tooth with the other end looped over her fist), pain killers and prayer. In this particular instance the medicine had proved ineffective; there wasn't enough enamel left to hook a string on, and the prayers were being ignored because the Balancing Angel was blocking their passage.

2   I lived a few days and nights in blinding pain, not so much toying with as seriously considering the idea of jumping in the well, and Momma decided I had to be taken to a dentist. The nearest Negro dentist was in Texarkana, twenty-five miles away, and I was certain that I'd be dead long before we reached half the distance. Momma said we'd go to Dr. Lincoln, right in Stamps, and he'd take care of me. She said he owed her a favor.

3   I knew that there were a number of whitefolks in town that owed her favors. Bailey and I had seen the books which showed how she had lent money to Blacks and whites alike during the Depression, and most still owed her. But I couldn't aptly remember seeing Dr. Lincoln's name, nor had I ever heard of a Negro's going to him as a patient. However, Momma said we were going, and put water on the stove for our baths. I had never been to a doctor, so she told me that after the bath (which would make my mouth feel better) I had to put on freshly starched and ironed underclothes from inside out. The ache failed to respond to the bath, and I knew then that the pain was more serious than that which anyone had ever suffered.

4   Before we left the Store, she ordered me to brush my teeth and then wash my mouth with Listerine. The idea of even opening my clamped jaws increased the pain, but upon her explanation that when you go to a doctor you have to clean yourself all over, but most especially the part that's to be examined, I screwed up my courage and unlocked my teeth. The cool air in my mouth and the jarring of my molars dislodged what little remained of my reason. I had frozen to the pain, my family nearly had to tie me down to take the toothbrush away. It was no small effort to get me started on the road to the dentist. Momma spoke to all the passers-by,

but didn't stop to chat. She explained over her shoulder that we were going to the doctor and she'd "pass the time of day" on our way home.

5   Until we reached the pond the pain was my world, an aura that haloed me for three feet around. Crossing the bridge into whitefolks' country, pieces of sanity pushed themselves forward. I had to stop moaning and start walking straight. The white towel, which was drawn under my chin and tied over my head, had to be arranged. If one was dying, it had to be done in style if the dying took place in whitefolks' part of town.

6   On the other side of the bridge the ache seemed to lessen as if a whitebreeze blew off the whitefolks and cushioned everything in their neighborhood—including my jaw. The gravel road was smoother, the stones smaller and the tree branches hung down around the path and nearly covered us. If the pain didn't diminish then, the familiar yet strange sights hypnotized me into believing that it had.

7   But my head continued to throb with the measured insistence of a bass drum, and how could a toothache pass the calaboose, hear the songs of the prisoners, their blues and laughter, and not be changed? How could one or two or even a mouthful of angry tooth roots meet a wagonload of powhitetrash children, endure their idiotic snobbery and not feel less important?

8   Behind the building which housed the dentist's office ran a small path used by servants and those tradespeople who catered to the butcher and Stamps' one restaurant. Momma and I followed that lane to the backstairs of Dentist Lincoln's office. The sun was bright and gave the day a hard reality as we climbed up the steps to the second floor.

9   Momma knocked on the back door and a young white girl opened it to show surprise at seeing us there. Momma said she wanted to see Dentist Lincoln and to tell him Annie was there. The girl closed the door firmly. Now the humiliation of hearing Momma describe herself as if she had no last name to the young white girl was equal to the physical pain. It seemed terribly unfair to have a toothache and a headache and have to bear at the same time the heavy burden of Blackness.

10   It was always possible that the teeth would quiet down and maybe drop out of their own accord. Momma said we would wait. We leaned in the harsh sunlight on the shaky railings of the dentist's back porch for over an hour.

11   He opened the door and looked at Momma. "Well, Annie, what can I do for you?"

12   He didn't see the towel around my jaw or notice my swollen face.

13   Momma said, "Dentist Lincoln. It's my grandbaby here. She got two rotten teeth that's giving her a fit."

14   She waited for him to acknowledge the truth of her statement. He made no comment, orally or facially.

15   "She had this toothache purt' near four days now, and today I said, 'Young lady, you going to the Dentist.' "

16　"Annie?"

17　"Yes, sir, Dentist Lincoln."

18　He was choosing words the way people hunt for shells. "Annie, you know I don't treat nigra, colored people."

19　"I know, Dentist Lincoln. But this here is just my little grandbaby, and she ain't gone be no trouble to you . . ."

20　"Annie, everybody has a policy. In this world you have to have a policy. Now, my policy is I don't treat colored people."

21　The sun had baked the oil out of Momma's skin and melted the Vaseline in her hair. She shone greasily as she leaned out of the dentist's shadow.

22　"Seem like to me, Dentist Lincoln, you might look after her, she ain't nothing but a little mite. And seems like maybe you owe me a favor or two."

23　He reddened slightly. "Favor or no favor. The money has all been repaid to you and that's the end of it. Sorry, Annie." He had his hand on the doorknob. "Sorry." His voice was a bit kinder on the second "Sorry," as if he really was.

24　Momma said, "I wouldn't press on you like this for myself but I can't take No. Not for my grandbaby. When you come to borrow my money you didn't have to beg. You asked me, and I lent it. Now, it wasn't my policy. I ain't no moneylender, but you stood to lose this building and I tried to help you out."

25　"It's been paid, and raising your voice won't make me change my mind. My policy . . ." He let go of the door and stepped nearer Momma. The three of us were crowded on the small landing. "Annie, my policy is I'd rather stick my hand in a dog's mouth than in a nigger's."

26　He had never once looked at me. He turned his back and went through the door into the cool beyond. Momma backed up inside herself for a few minutes. I forgot everything except her face which was almost a new one to me. She leaned over and took the doorknob, and in her everyday soft voice she said, "Sister, go on downstairs. Wait for me. I'll be there directly."

27　Under the most common of circumstances I knew it did no good to argue with Momma. So I walked down the steep stairs, afraid to look back and afraid not to do so. I turned as the door slammed, and she was gone.

28　*Momma walked in that room as if she owned it. She shoved that silly nurse aside with one hand and strode into the dentist's office. He was sitting in his chair, sharpening his mean instruments and putting extra sting into his medicines. Her eyes were blazing like live coals and her arms had doubled themselves in length. He looked up at her just before she caught him by the collar of his white jacket.*

29　*"Stand up when you see a lady, you contemptuous scoundrel." Her tongue had thinned and the words rolled off well enunciated. Enunciated and sharp like little claps of thunder.*

30   *The dentist had no choice but to stand at R.O.T.C. attention. His head dropped after a minute and his voice was humble. "Yes, ma'am, Mrs. Henderson."*

31   *"You knave, do you think you acted like a gentleman, speaking to me like that in front of my granddaughter?" She didn't shake him, although she had the power. She simple held him upright.*

32   *"No, ma'am, Mrs. Henderson."*

33   *"No, ma'am, Mrs. Henderson, what?" Then she did give him the tiniest of shakes, but because of her strength the action set his head and arms to shaking loose on the ends of his body. He stuttered much worse than Uncle Willie. "No, ma'am. Mrs. Henderson, I'm sorry."*

34   *With just an edge of her disgust showing, Momma slung him back in his dentist's chair. "Sorry is as sorry does, and you're about the sorriest dentist I ever laid my eyes on." (She could afford to slip into the vernacular because she had such eloquent command of English.)*

35   *"I didn't ask you to apologize in front of Marguerite, because I don't want her to know my power, but I order you, now and herewith. Leave Stamps by sundown."*

36   *"Mrs. Henderson, I can't get my equipment . . ." He was shaking terribly now.*

37   *"Now, that brings me to my second order. You will never again practice dentistry. Never! When you get settled in your next place, you will be a vegetarian caring for dogs with the mange, cats with the cholera and cows with the epizootic. Is that clear?"*

38   *The saliva ran down his chin and his eyes filled with tears. "Yes, ma'am. Thank you for not killing me. Thank you, Mrs. Henderson."*

39   *Momma pulled herself back from being ten feet tall with eight-foot arms and said, "You're welcome for nothing, you varlet, I wouldn't waste a killing on the likes of you."*

40   *On her way out she waved her handkerchief at the nurse and turned her into a crocus sack of chicken feed.*

41   Momma looked tired when she came down the stairs, but who wouldn't be tired if they had gone through what she had. She came close to me and adjusted the towel under my jaw (I had forgotten the toothache; I only knew that she made her hands gentle in order not to awaken the pain). She took my hand. Her voice never changed. "Come on, Sister."

42   I reckoned we were going home where she would concoct a brew to eliminate the pain and maybe give me new teeth too. New teeth that would grow overnight out of my gums. She led me toward the drugstore, which was in the opposite direction from the Store. "I'm taking you to Dentist Baker in Texarkana."

43   I was glad after all that that I had bathed and put on Mum and Cashmere Bouquet talcum powder. It was a wonderful surprise. My toothache had quieted to solemn pain, Momma had obliterated the evil white man, and we were going on a trip to Texarkana, just the two of us.

44   On the Greyhound she took an inside seat in the back, and I sat beside her. I was so proud of being her granddaughter and sure that some of her magic must have come down to me. She asked if I was scared. I only shook my head and leaned over on her cool brown upper arm. There was no chance that a dentist, especially a Negro dentist, would dare hurt me then. Not with Momma there. The trip was uneventful, except that she put her arm around me, which was very unusual for Momma to do.

45   The dentist showed me the medicine and the needle before he deadened my gums, but if he hadn't I wouldn't have worried. Momma stood right behind him. Her arms were folded and she checked on everything he did. The teeth were extracted and she bought me an ice cream cone from the side window of a drug counter. The trip back to Stamps was quiet, except that I had to spit into a very small empty snuff can which she had gotten for me and it was difficult with the bus humping and jerking on our country roads.

46   At home, I was given a warm salt solution, and when I washed out my mouth I showed Bailey the empty holes, where the clotted blood sat like filling in a pie crust. He said I was quite brave, and that was my cue to reveal our confrontation with the peckerwood dentist and Momma's incredible powers.

47   I had to admit that I didn't hear the conversation, but what else could she have said than what I said she said? What else done? He agreed with my analysis in a lukewarm way, and I happily (after all, I'd been sick) flounced into the Store. Momma was preparing our evening meal and Uncle Willie leaned on the door sill. She gave her version.

48   "Dentist Lincoln got right uppity. Said he'd rather put his hand in a dog's mouth. And when I reminded him of the favor, he brushed it off like a piece of lint. Well, I sent Sister downstairs and went inside. I hadn't never been in his office before, but I found the door to where he takes out teeth, and him and the nurse was in there thick as thieves. I just stood there till he caught sight of me." Crash bang went the pots on the stove. "He jumped just like he was sitting on a pin. He said, 'Annie, I done tole you, I ain't gonna mess round in no niggah's mouth.' I said, 'Somebody's got to do it then,' and he said, 'Take her to Texarkana to the colored dentist' and that's when I said, 'If you paid me my money I could afford to take her.' He said, 'It's all been paid.' I tole him everything but the interest had been paid. He said, ' 'Twasn't no interest.' I said. ' 'Tis now. I'll take ten dollars as payment in full.' You know, Willie, it wasn't no right thing to do, 'cause I lent that money without thinking about it.

49   "He tole that little snippity nurse of his'n to give me ten dollars and make me sign a 'paid in full' receipt. She gave it to me and I signed the papers. Even though by rights he was paid up before, I figger, he gonna be that kind of nasty, he gonna have to pay for it."

50   Momma and her son laughed and laughed over the white man's evilness and her retributive sin.

51   I preferred, much preferred, my version.

READING RESPONSE JOURNAL

1. Write a summary of the reading.

2. How does this story relate to your life?

3. What more can you write about here?

4. How had Momma handled earlier toothaches?

5. Why did Momma think she could bring Maya to the white dentist in Stamps?

6. Why did Maya "stop moaning and start walking straight" when she reached the white neighborhood?

7. Why was Maya embarrassed when Momma said to the white nurse to tell the dentist that "Annie" was here?

8. Why does Angelou break into italicized type (a font or print that slants to the right) beginning at paragraph 28?

9. What is the last straw in her conversation with the dentist that forces Momma to confront him even further?

10. How does Momma justify her "retributive sin" in getting the $10 from the dentist?

11. Why did Maya prefer her version of events to Momma's?

WRITING FROM READING

Development by Contrast

Maya Angelou uses contrast to create an imaginary version of Momma's confrontation with Dentist Lincoln. Maya describes what she wished had happened, not what really happened. By using italicized type, Angelou tells the reader that what follows is different—it's not real, but exists only in the mind of the writer.

1. Think back to some confrontation you've had in your life and write two versions of what happened: first, what you *wished* you had said, and second, what you *really* said.
2. Dentist Lincoln's prejudice is shocking—even for his day. Think of the worst prejudice that you ever experienced or witnessed and write about it. Use the Reporter's Questions—who, what, when, where, and why—to make the incident clear.

COLLABORATIVE LEARNING ACTIVITY

Checking for Structure

After finishing your writing, read it to the group. Ask them to check if your writing has an obvious beginning, middle, and end.

WRITING TIPS

Using Clear Dialogue

Using good dialogue, or conversation, is important in telling a story well. To write good dialogue, make clear who the speaker is and use a new paragraph every time you change speakers. Notice that lines of dialogue are like human speech, sometimes short, sometimes longer:

"Annie?"

"Yes, sir, Dentist Lincoln."

He was choosing words the way people hunt for shells. "Annie, you know I don't treat nigra, colored people."

Now go back to your writing about your confrontation. Make sure you have a new paragraph for each new speaker and that you have made clear in every line who the speaker is.

VOCABULARY DEVELOPMENT

Look at the beginning of the first paragraph:

The Angel of the candy counter had found me out at last, and was exacting *excruciating* penance for all the stolen Milky Ways, Mounds, Mr. Goodbars and Hersheys with Almonds. I had two cavities that were rotten to the gums. The pain was beyond the *bailiwick* of crushed aspirins or oil of cloves.

What is the context, the situation, described here with the little girl?

The girl's "rotten cavities" were her "penance." How does that help you to figure out the meaning of "*excruciating* penance"? What do you think "excruciating" means?

Did the little girl find any relief for her toothache in aspirins or oil of cloves? If not, what does it mean that her "pain was beyond the *bailiwick*" of these two medicines? Try to guess what "bailiwick" means.

Look up these words in the dictionary to see how close you were to their meaning.

REVIEW

As a writer, you make things more powerful for your reader when you use dialogue, the speech of real people. Using dialogue also adds to human interest because we want to know what other people say.

JUST WALK ON BY: A BLACK MAN PONDERS HIS POWER TO ALTER PUBLIC SPACE

Brent Staples

This is an essay by a black man about how people in public, total strangers, perceive him because of his race and gender.

VOCABULARY IN CONTEXT

"*billowing* hair"—blowing, expanding

"*menacingly* close"—dangerously

"*unwieldy* inheritance"—hard to carry or adjust to

"*insomnia*"—inability to sleep

"*tyranny*"—control, threat, danger

"*indistinguishable* from the muggers"—not apparently different, appearing the same

"vast, *unnerving* gulf"—make scared or nervous

"an *errant* move"—wrong, mistaken

"*taut*"—tense

"*extols*"—praise

"*warrenlike*"—narrow, cramped

"*solace*"—comfort

"a fearsome *entity*"—object, thing

"*lethality*"—deadliness

"*attributed*"—assigned, gave

"*retrospect*"—looking back

"*consummation*"—completion, fulfillment

"*bravado*"—appearance of bravery

"*ad hoc posse*"—hastily formed gang

"*labyrinthine* halls"—like a puzzle or maze

"*cursory*"—quick, fast

"wide *berth*"—room, space

"*skittish*"—nervous, worried

"*congenial*"—friendly, agreeable

"late-evening *constitutionals*"—walks

PREREADING

1. Read the first and last paragraphs; with the help of the long title, predict what the essay will say.

Just Walk On By: A Black Man Ponders His Power to Alter Public Space

Brent Staples

1   My first victim was a woman—white, well dressed, probably in her early twenties. I came upon her late one evening on a deserted street in Hyde Park, a relatively affluent neighborhood in an otherwise mean, impoverished section of Chicago. As I swung onto the avenue behind her, there seemed to be a discreet, uninflammatory distance between us. Not so. She cast back a worried glance. To her, the youngish black man—a broad six feet two inches with a beard and billowing hair, both hands shoved into the pockets of a bulky military jacket—seemed menacingly close. After a few more quick glimpses, she picked up her pace and was soon running in earnest. Within seconds she disappeared into a cross street.

2   That was more than a decade ago. I was twenty-two years old, a graduate student newly arrived at the University of Chicago. It was in the echo of that terrified woman's footfalls that I first began to know the unwieldy inheritance I'd come into—the ability to alter public space in ugly ways. It was clear that she thought herself the quarry of a mugger, a rapist, or worse. Suffering a bout of insomnia, however, I was stalking sleep, not defenseless wayfarers. As a softy who is scarcely able to take a knife to a raw chicken—let alone hold it to a person's throat—I was surprised, embarrassed, and dismayed all at once. Her flight made me feel like an accomplice in tyranny. It also made it clear that I was indistinguishable from the muggers who occasionally seeped into the area from the surrounding ghetto. That first encounter, and those that followed, signified that a vast, unnerving gulf lay between nighttime pedestrians—particularly women—and me. And I soon gathered that being perceived as dangerous is a hazard in itself. I only needed to turn a corner into a dicey situation, or crowd some frightened, armed person in a foyer somewhere, or make an errant move after being pulled over by a policeman. Where fear and weapons meet—and they often do in urban America—there is always the possibility of death.

3   In that first year, my first away from my hometown, I was to become thoroughly familiar with the language of fear. At dark, shadowy intersections in Chicago, I could cross in front of a car stopped at a traffic light and elicit the *thunk, thunk, thunk, thunk* of the driver—black, white, male, or female—hammering down the door locks. On less traveled streets after dark, I grew accustomed to but never comfortable with people who crossed

to the other side of the street rather than pass me. Then there were the standard unpleasantries with police, doormen, bouncers, cabdrivers, and others whose business is to screen out troublesome individuals *before* there is any nastiness.

4   I moved to New York nearly two years ago and I have remained an avid night walker. In central Manhattan, the near-constant crowd cover minimizes tense one-on-one street encounters. Elsewhere—visiting friends in SoHo, where sidewalks are narrow and tightly spaced buildings shut out the sky—things can get very taut indeed.

5   Black men have a firm place in New York mugging literature. Norman Podhoretz in his famed (or infamous) 1963 essay, "My Negro Problem—And Ours," recalls growing up in terror of black males; they "were tougher than we were, more ruthless," he writes—and as an adult on the Upper West Side of Manhattan, he continues, he cannot constrain his nervousness when he meets black men on certain streets. Similarly, a decade later, the essayist and novelist Edward Hoagland extols a New York where once "Negro bitterness bore down mainly on other Negroes." Where some see mere panhandlers, Hoagland sees "a mugger who is clearly screwing up his nerve to do more than just *ask* for money." But Hoagland has "the New Yorker's quick-hunch posture for broken-field maneuvering," and the bad guy swerves away.

6   I often witness that "hunch posture," from women after dark on the warrenlike streets of Brooklyn where I live. They seem to set their faces on neutral and, with their purse straps strung across their chests bandolier style, they forge ahead as though bracing themselves against being tackled. I understand, of course, that the danger they perceive is not a hallucination. Women are particularly vulnerable to street violence, and young black males are drastically overrepresented among the perpetrators of that violence. Yet these truths are no solace against the kind of alienation that comes of being ever the suspect, against being set apart, a fearsome entity with whom pedestrians avoid making eye contact.

7   It is not altogether clear to me how I reached the ripe old age of twenty-two without being conscious of the lethality nighttime pedestrians attributed to me. Perhaps it was because in Chester, Pennsylvania, the small, angry industrial town where I came of age in the 1960s, I was scarcely noticeable against a backdrop of gang warfare, street knifings, and murders. I grew up one of the good boys, had perhaps a half-dozen fistfights. In retrospect, my shyness of combat has clear sources.

8   Many things go into the making of a young thug. One of those things is the consummation of the male romance with the power to intimidate. An infant discovers that random flailings send the baby bottle flying out of the crib and crashing to the floor. Delighted, the joyful babe repeats those motions again and again, seeking to duplicate the feat. Just so, I recall the points at which some of my boyhood friends were finally seduced by the perception of themselves as tough guys. When a mark cowered and surrendered his money without resistance, myth and real-

ity merged—and paid off. It is, after all, only manly to embrace the power to frighten and intimidate. We, as men, are not supposed to give an inch of our lane on the highway; we are to seize the fighter's edge in work and in play and even in love; we are to be valiant in the face of hostile forces.

9   Unfortunately, poor and powerless young men seem to take all this nonsense literally. As a boy, I saw countless tough guys locked away; I have since buried several, too. They were babies, really—a teenage cousin, a brother of twenty-two, a childhood friend in his mid-twenties—all gone down in episodes of bravado played out in the streets. I came to doubt the virtues of intimidation early on. I chose, perhaps even unconsciously, to remain a shadow—timid, but a survivor.

10   The fearsomeness mistakenly attributed to me in public places often has a perilous flavor. The most frightening of these confusions occurred in the late 1970s and early 1980s when I worked as a journalist in Chicago. One day, rushing into the office of a magazine I was writing for with a deadline story in hand, I was mistaken for a burglar. The office manager called security and, with an ad hoc posse, pursued me through the labyrinthine halls, nearly to my editor's door. I had no way of proving who I was. I could only move briskly toward the company of someone who knew me.

11   Another time I was on assignment for a local paper and killing time before an interview. I entered a jewelry store on the city's affluent Near North Side. The proprietor excused herself and returned with an enormous red Doberman pinscher straining at the end of a leash. She stood, the dog extended toward me, silent to my questions, her eyes bulging nearly out of her head. I took a cursory look around, nodded, and bade her good night. Relatively speaking, however, I never fared as badly as another black male journalist. He went to nearby Waukegan, Illinois, a couple of summers ago to work on a story about a murderer who was born there. Mistaking the reporter for the killer, police hauled him from his car at gunpoint and but for his press credentials would probably have tried to book him. Such episodes are not uncommon. Black men trade tales like this all the time. . . .

12   I began to take precautions to make myself less threatening. I move about with care, particularly late in the evening. I give a wide berth to nervous people on subway platforms during the wee hours, particularly when I have exchanged business clothes for jeans. If I happen to be entering a building behind some people who appear skittish, I may walk by, letting them clear the lobby before I return, so as not to seem to be following them. I have been calm and extremely congenial on those rare occasions when I've been pulled over by the police.

13   And on late-evening constitutionals along streets less traveled by, I employ what has proved to be an excellent tension-reducing measure: I whistle melodies from Beethoven and Vivaldi and the more popular classical composers. Even steely New Yorkers hunching toward nighttime destinations seem to relax, and occasionally they even join in the tune. Virtually everybody seems to sense that a mugger wouldn't be warbling

bright, sunny selections from Vivaldi's *Four Seasons.* It is my equivalent of the cowbell that hikers wear when they know they are in bear country.

READING RESPONSE JOURNAL

1. Write a one-paragraph summary of the article.

2. How does the essay relate to your life?

3. Is there more to write on?

4. How does the writer fool us in his first sentence?

5. What does Staples mean by the "unwieldy inheritance I'd come into—the ability to alter public space in ugly ways"?

6. How did Staples's ability to cause fear in public become a danger to him?

7. How does Staples explain his lack of aggression?

8. How does Staples believe that thugs are made?

9. What personal examples does Staples give of bad results of street bravado?

10. What powerful examples of personal danger from being a black man in public does Staples give?

11. What steps does Staples take today to seem nonthreatening?

WRITING FROM READING

Getting the Reader's Attention

It is important for a writer to get the reader's attention in the beginning of a paper. How does Staples accomplish this? An attention-getting incident or story can be a great way to begin a serious essay, like one on racism. If you are writing a paper on racism, think of an incident or story that you could lead with.

Notice that in Staples's essay, his thesis concludes the account of his first "victim": "That first encounter, and those that followed, signified that a vast, unnerving gulf lay between nighttime pedestrians—particularly women—and me."

The point here is that the example, incident, or story comes first—before the thesis.

1. In writing a paper on racism, try to follow Staples's pattern: an example or story before your thesis.

   To get started, try to think of any street danger you have ever experienced. Were you, one of your family, or one of your friends ever threatened in public or perceived as a threat? Prewrite about your incident, perhaps using the Reporter's Questions of who, what, when, where, and why. Then after some more thinking and prewriting, write a longer paper detailing your example of street danger. Like Staples, develop a thesis that shapes the story and examples you use.

2. Staples certainly gets our attention and sympathy in this essay, but let's look further at the situation. From the "victim's" perspective, how do you deal with a tall black man who appears to be following you on some deserted street? Explain what strategies you might use if you were Staples's first "victim" as in paragraph 1? Prewrite about this before writing a longer paper.

COLLABORATIVE LEARNING ACTIVITY

Brainstorming as a Group

Staples's essay is disturbing, but enlightening. Perhaps as a group you could brainstorm about some of the racial incidents you have experienced, heard about, or learned from the news. Try to pick out one such incident, prewrite about it, and share it with your group. It may be useful to talk your story through with your group before doing any writing.

WRITING TIPS

Suggesting Solutions

As grim as Staples's account is, he ends his paper with some solutions to his dilemma: trying to appear nonthreatening in crowds, being affable to police, and even whistling classical tunes. This is a natural order—that of problem-solution—but one that you have to teach yourself to use whenever you are describing problems. If you can't think of solutions, you should say that.

VOCABULARY DEVELOPMENT

Staples describes a place where he once lived: "Hyde Park, a relatively *affluent* neighborhood in an otherwise mean, *impoverished* section of Chicago." What do these italicized words mean? Knowing one of them helps with the meaning of the other. If you know that "impoverished" means "poor," then what must "affluent" mean?

Staples explains his trouble walking the streets: "As I swung onto the avenue behind her, there seemed to be a *discreet,* uninflammatory distance between us." If we know what *uninflammatory* means, it will help us to figure out *discreet.* For example, what is an "inflammatory" speech? It is speech that arouses excitement or anger. The prefix *un-* does what to the meaning of a word? *Inflammatory*—"arousing anger"; *uninflammatory*—"*not* arousing anger." So, the distance between Staples and the woman walking ahead of him is "safe"—"uninflammatory." And the meaning of *discreet* is closely related, "safe, careful, cautious."

REVIEW

Strong stories or incidents at the beginning of a paper will get the reader's attention and should lead to a clear thesis that expresses the point of your attention-getting examples.

NATIVE AMERICAN PREJUDICE, from *BLUE HIGHWAYS*

William Least Heat Moon

William Least Heat Moon, a college English teacher of part–Native American ancestry, decided to walk away from his job and life to discover himself on America's backroads. His book *Blue Highways* is his journal of his travels. In this part of his journey, he makes his way through "Indian country," the Navajo and Hopi reservations in Utah, New Mexico, Colorado, and Arizona where he confronts questions about his Indian heritage.

VOCABULARY

"*Anglo(s)*"—Indian term for "white(s)"

"*BIA*"—abbreviation for "Bureau of Indian Affairs," the government agency responsible for Indian matters.

"*intricately*"—"carefully, in a complex way"

"*migrations*"—"movements from place to place"

"*a world as technological* as medicine is"—"built on technology, use of machines like computers"

PREREADING

1. Read the first paragraph of this selection. Predict what the following paragraphs will say.
2. Now read the first two paragraphs of the second part of this selection (paragraphs 5 and 6) and predict what will follow.

Native American Prejudice, from *Blue Highways*

William Least Heat Moon

1 Tuba City, founded by Mormon missionaries as an agency and named after a Hopi chieftain although now mostly a Navajo town, caught the sandstorm full face. As I filled the gas tank, I tried to stay behind the van, but gritty gusts whipped around the corners and stung me and forced my eyes shut. School was just out, and children, shirts pulled over their heads, ran for the trading post, where old Navajo men who had been sitting outside took cover as the sand changed the air to matter. I ducked in too. The place was like an A&P, TG&Y, and craft center.

2   In viridescent velveteen blouses and violescent nineteenth-century skirts, Navajo women of ample body, each laden with silver and turquoise bracelets, necklaces, and rings—not the trading post variety but heavy bands gleaming under the patina of long wear—reeled off yards of fabric. The children, like schoolkids anywhere, milled around the candy; they spoke only English. But the old men, now standing at the plate glass windows and looking into the brown wind, popped and puffed out the ancient words. I've read that Navajo, a language related to that of the Indians of Alaska and northwest Canada, has no curse words unless you consider "coyote" cursing. By comparison with other native tongues, it's remarkably free of English and Spanish; a Navajo mechanic, for example, has more than two hundred purely Navajo terms to describe automobile parts. And it might be Navajo that will greet the first extraterrestrial ears to hear from planet Earth: on board each *Voyager* spacecraft traveling toward the edge of the solar system and beyond is a gold-plated, long-playing record; following an aria from Mozart's *Magic Flute* and Chuck Berry's "Johnny B. Goode," is a Navajo night chant, music the conquistadors heard.

3   Intimidated by my ignorance of Navajo and by fear of the contempt that full-bloods often show lesser bloods, I again failed to stir a conversation. After the storm blew on east, I followed the old men back outside, where they squatted to watch the day take up the weather of an hour earlier. To one with a great round head like an earthen pot, I said, "Is the storm finished now?" He looked at me, then slowly turned his head, while the others examined before them things in the air invisible to me.

4   I took a highway down the mesa into a valley of the Painted Desert, where wind had textured big drifts of orange sand into rills. U.S. 89 ran north along the Echo Cliffs. Goats grazed in stubble by the roadsides, and to the west a horseman moved his sheep. Hogans here stood alone; they were not ceremonial lodges but homes. For miles at the highway edges sat little cardboard and scrapwood ramadas, each with a wind-blasted sign advertising jewelry and cedar beads. In another era, white men came in wagons to trade beads to Indians; now they came in station-wagons and bought beads. History may repeat, but sometimes things get turned around in the process. . . .

5   In the cafeteria of Southern Utah State College, I bought a breakfast of scrambled eggs, pancakes, bacon, oatmeal, grapefruit, orange juice, milk, and a cinnamon roll. A celebration of being alive. I was full of victory.

6   Across the table sat an Indian student named Kenrick Fritz, who was studying chemistry and wanted to become a physician. He had grown up in Moenkopi, Arizona, just across the highway from Tuba City. I said, "Are you Navajo or Hopi?"

7   "Hopi. You can tell by my size. Hopis are smaller than Navajos."

8   His voice was gentle, his words considered, and smile timid. He seemed open to questions. "Fritz doesn't sound like a Hopi name."

9   "My father took it when he was in the Army in the Second World War. Hopis usually have Anglo first names and long Hopi last names that are hard for other people to pronounce."

10   I told him of my difficulty in rousing a conversation in Tuba City. He said, "I can't speak for Navajos about prejudice, but I know Hopis who believe we survived Spaniards, missionaries, a thousand years of other Indians, even the BIA. But tourists?" He smiled. "Smallpox would be better."

11   "Do you—yourself—think most whites are prejudiced against Indians?"

12   "About fifty-fifty. Half show contempt because they saw a drunk squaw at the Circle K. Another half think we're noble savages—they may be worse because if an Indian makes a mistake they hate him for being human. Who wants to be somebody's ideal myth?"

13   "My grandfather used to say the Big Vision made the Indian, but the white man invented him."

14   "Relations are okay here, but I wouldn't call them good, and I'm not one to go around looking for prejudice. I try not to."

15   "Maybe you're more tolerant of Anglo ways than some others."

16   "Could be. I mean, I *am* studying to be a doctor and not a medicine man. But I'm no apple Indian—red outside and white underneath. I lived up in Brigham City, Utah, when I went to the Intermountain School run by the BIA. It was too easy though. Too much time to goof around. So I switched to Box Elder—that's a public school. I learned there. And I lived in Dallas a few months. What I'm saying is that I've lived on Hopi land and I've lived away. I hear Indians talk about being red all the way through criticizing others for acting like Anglos, and all the time they're sitting in a pickup at a drive-in. But don't tell them to trade the truck for a horse."

17   "The Spanish brought the horse."

18   He nodded. "To me, being Indian means being responsible to my people. Helping with the best tools. Who invented penicillin doesn't matter."

19   "What happens after you finish school?"

20   "I used to want out of Tuba, but since I've been away, I've come to see how our land really is our Sacred Circle—it's our strength. Now, I want to go back and practice general medicine. At the Indian hospital in Tuba where my mother and sister are nurse's aides, there aren't any Indian M.D.'s, and that's no good. I don't respect people who don't help themselves. Hopi land is no place to make big money, but I'm not interested anyway."

21   "You don't use the word *reservation.*"

22   "We don't think of it as a reservation since we were never ordered there. We found it through Hopi prophecies. We're unusual because we've always held onto our original land—most of it anyway. One time my grandfather pointed out the old boundaries to me. We were way up on a mesa. I've forgotten what they are except for the San Francisco Peaks. But in the last eighty years, the government's given a lot of our land to Navajos, and now we're in a hard spot—eight thousand Hopis are surrounded and outnumbered twenty-five to one. I don't begrudge the Navajo anything, but I think Hopis

should be in on making the decisions. Maybe you know that Congress didn't even admit Indians to citizenship until about nineteen twenty. Incredible— live someplace a thousand years and then find out you're a foreigner."

23   "I know an Osage who says, 'Don't Americanize me and I won't Americanize you.' He means everybody in the country came from someplace else."

24   "Hopi legends are full of migrations."

25   "Will other Hopis be suspicious of you when you go home as a doctor?"

26   "Some might be, but not my family. But for a lot of Hopis, the worst thing to call a man is *kahopi,* 'not Hopi.' Nowadays, though, we all have to choose either the new ways or the Hopi way, and it's split up whole villages. A lot of us try to find the best in both places. We've always learned from other people. If we hadn't, we'd be extinct like some other tribes."

27   "Medicine's a pretty good survival technique."

28   "Sure, but I also like Jethro Tull and the Moody Blues. That's not survival."

29   "Is the old religion a survival technique?"

30   "If you live it."

31   "Do you?"

32   "Most Hopis follow our religion, at least in some ways, because it reminds us who we are and it's part of the land. I'll tell you, in the rainy season when the desert turns green, it's beautiful there. The land is medicine too."

33   "If you don't mind telling me, what's the religion like?"

34   "Like any religion in one way—different clans believe different things."

35   "There must be something they all share, something common."

36   "That's hard to say."

37   "Could you try?"

38   He thought a moment. "Maybe the idea of harmony. And the way a Hopi prays. A good life, a harmonious life, is a prayer. We don't just pray for ourselves, we pray for all things. We're famous for the Snake Dances, but a lot of people don't realize those ceremonies are prayers for rain and crops, prayers for life. We also pray for rain by sitting and thinking about rain. We sit and picture wet things like streams and clouds. It's sitting in pictures."

39   He picked up his tray to go. "I could give you a taste of the old Hopi Way. But maybe you're too full after that breakfast. You always eat so much?"

40   "The mountain caused that." I got up. "What do you mean by 'taste'?"

41   "I'll show you."

42   We went to his dormitory room. Other than several Kachina dolls he had carved from cottonwood and a picture of a Sioux warrior, it was just another collegiate dorm room—maybe cleaner than most. He pulled a shoebox from under his bed and opened it carefully. I must have been watching a little wide-eyed because he said, "It isn't live rattlesnakes." From the box he took a long cylinder wrapped in waxed paper and held

it as if trying not to touch it. "Will you eat this? It's very special." He was smiling. "If you won't, I can't share the old Hopi Way with you."

43   "Okay, but if it's dried scorpions, I'm going to speak with a forked tongue."

44   "Open your hands." He unwrapped the cylinder and ever so gently laid across my palms an airy tube the color of a thunderhead. It was about ten inches long and an inch in diameter. "There you go," he said.

45   "You first."

46   "I'm not having any right now."

47   So I bit the end off the blue-gray tube. It was many intricately rolled layers of something with less substance than butterfly wings. The bite crumbled to flakes that stuck to my lips. "Now tell me what I'm eating."

48   "Do you like it?"

49   "I think so. Except it disappears like cotton candy just as I get ready to chew. But I think I taste corn and maybe ashes."

50   "Hopis were eating that before horses came to America. It's piki. Hopi bread you might say. Made from blue-corn flour and ashes from grease-wood or sagebrush. Baked on an oiled stone by my mother. She sends piki every so often. It takes time and great skill to make. We call it Hopi corn-flakes."

51   "Unbelievably thin." I laid a piece on a page of his chemistry book. The words showed through.

52   "We consider corn our mother. The blue variety is what you might call our compass—wherever it grows, we can go. Blue corn directed our migrations. Navajos cultivate a yellow species that's soft and easy to grind, but ours is hard. You plant it much deeper than other corns, and it survives where they would die. It's a genetic variant the Hopi developed."

53   "Why is it blue? That must be symbolic."

54   "We like the color blue. Corn's our most important ritual ingredient."

55   "The piki's good, but it's making me thirsty. Where's a water fountain?"

56   When I came back from the fountain, Fritz said, "I'll tell you what I think the heart of our religion is—it's the Four Worlds."

57   Over the next hour, he talked about the Hopi Way, and showed pictures and passages from *Book of the Hopi.* The key seemed to be emergence. Carved in a rock near the village of Shipolovi is the ancient symbol for it:

With variations, the symbol appears among other Indians of the Americas. Its lines represent the course a person follows on his "road of life" as he passes through birth, death, rebirth. Human existence is essentially a series of journeys, and the emergence symbol is a kind of map of the wandering soul, an image of a process; but it is also, like most Hopi symbols and ceremonies, a reminder of cosmic patterns that all human beings move in.

58   The Hopi believes mankind has evolved through four worlds: the first a shadowy realm of contentment; the second a place so comfortable the people forgot where they had come from and began worshipping material goods. The third world was a pleasant land too, but the people, bewildered by their past and fearful for their future, thought only of their own earthly plans. At last, the Spider Grandmother, who oversees the emergences, told them: "You have forgotten what you should have remembered, and now you have to leave this place. Things will be harder." In the fourth and present world, life is difficult for mankind, and he struggles to remember his source because materialism and selfishness block a greater vision. The newly born infant comes into the fourth world with the door of his mind open (evident in the cranial soft spot), but as he ages, the door closes and he must work at remaining receptive to the great forces. A human being's grandest task is to keep from breaking with things outside himself.

59   "A Hopi learns that he belongs to two families," Fritz said, "his natural clan and that of all things. As he gets older, he's supposed to move closer to the greater family. In the Hopi Way, each person tries to recognize his part in the whole."

60   "At breakfast you said you hunted rabbits and pigeons and robins, but I don't see how you can shoot a bird if you believe in the union of life."

61   "A Hopi hunter asks the animal to forgive him for killing it. Only life can feed life. The robin knows that."

62   "How does robin taste, by the way?"

63   "Tastes good."

64   "The religion doesn't seem to have much of an ethical code."

65   "It's there. We watch what the Kachinas say and do. But the Spider Grandmother did give two rules. To all men, not just Hopis. If you look at them, they cover everything. She said, 'Don't go around hurting each other,' and she said, 'Try to understand things.' "

66   "I like them. I like them very much."

67   "Our religion keeps reminding us that we aren't just will and thoughts. We're also sand and wind and thunder. Rain. The seasons. All those things. You learn to respect everything because you *are* everything. If you respect yourself, you respect all things. That's why we have so many songs of creation to remind us where we came from. If the fourth world forgets that, we'll disappear in the wilderness like the third world, where people decided they had created themselves."

68   "Pride's the deadliest of the Seven Deadly Sins in old Christian theology."

69   "It's *kahopi* to set yourself above things. It causes divisions."

70   Fritz had to go to class. As we walked across campus, I said, "I guess it's hard to be a Hopi in Cedar City—especially if you're studying biochemistry."

71   "It's hard to be a Hopi anywhere."

72   "I mean, difficult to carry your Hopi heritage into a world as technological as medicine is."

73   "Heritage? My heritage is the Hopi Way, and that's a way of the spirit. Spirit can go anywhere. In fact, it has to go places so it can change and emerge like in the migrations. That's the whole idea."

READING RESPONSE JOURNAL

1. Now having finished both parts of the reading, write a one- or two-paragraph summary of them.

2. Does anything in this selection relate to your life? If so, do some prewriting about it.

3. Do you find any more to write on? What interests you here?

4. As Least Heat Moon tries to question the old Navajo man, what feelings does he have?

5. How does Fritz, the young Hopi student, reply when William asks if he thinks whites are prejudiced against Native Americans?

6. What's an "apple Indian"?

7. How does Fritz wish to spend his life?

8. William takes some *piki*, Hopi bread. What are its ingredients?

9. What two rules did the Spider Grandmother give the Hopis?

WRITING FROM READING

Using Dialogue

When William recounts his attempt to speak with the old Navajo man, he uses dialogue to make this scene more real: "To one with a great round head like an earthen pot, I said, 'Is the storm finished now?' He looked at me, then slowly turned his head, while the others examined before them things in the air invisible to me." Even though William uses only one line of dialogue here, notice how effective it is in making the description more human and real to us.

In your descriptive writing, try to use dialogue, the exact words of speech, to bring life to your work.

1. Because he is part Indian, Least Heat Moon is concerned with prejudice and the role of Native Americans in a white man's world. What thoughts and feelings do you have about Native Americans in today's America? Prewrite about your ideas and then write a longer paper on your thoughts.

2. Some of us from large cities have probably never met any Native Americans, but if you have had experience meeting Native Americans where cultural differences stood out, describe your thoughts. If you can, include some dialogue.

3. In the first part of this selection, Least Heat Moon reveals that he has "fear of the contempt that full-bloods often show lesser bloods." Do you have any doubts or feelings of embarrassment about your background? All of us can sometimes worry about our parents or our economic status. What are your worries about your background? This is a personal question, and it might take some thinking. Prewrite about it first and then write a longer paper on it, remembering to use some dialogue to give your writing more zest.

COLLABORATIVE LEARNING ACTIVITY

Exploring Stereotypes

For whichever assignment you chose to write about, share your prewriting with your group. Listen carefully to each reader and make constructive comments.

Think of all the stereotypes about Native Americans that our culture has absorbed from western movies and other media. Make a master list from your group. Try to give specific examples you can recall from movies, television shows, and books.

WRITING TIPS

Use the Reporter's Questions

In writing stories, check to see if you've answered the Reporter's Questions—who, what, when, where, and why.

VOCABULARY DEVELOPMENT

The first sentence of paragraph 2 from this selection has some difficult vocabulary: "In *viridescent* velveteen blouses and *violescent* nineteenth-century skirts, Navajo women of ample body, each laden with silver and turquoise bracelets, necklaces, and rings—not the trading post variety but heavy bands gleaming under the *patina* of long wear—reeled off yards of fabric."

Viridescent is a very difficult word, probably impossible to define from context. It means "green or slightly green."

Violescent means "shading off toward a violet color" *(Webster's New World Dictionary).*

"*Patina* of long wear": If the silver bracelets "gleam" from "long wear," can you guess the meaning of *patina*?

Patina means "shine."

REVIEW

Using dialogue well and appropriately energizes your writing.

LEARNING FROM RACISM, from *THE COLOR OF WATER: A BLACK MAN'S TRIBUTE TO HIS WHITE MOTHER*

James McBride

This reading is a selection from a book that is both a biography of the writer's mother and his own autobiography.

VOCABULARY IN CONTEXT

"her words flying together like *gibberish*"—nonsense words; sounds of no meaning

"*antebellum* South"—pre–Civil War

PREREADING

1. The author's first paragraph tells us what his story will contain. What else do you think the book might say?

Learning from Racism, from *The Color of Water: A Black Man's Tribute to His White Mother*

James McBride

1 As a boy, I never knew where my mother was from—where she was born, who her parents were. When I asked she'd say, "God made me." When I asked if she was white, she'd say, "I'm light-skinned," and change the subject. She raised twelve black children and sent us all to college and in most cases graduate school. Her children became doctors, professors, chemists, teachers—yet none of us even knew her maiden name until we were grown. It took me fourteen years to unearth her remarkable story— the daughter of an Orthodox Jewish rabbi, she married a black man in 1942—and she revealed it more as a favor to me than out of any desire to revisit her past. Here is her life as she told it to me, and betwixt and between the pages of her life you will find mine as well. . . .

2 Whenever she [mother] stepped out of the house with us, she went into a sort of mental zone where her attention span went no farther

than the five kids trailing her and the tightly balled fist in which she held her small bit of money, which she always counted to the last penny. She had absolutely no interest in a world that seemed incredibly agitated by our presence. The stares and remarks, the glances and cackles that we heard as we walked about the world went right over her head, but not over mine. By age ten, I was coming into my own feelings about myself and my own impending manhood, and going out with Mommy, which had been a privilege and an honor at age five, had become a dreaded event. I had reached a point where I was ashamed of her and didn't want the world to see my white mother. When I went out with my friends, I'd avoid telling her where we were playing because I didn't want her coming to the park to fetch me. I grew secretive, cautious, passive, angry, and fearful, always afraid that the baddest cat on the block would call her a "honky," in which case I'd have to respond and get my ass kicked. "Come and let's walk to the store," she said one afternoon.

3   "I can go by myself," I said. The intent was to hide my white mom and go it alone.

4   "Okay," she said. She didn't seem bothered by my newfound independence. Relieved, I set off to a neighborhood grocery store. The store owner was a gruff white man who, like many of the whites in St. Albans, was on his way out as we blacks began to move in. He did not seem to like black children and he certainly took no particular liking to or interest in me. When I got home, Mommy placed the quart of milk he sold me on the table, opened it up, and the smell of sour milk filled the room. She closed the carton and handed it to me. "Take it back and get my money back."

5   "Do I have to?"

6   "Take it back." It was an order. I was a Little Kid in my house, not a Big Kid who could voice opinions and sway the master. I had to take orders.

7   I dragged myself back to the store, dreading the showdown I knew was coming. The owner glared at me when I walked in. "I have to return this," I said.

8   "Not here," he said. "The milk is opened. I'm not taking it back."

9   I returned home. Ten minutes later Mommy marched into the store, doing her "madwalk," the bowlegged strut that meant thunder and lightning was coming—body pitched forward, jaw jutted out, hands balled into tight fists, nose red, stomping like Cab Calloway with the Billy Eckstein band blowing full blast behind him. I followed her sheepishly, my plan to go it alone and hide my white mother now completely awash, backfired in the worst way.

10   She angrily placed the milk on the counter. The merchant looked at her, then at me. Then back at her. Then at me again. The surprise written on his face changed to anger and disgust, and it took me completely

by surprise. I thought the man would see Ma, think they had something in common, then give her the dough and we'd be off. "That milk is sold," he said.

11   "Smell it," Ma said. "It's spoiled."

12   "I don't smell milk. I sell milk."

13   Right away they were at each other, I mean really going at it. A crowd of black kids gathered, watching my white mother arguing with this white man. I wanted to sink into the floor and disappear. "It's okay, Ma . . ." I said. She ignored me. In matters of money, of which she had so little, I knew it was useless. She was going full blast—". . . fool . . . think you are . . . idiot!"—her words flying together like gibberish, while the neighborhood kids howled, woofing like dogs and enjoying the show.

14   After a while it was clear the man was not going to return her money, so she grabbed my hand and was heading toward the door, when he made another remark, something that I missed, something he murmured beneath his breath so softly that I couldn't hear, but it made the crowd murmur "Ooohhhh." Ma stiffened. Still holding the milk in her right hand, she turned around and flung it at him like a football. He ducked and the milk missed him, smashing into the cigarette cabinet behind him and sending milk and cigarettes splattering everywhere.

15   I could not understand such anger. I could not understand why she didn't just give up the milk. Why cause a fuss? I thought. My own embarrassment overrode all other feelings. As I walked home, holding Mommy's hand while she fumed, I thought it would be easier if we were just one color, black or white. I didn't want to be white. My siblings had already instilled the notion of black pride in me. I would have preferred that Mommy were black. Now, as a grown man, I feel privileged to have come from two worlds. My view of the world is not merely that of a black man but that of a black man with something of a Jewish soul. I don't consider myself Jewish, but when I look at Holocaust photographs of Jewish women whose children have been wrenched from them by Nazi soldiers, the women look like my own mother and I think to myself, *There but for the grace of God goes my own mother—and by extension, myself.* When I see two little Jewish old ladies giggling over coffee at a Manhattan diner, it makes me smile, because I hear my own mother's laughter beneath theirs. Conversely, when I hear black "leaders" talking about "Jewish slave owners" I feel angry and disgusted, knowing that they're inflaming people with lies and twisted history, as if all seven of the Jewish slave owners in the antebellum South, or however few there were, are responsible for the problems of African-Americans now. Those leaders are no better than their Jewish counterparts who spin statistics in marvelous ways to make African-Americans look like savages, criminals, drags on society, and "animals" (a word quite popular when used to describe blacks these days). I don't belong to any of those groups. I belong to the world of one God, one people.

READING RESPONSE JOURNAL

1. Summarize the reading.

2. What food for thought does the reading provide?

3. What other ideas does the reading inspire in you?

4. How did the incident with the storekeeper "backfire" on the young man?

5. Why did the son want to "hide" his white mother?

6. What contrast does the writer draw between his thoughts as a young man about being biracial and his adult views on this?

WRITING FROM READING

Writing as Reflection

James McBride's writing about his mother and himself allows him to learn from his past, to extract truth from his life as a youth in preparation for adult living.

What events from your past have you learned from? Writing about your past can help you understand yourself and the reasons why you are the person you are today.

1. Look back at an incident in your life when a parent may have embarrassed you as a child. Describe the event as you remember it—using

the Reporter's Questions. Then step back from your youth to re-examine the incident as an adult and contrast your new feeling about the event with the old.

2. Race is such a volatile issue in America that we are not surprised about young James McBride's intense feelings about it; in his case, he wished to be from one race, not two. Looking back later, though, he has changed:

> Now as a grown man, I feel privileged to have come from two worlds. My view of the world is not merely that of a black man but that of a black man with something of a Jewish soul.

Have *your* feelings about race changed from when you were younger? Explain the changes in your thinking about race and the reasons for it. You may choose to develop your ideas by comparison and contrast, first describing your "old" thinking and then the "new."

3. The writer forms generalizations about racists among blacks and Jews:

> When I hear black "leaders" talking about "Jewish slave owners" I feel angry and disgusted, knowing that they're inflaming people with lies and twisted history, as if all seven of the Jewish slave owners in the antebellum South, or however few there were, are responsible for the problems of African-Americans now. Those leaders are no better than their Jewish counterparts who spin statistics in marvelous ways to make African-Americans look like savages, criminals, drags on society, and "animals" (a word quite popular when used to describe blacks these days).

What generalizations about race can *you* draw from your life experiences? McBride sees prejudice in two vastly different groups: black leaders and Jewish spokespersons. What racist attitudes make themselves apparent to you today? Write about your thoughts on racism in America today.

COLLABORATIVE LEARNING ACTIVITY

Reading for Quotations

In your group, take turns reading McBride's excerpt out loud to note how effectively he uses quotations in the confrontation with the shopkeeper. Try to use quotes to spark the incidents you relate.

WRITING TIPS

Using Foreshadowing

Foreshadowing is the writer's hint or advanced notice of what is to follow. It can also function like a transition, as in McBride's narrative: "I dragged myself back to the store, dreading the showdown I knew was coming." This sentence foreshadows the explosion when McBride's mother gets involved. This device also keeps the reader's interest as we wait for the confrontation. As a writer, think of using foreshadowing to signal something important coming.

REVIEW

A natural way of developing your ideas is to contrast the new with the old.

THE QUIET RIOT NEXT DOOR

Alex Kotlowitz

Kotlowitz writes an article about Chicago's West Side in 1996, the site and time of the Democratic National Convention. He had previously written a book, *There Are No Children Here*, about the people trapped in public housing on Chicago's West Side.

VOCABULARY IN CONTEXT

"*fusillade*"—barrage of gunfire

"*discernible* noise"—able to be heard

"*unraveling*"—unwinding, falling apart

"*frenetic* time"—very busy, hassled

"*edifice*"—building

"*staccato* report of pistols"—single reports of gunfire

"*daunting* forces"—overwhelming

"*paucity*" of resources—very few, scarcity

"*distraught*"—discouraged, depressed

"*cohesive* urban *agenda*"—unified; plan

PREREADING

1. Read the title. Isn't it odd? What's a "quiet riot"? The riot is "next door" to what? What does this title tell us the essay will be about?
2. Now read the first two paragraphs and last two paragraphs. What they have in common tells us much about the article. Predict what the article will say.

The Quiet Riot Next Door

Alex Kotlowitz

1   It doesn't seem that long ago that I first ventured into the Horner Homes, a stretch of red brick, mid- and high-rise buildings known to the kids as "the Hornets."

2   It was a weekday afternoon in early June 1987, and as I arrived at the local Boys and Girls Club, a squat, haggard-looking structure, the area outside was eerily still. Adults were just beginning to emerge, cautiously, from the dark, concrete high-rise breezeways. Children soon

followed, slowly and vigilantly setting forth from the safety of the club. I asked a group of kids, maybe 11- and 12-year-olds, what had happened. Breathlessly they told me that gang members, armed with handguns and Uzis, had shot at each other from two facing high-rises, like warring ships at sea. No one, it appeared, had been injured.

3   I didn't fully believe their story, so I called the police department the next morning.

4   "If such an incident occurred it would have been discussed with the police superintendent at his morning meeting, and nothing of the sort was brought up," I was told by the department's media-relations director. "I can assure you it didn't happen."

5   But when I went back to Horner later that day, the children insisted it had happened just as they said, so I talked with the beat cops. They described it just as the children had. In fact, the police initially had thought they were the target of the fusillade and had taken cover under their patrol cars.

6   At first this episode bemused me. Then well into the summer—after I'd tasted the same elevated anxiety the kids felt every day—it began to anger me. Not only did that shootout officially not happen, but afterward no adults came to these children to assure them that they would do what they could to make sure such an incident didn't happen again. Nobody.

7   As the Democrats gather just two blocks from where this gun battle occurred, they might contemplate how they could break that ringing silence. When they leave the convention center late at night, they might listen for the most discernible noise in the lives of these kids, the unmistakable, unrhythmic, unwanted pop, pop, pop of gunfire.

8   In the summer of 1968, *Look* magazine ran an article about Chicago titled "City in a bind." It was not about Mayor Richard J. Daley's fears that young, anti-war protesters might disrupt the upcoming Democratic convention. It was, instead, about the city's West Side, the site of three major riots in four years, including the burning and looting that took place along Madison Street just a few months earlier, in the wake of Dr. Martin Luther King Jr.'s assassination. The piece implied that with the approaching convention there was still a general unease among the city's ghetto residents. The article pointed out that the unemployment rate for Chicago blacks was 8.2 percent, nearly three times that of the city's whites, and that the ghetto schools produced more dropouts than graduates. What struck me, though, as I recently read this article, was not how little these West Side neighborhoods had changed in the past 28 years, but how, in fact, they've collapsed even more.

9   The unemployment rate is well into double digits; the average dropout rate for West Side schools is 59 percent, and as high as 70 percent at the Austin Community Academy. And though we haven't had the mass disturbances of the 1960s, one could certainly make the case that the slow, continual unraveling of these communities and the slow,

continual sapping of the children's spirits has, in the end, had the same effect. A few years back, Fred Harris, a former U.S. senator and member of the Kerner Commission, aptly called such unraveling "quiet riots."

10   I'm sure it's a frenetic time for delegates and other visitors, but if they have a few hours free, let me suggest a tour of Chicago's West Side, a 15-square-mile collage of graystones, brownstones and public housing high-rises, all as worn and tired as their occupants. Some might call it Chicago's underbelly, or its residents the underclass, but they are our neighbors, and as such their worries and fears should be our worries and fears. Their struggles and dreams should be ours as well.

11   Start at Rockwell Gardens, one of the city's smaller and less-imposing public-housing complexes. It's half a mile west of the United Center. On two plastic crates in front of the 13-story edifice on Adams Street are usually seated a young woman in a white-and-blue uniform and a young man in jeans and a Tommy Hilfiger polo shirt. They are the building's protectors: one a private security guard, the other a member of the Black Gangster Disciples, a street gang. Just tell them you've come to visit Brenda and Millie, and they'll let you in without any hassles.

12   I met Brenda Stephenson and Millie Wortham that first summer I spent at Horner. As stormy as Horner was, Rockwell Gardens was considerably worse. The complex, in fact, had one of the highest violent-crime rates in the city. Still does. But Millie, impulsive and vocal, and Brenda, cautious and even-tempered, always seem to be in full bloom, bedecked in colorful, hip-hugging dresses in the summer, floppy hats and dazzling pantsuits in the winter. And they are always spirited.

13   Once, as I sat talking with Millie and Brenda in a first-floor apartment, shooting erupted outside. We threw ourselves onto the tiled floor and lay there for three to five minutes, listening to the staccato report of pistols. When the battle ended, they escorted me to my car. The police who had rushed there with guns drawn had ticketed me for parking on the wrong side of the road. Brenda and Millie laughed at my sputtering ire.

14   Brenda and Millie, both of whom grew up here, work for West Side Future, an organization that aids young moms. The two dispense bags of baby accessories, homespun advice and plenty of good cheer. I went on a home visit recently with Brenda, and as we were leaving the apartment of a 19-year-old mom, Brenda whipped around and asked of her, "Are you pregnant?" "No way," the young woman replied. "Just thought I'd ask when your guard was down," laughed Brenda, who then kissed the teenager's son before skipping out the door.

15   The Democrats should listen to Brenda and Millie. They've got it figured out. They cultivate a sense of responsibility in the young moms; they teach them how to take care of themselves and their children. They don't excuse the sometimes destructive choices people make. A mother turns to drugs. Fine, get into rehab—and in the meantime find another home for the kids.

16   But Brenda and Millie are also painfully aware of the daunting forces bearing down on these families—and the paucity of resources. Don't whip away the safety net, they tell me. Don't pull away what little their neighborhood has.

17   Last month, Millie called me, distraught. Did I know where she could get a deal on T-shirts? She was accompanying 18 children (last year they had enough money to send 40) to a weeklong YMCA camp. Did I know where she could get assistance to help pay the $250 for uniforms and books so that some teens could attend a prenursing program? The two are always scraping, pulling together what they can for the kids. They organize fundraisers—dances, car washes, bake sales—to buy tickets for the kids to the circus and ice show. They plead with whoever will listen to start an arts, music and dance program in the community because the schools no longer provide any of that.

18   "We need someone to help us to help our community to grow," says Millie, who isn't asking for handouts, just a hand.

19   Not far from here, I once counted 17 liquor stores in a 12-block stretch. Not much else in the way of legal enterprise. And not much in the way of jobs. Indeed, one of the more noticeable business expansions on Madison Street in recent years has been Corbin Colonial Funeral Chapel. In some neighborhoods as much as 60 percent of the housing is abandoned, much of it used by drug pushers and users. Some of these vacant homes are known as "violation buildings," where gang members mete out punishment to associates who have violated their trust.

20   It's easy to despair when spending time amid the rubble of the West Side, but there are people, like Millie and Brenda, who persist—quietly, fearlessly, even optimistically. They include Paul Adams and Mary Nelson, and both are worth meeting.

21   Adams, a gruff, no-nonsense educator, kept Providence-St. Mel High School from closing when the Roman Catholic Archdiocese cut it adrift in 1978. Mostly through private donations, he has kept it open, a place where a student who makes it through four years is virtually guaranteed entrance into college. But many don't make it. They don't cut it academically. They are swept away by the gangs. Or they fall prey to another youngster's ferocious rage. One 9th grader I had known from Horner, Terrell Collins, a straight-A student, was shot point-blank in the head and chest a few blocks from the stadium. His killer, who mistook Terrell for a rival gang member, was 18 years old. Nonetheless, Adams pushes ahead. He just hired as principal a 15-year veteran of Phillips Academy in Andover, Mass., one of the nation's premier prep schools, and has expanded the school to include 1st through 8th grades.

22   Farther west, tucked away among the scrap yards and the railroad tracks of what was once a humming industrial belt, is a small, unassuming brownstone that houses Bethel New Life. Bethel is among a slew of non-profit housing groups that sprung up in the 1980s as the federal government pulled back from its commitment to the urban poor. Nelson,

who lives in the neighborhood, is giving a tour to the Minnesota delegates. In addition to showing them Bethel's newly constructed single-family homes, she plans to take them to a hospital Bethel is converting into 125 units of elderly housing, to a new, 80-child day-care center, to a cultural and performing arts center under construction, and to an area in which Bethel, acting as a developer, is hoping to lure new business, including what would be the West Side's only movie theater. What the Minnesota delegation probably won't see is Nelson's extraordinary effort to rebuild a spiritual sense of community, including late-night rallies to challenge the brazen street corner drug dealing.

23   But if one wants to see the most noticeable transformation, one need look no farther than Horner and the surrounding neighborhood. With the completion of the United Center two years ago, this neighborhood, in real estate parlance, has become "hot." Nearby homes are selling for an astonishing $400,000. And Henry Cisneros, a lone voice in the Clinton administration for a cohesive urban agenda, has leveraged Horner's now-prime location, luring private developers into a partnership with the Chicago Housing Authority. He wants to redefine public housing by attracting working people back into Horner, building low-rise units and town homes among the high-rises.

24   I drove around the area with Millie and Brenda recently. The worst has been pulled down, most notably three high-rises at Horner and dozens of abandoned homes nearby. And, as Brenda and Millie marvel, out of the ashes have risen new single-family homes, a new library, a new Boys and Girls Club, a new playground, and new street lamps, as well as planters along Madison Street, a bank branch, traffic islands and more than 1,000 birch, pear, honey locust, ginkgo, and maple trees. They also point to the razed storefronts along Madison; some businesses, including the neighborhood's pawn shop, have been relocated well west of the United Center.

25   The more cynical among us might conclude that the Democratic convention has been the catalyst for such rebuilding and beautification. So be it. To Millie and Brenda—who with disbelief and joy point to the wood-chip-covered vacant lots and to the new elevators at Horner, whose previous unreliability had come to symbolize public housing's decline—it is only evidence that with political will and muscle, there is much that can be done. Nonetheless, they caution that there is still much missing. There are still few jobs. The schools still don't prepare their students for the work force or college. The beat cops are still too busy battling the gangs and drug dealers to befriend the kids. And many of the parents, sunken and despondent, are not nurturing of their youngsters. As a result the neighborhood children certainly don't feel as rejuvenated as the real estate. Most of the boys I met while working on my book quit school long ago and are either running with a gang or selling reefer or crack cocaine. They are without much sense of future. Many are depressed. A few are in prison. And at least one, Terrell, is dead.

26   "You can't only beautify the outside when the inside ain't right," says Millie.

27   A few weeks ago, Brenda and I visited a family living in an 11th-floor apartment at Horner, two blocks directly north of the United Center. They urged us to get inside—quickly. There had, just a few minutes earlier, been a blazing gun battle in the playground below. I peeked out the window and, except for an elevated train rattling by, it was oddly quiet. I couldn't spot anyone. Not a soul. This time, though, I didn't call the police to verify their story. I knew.

READING RESPONSE JOURNAL

1. Having finished this long reading, write a summary, perhaps in two paragraphs.

2. Can you tie in this reading in any way to your life?

3. Can you find anything else in this article to write about?

4. Why does Kotlowitz begin his article with a flashback about the unreported shooting?

5. What does Kotlowitz say about the current West Side from the time of the 1968 riots?

6. According to Kotlowitz, what did former Senator Fred Harris refer to as "quiet riots"?

7. Why does Kotlowitz wish the convention delegates would tour Chicago's West Side?

8. What is a "violation building"?

9. What would Brenda Stephenson and Millie Wortham do to help West Side residents?

10. How have Paul Adams and Mary Nelson helped West Side residents?

11. Why does Kotlowitz recount the story of Terrell Collins?

12. Why has Chicago's West Side recently become a "hot" area for real estate?

13. Despite the physical rebuilding of the West Side, what continuing problems concern Brenda Stephenson and Millie Wortham?

14. Why does Kotlowitz conclude his essay with the report of another gun battle?

WRITING FROM READING

Using Multiple Sources

In his essay, Kotlowitz shows he has done his homework as a writer in gathering information from many sources. For example, he spends time with children in the housing project, calls the police station, talks with beat cops, accompanies Brenda and Millie from West Side Future on their rounds, interviews educator Paul Adams and Bethel New Life spokesperson Mary Nelson, and even counts the liquor stores in the area.

As you do the writing assignments that follow, try to get some other sources for information, perhaps by interviewing friends and acquaintances or by searching the Internet.

1. Kotlowitz's essay could be very depressing, but instead he finds much hope in the people who work for the good of the West Side. Think of some people who have done good things for your community. Prewrite about them, get some more information from interviews or on the Internet, and then write a paper telling about them and their accomplishments.
2. A tragic death like Terrell Collins's has become an all-too-common occurrence today in urban America. Do you have a similar story, someone you know who has been cut down or terrorized by random violence? Prewrite about your story; then get some added information from interviews and the Internet and write a fuller account giving enough details to let your readers know the story.

COLLABORATIVE LEARNING ACTIVITY

Compiling a Portfolio of Community Heroes

Let's focus on assignment 1 in Writing from Reading by having the members of your group list people who have been a positive force in their city or community. Each group member could give a brief account of the person's service to the community, and the group would then have a portfolio of solid citizens who benefit others.

WRITING TIPS

Knowing the Territory

Knowing the facts is important for a writer. It proves to the reader that the writer knows what he or she is talking about. Describing the West Side's problems, Kotlowitz informs us that he knows the territory: "Not far from here, I once counted 17 liquor stores in a 12-block stretch." This fact shows us Kotlowitz has done his research. In your paper about your local hero or the paper you wrote on urban violence, you must prove you know what you're talking about—by giving facts and details, perhaps names of people or places or specific actions. By doing this, you show that you, too, know the territory.

VOCABULARY DEVELOPMENT

You can guess the meaning of some new vocabulary words from their context, the words and meanings around them. The first four paragraphs of Alex Kotlowitz's essay "The Quiet Riot Next Door" speak of a reported gun battle between two rival gangs in a Chicago housing project. In paragraph 5, Kotlowitz tells us, "the police initially had thought they were the target of the *fusillade* and had taken cover under their patrol cars." Can you guess what the word *fusillade* means? Why were the police hiding under their cars? If you guessed that *fusillade* means a "barrage of gunfire," you would be right. The clues about the gang fight and the police protecting themselves help us with the meaning of this new word.

Two paragraphs later, Kotlowitz suggests that delegates to the Democratic National Convention should pay attention to the sounds of the West Side: "When they leave the convention center late at night, they might listen for the most *discernible* noise in the lives of these kids [from West Side public housing], the unmistakable, unrhythmic, unwanted pop, pop, pop of gunfire." The context of *discernible* is a description of the gunfire the public housing children hear constantly. What does "most *discernible* noise" mean? The "most clearly heard" sound is of guns. The root word of *discernible* is *discern* as in "he tried to discern—learn—where the shots were coming from." What does the suffix or ending, *-ible*, mean in *discernible?* The suffix *-ible*—in some words *able*, like "work*able*" means "able to"; so *discernible* means "able to be learned, recognizable, easily discovered."

Describing the plight of Chicago's West Side, Kotlowitz points out that the double-digit unemployment rate and a school dropout rate as high as 70 percent are signs of the "slow, continual *unraveling* of these communities and the slow, continual sapping of the children's spirits." He compares this "unraveling" to the mass disturbances of the 1960s—inner city riots in Chicago, Detroit, New York, and other places. So, what happens when communities "unravel"? Unemployment, school dropouts, even riots may result—"a falling apart or coming apart" of the community.

Now you try to discover from their context what some difficult vocabulary words mean.

At the beginning of paragraph 10, Kotlowitz says, "I'm sure it's [days of the Convention] a *frenetic* time for delegates and other visitors, but if they have a few hours free, let me suggest a tour of Chicago's West Side."

The word *frenetic* may be new to you, but in the same sentence there is a clue about time. What is the clue? What kind of schedule must they have with only the possibility of some free hours? Try now to guess what *frenetic* means.

In the next paragraph, Kotlowitz sets this scene: "On two plastic crates in front of the 13-story *edifice* on Adams Street are usually seated a young woman in a white-and-blue uniform and a young man in jeans and a Tommy Hilfiger polo shirt." What does *edifice* mean? We are given clues—it has 13 stories and is on Adams Street.

Let's do one more word in context. Describing a visit to Rockwell Gardens (paragraph 13), Kotlowitz explains that "shooting erupted outside. We threw ourselves onto the tiled floor and lay there for three to five minutes, listening to the *staccato* report of pistols." What does *staccato* mean? We know it has to do with gunshots. What do gunshots sound like? Try to guess what *staccato* means. Only if you have no idea, should you use the dictionary. The *American Heritage College Dictionary* defines *staccato* as "Marked by or composed of abrupt disconnected sounds." In the context of a gunfight, *staccato* means "single reports of gunfire."

REVIEW

Notice how Kotlowitz incorporates a variety of sources in his essay: facts and statistics about the neighborhood, information from a magazine article, and stories from his interviews with those on the front line.

OFFENSIVE WORDS

William Raspberry

This article by William Raspberry is about racial stereotypes, both obvious and subtle.

VOCABULARY IN CONTEXT

"*traumatizing* racial encounters"—shocking, very disturbing
"*insidious*"—deceptive, deadly
"*stereotype*"—commonly accepted image
"*regentrification*"—urban renewal
"*salient* idea"—clear, important
"*gratuitous* racial or ethnic slur"—petty, pointless

PREREADING

1. Read the title and first and last paragraphs. Predict what this essay will say.

Offensive Words

William Raspberry

1 Robert Mallett, former city administrator for the District of Columbia, was a boy of 11 or 12 when he went to a restaurant with his parents. He went to use the restroom and, as he was leaving, passed a white man and his son entering the facility.

2   The man spotted an unflushed urinal (Mallett had flushed his) and proceeded to lecture his son on the nasty habits of "niggers."

3   "Tears welled up in my eyes," Mallett, now a D.C. lawyer, recalled. "My parents sensed that something was wrong when I returned to the table, but I insisted everything was all right. But after that, everytime I left a restroom, if I was alone, I flushed all the toilets. I was determined that no one would ever come behind me and find an unflushed toilet."

4   Indeed, he says, he stopped the practice only a half-dozen years ago, at age 33, when a friend caught him at it and wondered what on earth he was doing.

5   Mallett's sad-funny account is not exactly a "lynching story." (Michel McQueen told her ABC colleague Ted Koppel that all black people have "lynching stories"—accounts of traumatizing racial encounters). But in

some ways such "nothing" little incidents are more insidious than the hard-edge racial confrontations because they subtly shift the burden of the stereotype from perpetrator to victim.

6   Mallett told his story last week at a roundtable session sponsored by the National Conference (formerly the National Conference of Christians and Jews) to help media representatives and other opinion leaders understand the power of racial and ethnic stereotypes to poison race relations.

7   Chuck Stone, veteran journalist and now a distinguished professor of journalism at the University of North Carolina, said journalists are "an unwitting but powerful force in reinforcing and maintaining negative stereotypes."

8   Some of the most damaging stereotypes, Stone said in a 45-minute lecture that highlighted the session, are those that carry no calculated insult.

9   He cited several examples from a list the National Conference has compiled for the update of its book, "Building Bridges": reporters who say "welfare moms" when they mean poor black women; who write "taxpayers" but have in mind white men; who describe neighborhood change as "regentrification" when the salient idea is whitening.

10   "Stereotypes are like a supermarket," he said. "They are convenient, economical and useful. They do our thinking for us. We don't have to waste time trying to make sense of our ignorance. Stereotypes slice through the niceties of language, tide us over the loose ends we don't understand and wrap up, into a comfortable package, our narrow-mindedness about everything and everybody except ourselves.

11   Still, it's Mallett's sad little tale that sticks in my mind. The "lynching stories," like the gratuitous racial or ethnic slur, may leave you furious. (I'm thinking, for instance, of the black teenager forced to remove his new shirt and go home for the receipt because an employee at Eddie Bauer decided it must have been stolen, or the woman forced to undergo a strip-search at Victoria's Secret because she was suspected to be a thief.)

12   But the "nothing" stories are in some ways more powerful because they *don't* anger—merely make you deal with the stereotype directed against you. There's hardly a professional black man who hasn't, when encountering whites—especially white women—on isolated sidewalks, found himself forcing a smile to signal his harmlessness. Minority college students often find themselves behaving in ways calculated to avoid bringing discredit to *their* group. I've even known black people who pretended not to like watermelon because the stereotype says they love it.

13   And these are the sensitive, successful, determined-to-fit-in ones. How much deadlier the negative stereotypes can be for those who either lash out in violent anger against the perpetrator of the stereotypes or, perhaps worse, internalize the insult. I mean, for instance, young blacks who accept the notion that restrained behavior, careful speech and academic exertion are "white."

14   Stereotypes—including those perpetrated by the media—can be surprisingly powerful, whether they trigger racial hatred and violence or, as with Mallett, merely make us flush with embarrassment.

READING RESPONSE JOURNAL

1. Make a one-paragraph summary of the article.

2. Can you relate anything in the article to your own life?

3. Does the article provide you with any more thoughts for writing?

4. Why did Raspberry begin his article with Mallett's story?

5. Why does Raspberry mention that Mallett was a "former city administrator for the District of Columbia" and is "now a D.C. lawyer"?

6. Raspberry tells us that Mallett stopped flushing urinals "at age 33, when a friend caught him at it." What do you think the friend said to Mallett?

7. What is Raspberry's definition of "lynching stories" in paragraph 5?

8. What two examples of "lynching stories" about the treatment of blacks does Raspberry provide?

9. Explain how the several examples from "Building Bridges" are stereotypes:

   a. reporters who use "welfare moms" for "poor black women"
   b. writers who use "taxpayers" for white men
   c. reporters who use "regentrification" for "whitening"

10. What does Raspberry mean when he writes that "in some ways such 'nothing' little incidents are more insidious than the hard-edge racial confrontations because they *subtly shift the burden* of the stereotype from perpetrator to victim" (italics added)?

11. Raspberry gives examples of how "determined-to-fit-in" blacks fight stereotypes by smiling at white women to signal their harmlessness or pretending not to like watermelons. The stereotypes can be deadlier, he asserts, for those blacks "who lash out in violent anger" or "internalize the insult." As examples of those who internalize the stereotype, Raspberry points to "young blacks who accept the notion that restrained behavior, careful speech and academic exertion are 'white.'" Do you think Raspberry is correct when he claims here that some blacks see academics as a "white" thing? Can you give any examples of your view?

WRITING FROM READING

Using Sources Correctly

1. Try to imagine the scene when Mallett's friend "caught him" flushing urinals. Re-create their conversation in dialogue form.

2. Explain why Raspberry ends his article by claiming that stereotypes "trigger racial hatred or violence or, as with Mallett, merely makes us *flush* with embarrassment."

3. All of us, no matter what our race, may have our own personal "lynching stories" when we were victims of racial harassment. Were you ever involved with, or a victim of, a "lynching story"? If so, try to think back to that incident and brainstorm or freewrite about it.

   After you've read your prewriting to your peers, add to it by asking the five W's about your story: who, what, when, where, and why.

   Finally, take all your prewriting and use it to form discovery (rough) and final drafts of your own "lynching story."

4. (This is a longer assignment.) If you wrote a "lynching story" for the previous assignment, use it to form a thesis for a more developed essay. The essay will tell the "point" of your story, the larger meaning that you and others can draw from it. Note that in Raspberry's piece, the thesis is at the end:

   Stereotypes—including those perpetrated by the media—can be surprisingly powerful, whether they trigger racial hatred and violence or, as with Mallett, merely make us flush with embarrassment.

   Raspberry has prepared us for this thesis by his powerful examples of racial stereotypes. In your essay, use your story and examples to construct a strong thesis.

In writing papers for their classes, students must be able to use accurately the words and ideas of writers of newspaper and magazine articles, articles on the Internet, and books. These media are called sources. Students may analyze, agree with, argue with, and discuss the words and thoughts of writers on important topics. This section shows you correct ways to use quotations and ideas from sources (in your papers). For our examples, we'll use Raspberry's article, "Offensive Words."

Using Quotations

In the article, "Offensive Words," Raspberry argues, "Minority college students often find themselves behaving in ways calculated to avoid bringing discredit to *their* group." To use this quotation correctly in your paper, you must write the name of the author, Raspberry, as in the preceding sentence, and put quotation marks around his words. Notice the period goes before the end quotation mark.

Now you try using a quotation properly from the last paragraph of Raspberry's article. Identify the writer as Raspberry; use a word of introduction or framing, such as, *says, argues, writes;* and then put his words in quotation marks.

Here is a correct student sample of the quotation:

```
    Raspberry argues that "Stereotypes—including those
perpetrated by the media—can be surprisingly powerful,
whether they trigger racial hatred and violence or, as
with Mallett, merely make us flush with embarrassment."
```

It's important to use a variety of words to introduce quotes; for example, Raspberry *says, claims, holds, argues, maintains, writes, alleges,* and *points out.* Such an introduction is called framing, setting off the quotation from your words.

Using Summaries

Two other kinds of writing important to students are the summary and the paraphrase, both of which allow you to explain the thoughts of an author without using his or her exact words. Also, the summary and paraphrase show that you *understand what you are reading* since you can explain it in your own words. At times it is difficult to find words to replace those in the original material. You can get help in doing this from a thesaurus, a dictionary of synonyms. But know that this reprocessing of language—while valuable to your own learning—is not easy.

In a summary, you tell in much fewer words—and again in your *own* words—what a longer piece of writing says. As in direct quotations, use the writer's name and a word of introduction, such as *Raspberry maintains.*

Here are some sentences from paragraph 10 of Raspberry's article in which he quotes journalism professor Chuck Stone. Read them carefully:

"Stereotypes are like a supermarket," he said. "They are convenient, economical and useful. They do our thinking for us. We don't have to waste time trying to make sense of our ignorance. Stereotypes slice through the niceties of language, tide us over the loose ends we don't understand and wrap up, into a comfortable package, our narrow-mindedness about everything and everybody except ourselves."

Write Stone's ideas in your own words.
This is a sample student summary of paragraph 10:

```
    According to Stone, stereotypes are unexamined
shortcuts to real thinking about race.
```

Here is another paragraph from Raspberry's article. Read it and then try to summarize it:

But the "nothing" stories are in some ways more powerful because they *don't* anger—merely make you deal with the stereotype directed against you. There's hardly a professional black man who hasn't, when encountering whites—especially white women—on isolated sidewalks, found himself forcing a smile to signal his harmlessness. Minority college students often find themselves behaving in ways calculated to avoid bringing discredit to *their* group. I've even known black people who pretended not to like watermelon because the stereotype says they love it.

Now try to summarize this paragraph.

To check yourself, here is a sample student summary of the paragraph:

```
Raspberry points out that some incidents force
victims of stereotypes to confront those unfair
images; for example, black men may try to always
present themselves as nonthreatening.
```

Now try a longer summary. Try to write in one paragraph what Raspberry's point is in his article "Offensive Words."

Here is a sample student summary of the entire article:

Raspberry criticizes writers in the media for using negative stereotypes to describe blacks. For example, some reporters use the term "welfare moms" when they mean "poor black women."

Your summary may be different from the sample, as long as you include the idea that Raspberry is critical of the media for using unfair stereotypes for blacks.

Using Paraphrases

A paraphrase is a student's rewording of a sentence or two, nothing longer. The paraphrase has roughly the same number of words as the original writer's work. As with the quotation and summary, use the author's name with a word of introduction.

Taking a sentence from Raspberry's article, we've quoted it (on the left) here and put a sample student paraphrase on the right:

Quotation	Paraphrase
Raspberry writes, "How much deadlier the negative stereotypes can be for those who either lash out in violent anger against the perpetrator of the stereotypes or, perhaps worse, internalize the insult."	Raspberry holds that negative racial images are much more harmful for those who strike out furiously against users of racial stereotypes or, maybe worse, believe the slanted racial messages.

The student substitutes *negative racial images* for "negative stereotypes," *users* for "perpetrator," *believe* for "internalize," and *slanted racial messages* for "insult."

Notice the student keeps the word *negative* and uses *racial stereotypes* for "stereotypes." In a summary or paraphrase, students are allowed to use two or three words from the original writing, but never more than that.

Now try some paraphrases of your own, first this sentence from Raspberry: "I mean, for instance, young blacks who accept the notion that restrained behavior, careful speech and academic exertion are 'white.'"

Write this idea in your words:

1. Raspberry thinks

Let's do another one, Raspberry's concluding sentence: "Stereotypes—including those perpetrated by the media—can be surprisingly powerful, whether they trigger racial hatred and violence or, as with Mallett, merely make us flush with embarrassment."

Now you try it, remembering to use Raspberry's name:

2.

As a self-check, here are sample paraphrases of the two you've been asked to do.

1. For example, Raspberry thinks of young blacks who come to believe that courteous, polite behavior, proper speech, and efforts and success in school are only "white" activities.
2. Raspberry maintains that negative racial images, especially those in the media, can be very influential, whether they stir up racial outbursts or, as in the case of Mallett, make us feel bad about ourselves.

COLLABORATIVE LEARNING ACTIVITY

Listening for a Thesis

Share your writing about "lynching stories" that may have happened to you or that you know about. Listen to your peers' papers for a thesis, a conclusion that they have drawn from their stories. If the other students need help in developing a thesis from their stories, suggest some possible thesis statements to them.

WRITING TIPS

Using Details and Specifics

In his article, Raspberry recounts embarrassing racial incidents at Eddie Bauer and Victoria's Secret. Using the names of the stores adds concreteness and definiteness to his story. In your own writing, try to use names, locations, maybe even addresses, to make your story more real. Also, notice that even in an essay, Raspberry uses a story to grab our attention right away. In your writing, too, stories are valuable for making a point.

REVIEW

Be careful with quotes, paraphrases, and summary. Be sure not to copy an author's words without indicating that you are quoting directly from that author.

MEMORIES IN BLOOD

Ellis Cose

The article "Memories in Blood" by Ellis Cose, from *Newsweek* (December 8, 1997), concerns a controversial subject: should a monument or memorial to American slavery be built on the Washington Mall?

VOCABULARY IN CONTEXT

"*implicit* assumption"—suggested, not directly stated

"*neurophysiologist*"—a doctor who treats the nervous system

"*gleaned*"—gotten from, learned

"huge, racial *disparity*"—gap, difference

"*ruminating*"—thinking about, considering

"*post-apartheid*"—period since racial segregation ended

PREREADING

1. Read the title and the first and last paragraphs to predict what the essay will explain.

Memories in Blood

Ellis Cose

1 Writing in *Essence* magazine, "Amistad" [the movie about a rebellion by blacks aboard a slave ship] midwife Debbie Allen described the Joseph Cinqué saga as "a little drop in a big bucket of blood memory we need to share with the world." Allen's implicit assumption is that "Amistad" is not enough, that we need to reach deeper into that bucket if we are to under-

2 stand America.

    S. Allen Counter, neurophysiologist, Harvard University professor and head of the Harvard Foundation, believes that nothing less than a national monument to slavery can transmit the essence of those blood memories across the generations. For years he has sought backing for a memorial on the Washington Mall that would showcase the hold of a slave ship with 300-plus men, women and children packed inside. Such a monument, he contends, "would answer all the questions," by providing some sense of the immensity of the pain endured and horror perpetrated in forging and preserving the Union. And if placed in the heart of the nation's capital, a city that was legally segregated well into this century, the memorial's lesson could not be easily overlooked.

3   Certainly, as Allen suggests, the Amistad story does not answer "all the questions" about slavery. Indeed, in some sense it is not much about slavery at all, but about heroic men who chose mutiny over slavery and, in the end, won freedom on a technicality. But is it really important for this generation of Americans to know much more about slavery than can be gleaned from a movie or two?

4   John Powell, head of the Institute of Race and Poverty at the University of Minnesota Law School, insists that it is. If we are to make sense of our country, he says, we must understand that peculiar institution and its aftereffects. The acceptance of slavery was an essential compromise that allowed the United States to be born, he points out, and thus set the terms for what it has become: "The enslavement of blacks really created freedom for whites."

5   Some scholars see slavery's legacy not simply in political-moral terms but in economic ones. In "Black Wealth, White Wealth," sociologists Melvin Oliver and Tom Shapiro documented the huge racial disparity in accumulated resources. Middle-class blacks, they calculated, earn 70 percent of the income of middle-class whites but possess only 15 percent of the wealth. The basic reason, they argue, is slavery—which denied generations of blacks the possibility of acquiring any substantial assets. Following the Civil War, that inequality was compounded by decades of discriminatory policies that, among other things, denied most blacks access to land settled upon by white homesteaders, and that made it difficult for blacks to own and operate businesses.

6   As a factual matter, Oliver and Shapiro are right. But what does that have to do with anybody today? The slaves are all dead, as are those who enslaved them. Isn't there some generational statute of limitations? In ruminating on post-apartheid South Africa, Mamphela Ramphele, vice chairman of the University of Cape Town, observed, "There are limits to the extent to which one can correct for past wrongs. One may have to make peace with the past."

7   If black South Africans, whose oppression is so recent that it burns within their memories, can talk about accepting the unfairness of history, why can't black Americans? Powell believes that such an argument misses an important point. "I would be very happy to forget about slavery," he says, "if we could also forget about the Declaration of Independence and the Constitution." For slavery (and the policies developed in its wake) continues, like those documents, to define a large part of America—in terms not only of attitudes and resources but also of life possibilities. Until the country comes to terms with that, maintains Powell, there will not be a "serious process of healing." Like Counter, Powell believes a memorial would be a monumental help, provided that it is not merely a shallow or symbolic gesture.

8   The Counter-Powell hope, in essence, is that a better understanding of American history will somehow affect the way we see—and presumably

implement—social policy today. If we can make the connection between slavery and, say, inner-city poverty, we will be better prepared to combat it. And we may also be more willing to do so.

9   I am not convinced that the will to resolve social inequality has much to do with a sophisticated understanding of history. Nor am I persuaded that a monument on the Mall will lead to a massive reawakening of American consciousness. Counter and Powell, however, are fundamentally correct in their insistence that the past matters. And they are right to search for ways to remind us of that; just as the creators of the new Museum of African-American History in Detroit were right to showcase the American tragedy of slavery. The reason is not that such knowledge will necessarily lead to good policymaking, but that ignorance will surely lead to bad.

READING RESPONSE JOURNAL

1. This is a complex article to summarize because it describes conflicting opinions, but do your best to make a general one-paragraph summary.

2. What does writer Cose mean by saying "Allen's implicit assumption is that 'Amistad' is not enough"?

3. Explain the thoughts of S. Allen Counter about the need for a memorial to slavery on the Washington Mall.

4. What is John Powell's view about our need to remember slavery?

5. According to sociologists Melvin Oliver and Tom Shapiro, what is the reason blacks today have less accumulated wealth than whites?

6. What does Cose mean when he asks if there is a "generational statute of limitations" on America's responsibility for slavery?

7. Why does Cose compare America's racial problems with those of South Africa?

8. What is the meaning of South African Mamphela Ramphele's statement, "There are limits to the extent to which one can correct for past wrongs. One may have to make peace with the past"?

9. To those who say blacks should forget about slavery, John Powell responds, "I would be very happy to forget about slavery if we could also forget about the Declaration of Independence and the Constitution." What does Powell mean here?

10. What does writer Cose see as the "hope" of S. Allen Counter and John Powell?

11. After analyzing the perspectives of several prominent authorities about America's relationship with slavery, the author of this essay, Ellis Cose, explains his own position in the very last paragraph: "The reason [that it's important for Americans to know about slavery] is not that such knowledge will necessarily lead to good policymaking, but that ignorance will surely lead to bad." In your own words, briefly explain what Cose means.

WRITING FROM READING

Writing a Synthesis Paper

A "synthesis" is a view or opinion compiled from different sources. College students are frequently asked to write papers in which they have to explain and evaluate different points of view—sometimes in order to form an opinion of their own. Such work requires careful reading and writing.

Before writing *your* thoughts about the question of America's need to know the history of slavery, look back at the article to identify the opinions of those Cose cites. Briefly summarize the thoughts of the following authorities Cose uses:

Debbie Allen (producer of *Amistad*):
S. Allen Counter
John Powell
Melvin Oliver and Tom Shapiro
Mamphela Ramphele
Ellis Cose (last paragraph)

With which of these opinions do you agree? Write down the authority's name and what he or she said that you agree with.

If you disagree with some of these experts, write down their names and your specific points of disagreement.

What you've written thus far is a *synthesis*, that is, an idea formed after considering and analyzing several other points of view. This synthesis can now be used as the thesis or main idea for a paper of your own.

Let's try to focus more on *your* thoughts about the question of America's need to remember the history of slavery—by building a memorial on the Washington Mall or by some other means. You have read Cose's article and the opinions of those he cites. And you have already written what you agree and disagree with. Take your statement—your synthesis—and rewrite it into a tentative thesis, a strong one-sentence opinion about your beliefs on this question. This is a *tentative* thesis statement because you may later wish to change it or refine it. Your thesis will help guide the rest of your prewriting and writing.

With your tentative thesis, let's do some prewriting. At this point you probably have many thoughts about *Amistad* and America's history of slavery. Write down some of your thinking, going as fast as you can and not worrying about spelling or punctuation. Make no scratch-outs—just keep going forward.

After doing your prewriting, look again at your tentative thesis. See if you wish to change it or leave it as it is. Write your thesis (tentative or revised) again.

With your thesis now in place and with some thoughts from your prewriting, start to write a paper about America's responsibilities for slavery and its legacy. Remember you can use the ideas of the authorities Ellis Cose cites by quoting or paraphrasing them with their names attached.

COLLABORATIVE LEARNING ACTIVITY

Listening to Your Own Work

After sharing your prewriting and discovery drafts with your group members, try this with your final draft. Give it to one of your group members and have him or her read it out loud back to you. Perhaps even close your eyes to focus attention even better.

As you listen to your paper, think about these questions: Do I have a clear thesis? Is my conclusion appropriate? What do I learn from hearing my own work?

WRITING TIPS

Documenting Sources

Writer Ellis Cose is careful to identify and establish the credentials of each authority he cites in his article: Debbie Allen, *Amistad*'s producer, writes for *Essence* magazine; S. Allen Counter is a Harvard neurophysiologist and head of the Harvard Foundation; John Powell directs the Institute of Race and Poverty at the University of Minnesota Law School; Melvin Oliver and Tom Shapiro are sociologists and co-authors of the book *Black Wealth, White Wealth*; and Mamphela Ramphele serves as vice chairman of the University of Cape Town. Cose wants his *Newsweek* readers to know that he has chosen "experts" on the questions of America's obligation to remember slavery; the ideas of these authorities provide the focus for Cose's discussion.

Just as Cose takes great pains to tell us about his sources, so should you as a writer identify *your* sources by telling their names, affiliations or titles, their articles or books, and the page numbers where you found your information. This process is called citing or footnoting.

REVIEW

Train yourself to use and give credit to sources, whether from newspapers, magazines, books, videos, the Internet, personal interviews, or speeches.

Word Demons

WHERE, WERE

Where is an adverb telling place, as in "Put the book *where* it belongs" and "*Where* is the money?"

Were is a past-tense form of the verb *to be*, used with plural and second-person singular subjects, as in "The Russians *were* stunned" and "You *were* interested."

Your test for which word to use is "place": *were* has nothing to do with "place," or *where* something is.

Practice

Write a sentence in which you use *where* and *were* correctly.

Complete the following sentences with either *were* or *where:*

1. The investigator wanted to know _____ the transcript of the trial was.
2. Several star witnesses _____ not called to testify.
3. _____ the legal confrontations as annoying as those from earlier in the trial?
4. The jurors _____ disgruntled about the lengthy delays in calling witnesses.
5. The judge's comments to the jury _____ not helpful to the defense.

THAN, THEN

Although these words are often pronounced alike, they have different spellings and different meanings. *Than* is used in comparisons: "Michael

Jordan is greater *than* any other basketball player" and "Golf is slower *than* tennis."

Then is an adverb telling time, as in "*Then* the killer tornado struck" and "The song *then* ended." *Then* always tells "time when."

Practice

Write a sentence in which you use *than* and *then* correctly.

Complete the following sentences with either *than* or *then.*

1. The movie *Titanic* was more popular in 1998 _____ any other film.
2. More flashbacks are used in *Titanic* _____ in most movies.
3. At the time of the construction of HMS *Titanic,* the owners thought it would last forever; _____ tragedy struck.
4. In its day, the *Titanic* was more powerful _____ any other ship.
5. It was several hours before neighboring ships learned of the *Titanic's* disaster. Only _____ were some of the passengers saved.

ARE, OUR

These words are often misused because they sound so much alike. *Are* is a verb, a form of *to be* or *am,* as in "There *are* many good films in the audio-visual department."

Our is a pronoun meaning "belonging to us," as in "*Our* business interests are booming." *Our* answers the question "to whom does something belong?"

One way to tell these two words apart is that *our* always answers the question "whose": *Whose* business interests are they? The answer is "*Our* business interests."

Practice

Write a sentence, or perhaps two sentences, in which you use *are* and *our* correctly.

Complete the following sentences with either *are* or *our:*

1. The remains of the *Titanic* _____ resting at the bottom of the sea near Newfoundland.
2. _____ curiosity is often piqued by information about a famous disaster like the *Titanic.*
3. _____ film history in America includes at least two portrayals of the destruction of the *Titanic.*
4. Why _____ natural disasters so compelling to humans?
5. The descendants of *Titanic* passengers _____ still making claims about the ownership of articles found in the shipwreck.

UNIT VI

Defining Family in Modern America

> The writers you study in this unit struggle with important questions of family life, marriage, gender roles, and expectations in our country today. The readings will provide you with food for thought, so that you may write to define for yourself your role in society.

FATHERS PROVIDE BRIDGE OVER THE "RIVER OF GOO"

Kathleen Parker

This article defines fatherhood in America from a specific perspective: the importance of the writer's father in her own life.

VOCABULARY IN CONTEXT

"that *metaphorical* crossover time"—symbolic, transitional

"before feminists revived *Ophelia* to decry female oppression"— learn about Ophelia's tragic story in Shakespeare's *Hamlet* and the 1994 book *Reviving Ophelia* by Mary Pipher

"girls need a good *boatswain* and his name is Dad"—officer on a ship responsible for deck and crew

PREREADING

1. Read the title and the first and last paragraphs, and then predict what the full article will say.

Fathers Provide Bridge over the "River of Goo"

Kathleen Parker

1 Columnist Leonard Pitts Jr. wrote recently of standing watch over the "River of Goo"—that metaphorical crossover time when clever, energetic, self-confident daughters reach adolescence and become someone their dads never knew before.

2 Where once they raced from place to place, they now slouch along sidewalks. Where once they eagerly raised their hands to answer questions in class, they sit silently hoping the boys won't think they're too smart. Where once they played joyfully with abandon, they now lurk dolefully in front of mirrors, comparing themselves to models who quit playing (and eating) long ago.

3 I remember well the River of Goo. Girls of my generation reached it around age 11 or 12, maybe earlier now. We, too, sulked and slouched and starved ourselves trying to be someone desirable. Girls were envying others' flat tummies long before feminists revived Ophelia to decry female oppression. So there's nothing new about the River of Goo, only our attention to it.

4 The attention is good, if talking about girls' loss of self-esteem during adolescence mends a few souls. But talking about self-esteem by way of school programs and role models and societal stereotypes is missing the boat. The River of Goo is navigable, but girls need a good boatswain and his name is Dad.

5 No single influence is more important to a girl's self-esteem and her future than her father. Studies support this notion, including a recent one out of England by a researcher named Adrienne Katz. In her "Can-Do Girls" report, published last year, Katz found that girls with the highest self-esteem and self-confidence had a strong father-daughter relationship.

6 But my belief in the importance of fathers isn't scientific; it's personal. My father raised me from the time I was 3, after my mother died. Here's what I know about fathers and daughters and the River of Goo.

7 My father didn't raise me to be a girl. He just raised me. He clocked me when I ran and praised me when I beat the neighborhood boys. He rarely told me I was pretty, even though every father thinks his daughter is. What I remember most is his telling me: "Looks aren't important. It's what you do that matters. Now go read a book."

8 "Look it up," he always said when I asked a word's meaning. He never would tell me himself. To look it up was to learn it.

9 "Do everything you can," he said. "Go everywhere, experience everything." I left home at 17 and never went home again except to visit.

10   "Think for yourself," he said. Once I was a teen, my father never told me what I could or couldn't do. He told me his opinion, then dropped the burden of decision in my lap. Of course, I always did what he wanted. How could I not? He was right.

11   "Be slow to know," he said about boys. "Don't give yourself away, hold your cards close, keep yourself to yourself." He taught me to play poker so I could keep a straight face, and to shoot a gun, so I could if I had to.

12   He took me on trips to learn to dine and dance. "Be a good listener," he said. That's all a man wants. "Leave the first time he raises a hand." He'll do it again.

13   "Peel the potatoes, Catalina," he said almost every night. He was Irish; I'm a master potato peeler. While I peeled, he cooked dinner and we talked about whatever came to mind. Can I do this? Should I do that?

14   "You can do anything," he said. Funny, I believed him.

15   I can't speak to the value of mothers to their daughters. I don't recommend growing up without one. But I can't fathom growing up without a father. They speak differently to daughters than mothers do. They allow you to take risks; they teach you your worth in the presence of men. They say things like "Chin up, Catalina, keep your eye on the ball."

16   I worry about the many girls growing up without fathers owing to divorce, divisive custody arrangements or the misguided decisions of some women to become single mothers. I'd wager that behind most women who successfully crossed the River of Goo was a man, and his name was Dad.

READING RESPONSE JOURNAL

1. After reading the whole article, write a one-paragraph summary of it.

2. What personal thoughts does the article stir in you? Brainstorm about them.

3. Does the article provide you with any other ideas to write about?

4. The writer defines the "River of Goo" as "that metaphorical crossover time when clever, energetic, self-confident daughters reach adolescence and become someone their dads never knew before." Paraphrase this definition.

5. What does Parker mean by "feminists revived Ophelia to decry female oppression"? Note that this sentence contains a play on words about the book *Reviving Ophelia.* Who was Ophelia and what happened to her?

6. In her metaphor of crossing the river as a journey, whom does Parker point to as the "boatswain," or guide, for young girls?

7. What research does Parker cite to support her claim that "No single influence is more important to a girl's self-esteem and future than her father"?

8. What influence did her father have in Parker's own life?

9. According to Parker, how do fathers "speak differently to daughters than mothers do"?

10. What worries for girls today does Parker mention?

11. How does Parker conclude her essay?

WRITING FROM READING

Using Specifics to Define and Describe

Parker's essay defines and describes her father's vital role in her own development. Note how she is specific in discussing her father's influence, relating to us his exact words and deeds:

> "Be slow to know," he said about boys. "Don't give yourself away, hold your cards close, keep yourself to yourself." He taught me to play poker, so I could keep a straight face, and to shoot a gun, so I could if I had to.

The essay also shows how Parker's father helped make her independent and self-reliant: "I left at 17 and never went home again except to visit."

1. If you are a female student, think of the "River of Goo" in your own life. Describe the troubles of adolescence and early womanhood—"goo" you crossed over. Then write about your father's help during that time. Like Parker, be specific and quote some of the advice your father gave you and the things he did for you. You might even make a brainstorming list of them to help you choose the ones to write about in your paper.

2. Unlike Parker's father, some dads are abusive to their daughters, verbally or even sexually, making their childhood a nightmare. If this trauma happened to you or someone close to you, write about it—as painful as it may be. You may wish to keep your paper confidential.

3. If you are a male student, look over what Parker's father said to her and then think about what advice *you* would give *your* daughter to help ease her way through the struggles of adolescence and later. Write about how you would act and how you would counsel your daughter. Again, like Parker, be specific.

4. Parker is troubled about the "misguided decisions of some women to become single mothers." Write your views on women who decide to become single mothers.

COLLABORATIVE LEARNING ACTIVITY

Listening for Specifics

In your group, brainstorm or freewrite about any of the questions raised in Writing from Reading. Ask your listeners if you have provided enough specifics to bring your characters and story to life.

WRITING TIPS

A Strong Conclusion

Parker ends her essay with a strong sentence: "I'd wager that behind most women who successfully crossed the River of Goo was a man, and his name was Dad." In your paper, try for a powerful, summarizing sentence, the kernel of your thoughts.

REVIEW

Details, specifics, and direct quotations add force to your writing.

THE STORY OF A SUCCESSFUL SINGLE MOM: HAD IT NOT BEEN FOR THE VILLAGE . . .

Bunnie Riedel

What follows is the story of a single mom who made it—with the help of the village, those people not our parents who sometimes show us the way.

VOCABULARY IN CONTEXT

> *"Afrocentric"*—of African origins
> "much-*maligned*"—criticized
> *"antithetical"*—the opposite
> *"admonition"*—warning
> *"forensics"*—speech and debate

PREREADING

1. Look at the title. Predict what the article will say.
2. Now read the first two and last two paragraphs. Suggest a tentative thesis for this article.

Had It Not Been for the Village . . .

Bunnie Riedel

1   These days the word "village" makes Republicans hiss and sneer and makes Democrats cheer wildly. Maybe it's because *village* has become the rallying cry for Republican-backed "parental rights" laws. Or maybe because the word is Afrocentric, as is the context from which "It takes a village to raise a child" is lifted. I don't know. I am sure, however, that parental rights proposals send chills down my spine and if it hadn't been for that much-maligned village, I would not be who I am today. In fact, I'd most likely be dead.

2   My youth was a living hell at best. I have the distinction of having had not one, but two mothers who were total failures.

3   My first mother was my biological mother. She became an itinerant farm worker, alcoholic, and finally, murder victim. I was her 12th child and there were three more to follow me. She left the Ozarks of Missouri while she was pregnant with me, with my older sister at her side, stopping just long enough in Tulsa to have me and then move on to California.

There she worked the fields, lived off the kindness of loser men and drank her once attractive self into complete ruin. When I was two, she became pregnant again and decided to give me (not my sister or the new baby) up for adoption to her two landlords. I didn't see my older sister, Debra, for another 20 years and I met the original 10 children (left behind in Missouri) 10 years after that.

4 My second mother, Naomi, thought of herself as being completely antithetical to the first and in many ways she was. She provided a home, clothes, great cooking and regular church attendance. I can count the number of times she hugged me on one hand and count even fewer times she told me she loved me. Our home looked fine from without but was a nightmare within. My father died when I was 8 and Naomi conveniently forgot his admonition that she was not to hit me. So hit me she did. With belts, coat hangers, kicks, hair- and ear-pulling, Naomi was determined to beat the hell out of me.

5 But more than the beatings, I'll never forget the things she said: "You'll never amount to anything." "You're so stupid." "Sometimes I would like to kill you." These verbal tirades were almost worse than the physical beatings because they would last for hours. I'll never forget the time I had a girlfriend spending the night and my mother woke me up at 4 a.m. and railed on me until 7. My friend will never forget it either. Even now, after 25 years, my old friend mentions that episode every time we see each other.

6 For me, and for so many children like me, the village became our life-saver. I would leave the house in the morning with swollen, red eyes (from crying myself to sleep the night before) and find haven for a few hours a day with adults who were actually kind, helpful and praised my accomplishments. School was my salvation. It was the teachers I encountered at public school who gave me a glimpse of what life could actually be like. In that glimpse, I saw a world beyond my mother's house, full of wonder and unafraid of inquiry. It was a world where discipline was administered with dignity and self-esteem was valued. Mrs. Nyberg, Mr. Wood, Mrs. Papadakis, Mr. Pessano, Mr. McDonald and Mrs. Edwards were people who broadened my horizons with ideas and information that were unattainable at home. They were people who gave me something to hold onto throughout those dark, ugly days and none of them knew that.

7 In my neighborhood, there were other examples of caring adults. My Girl Scout leader thought I had a keen, interesting mind and she told me so. The German woman down the street (with the six kids) taught me how to do the twist and offered me graham crackers and hot chocolate. My friend's aunt spent hours with me as I entered my teen years, talking to me like I was really a human being.

8 I used every excuse I could to go out into the village. I was active in after-school activities and clubs. I began working at 13. I went away to church camp. I excelled in drama, journalism and forensics. These are the things that kept me from drowning myself in drugs or alcohol. These people and activities kept me from killing myself that one awful night when I was 16 and I had reached the end of my rope. These people and activi-

ties gave me the courage to pack a bag and leave home at 17, two weeks before I was ready to start my first semester at the university my mother insisted I could not got to, even though I had a scholarship and grants that completely paid my way. If it hadn't been for that village . . .

9   Now, many years since Naomi's death and many miles from that home that was not a home, I count on my village as a parent. When my children were little, the village taught me simple things that I had not learned at home; how to breast feed, how to change diapers, how to teach my children to read, how to discipline without violence. As my children have become teenagers and I have become a single parent, the village has become even more critical to my family's health and well-being. There are those loving adults at our church who adore my children, give them new experiences and constant encouragement. There are those caring adults at their school who challenge them to stretch their imaginations and use their intellect. There are those adults in our neighborhood who wave and smile and provide a watchful eye of protection. As a single, custodial parent of children whose father is 3,000 miles away and rarely sees them, I count on the men in the village to provide examples to my son and daughter of what dedicated, responsible men look like.

10   I know firsthand that not every parent is wise, all-knowing and care-taking. Sometimes it is because they did not receive those things themselves as children; sometimes it is because they are hopelessly lost in their own egos.

11   Making fun of a promising and true statement, that it does indeed "take a village to raise a child," does not change bad parents into good ones, it only furthers political games at the expense of children. Writing into law that a parent's "rights" are absolute and inalienable (and thereby overturning almost 2,000 state child abuse statutes), will not strengthen families but lead to despair for the most vulnerable members of those families.

12   The village saved my life.

READING RESPONSE JOURNAL

1. Summarize the article.

2. What ideas from the article can you write about?

3. Does anything else from the article strike you?

4. In her first paragraph, Riedel quotes the African proverb "It takes a village to raise a child." Explain what this proverb means.

5. How does the essay define *village?*

6. We are often told that mental abuse is far worse for a child than physical abuse. What does Riedel say about that?

7. What real-life example does the writer use of how bad her second mother was? Why does Riedel mention that her "old friend" witnessed this incident?

8. In what two particular crises for Bunnie Riedel did the "village" save her?

9. How did the village again help Bunnie Riedel later in her life?

10. What two possible reasons does Riedel give for parents not being "wise, all-knowing and caretaking"?

11. What does Riedel say about those who poke fun at the village concept?

12. What does Riedel say is wrong about making laws of parents' rights that are "absolute and inalienable"?

WRITING FROM READING

Using Definition in a Personal Essay

This essay crackles with the emotional pain the writer has suffered. But consider the care Riedel takes to define and describe those who were *her* village:

> Mrs. Nyberg, Mr. Woody, Mrs. Papadakis, Mr. Pessano, Mr. McDonald and Mrs. Edwards were people who broadened my horizons with ideas and information that were unattainable at home.

> My Girl Scout leader thought I had a keen, interesting mind and she told me so.

> My friend's aunt spent hours with me as I entered my teen years, talking to me like I was really a human being.

In the writing assignments that follow, try to define for yourself and your audience those figures crucial to your development. Like Riedel, use specific examples.

1. Are there any examples of how the village helped in your development? Make a prewriting list of such people and examples, trying to define them by their effects on you.
2. Part of the "village" for most people is made up of relatives other than their parents. Riedel had no such relatives living close to her. Are there any relatives who make up *your* village? If so, make a prewriting list and then write a paper about the influence of your relatives. You may want to pick just one to define and describe at length.
3. This topic may be too personal for you to write about, but could you define, or explain in detail, the difficulties you have had in getting to college? Look at the obstacles Bunnie Riedel overcame: an alcoholic mother, the deaths of both her biological parents, and a stepmother who had forbidden her to go to a university "even though I had a scholarship and grants that completely paid my way." Most of us never had to face such strong obstacles in our lives. Prewrite about the problems you overcame and then write a paper explaining them more fully.

In addition to using definition in her essay, Riedel uses contrast to describe the chaotic life she had lived with her stepmother who "provided a home, clothes, great cooking and regular church attendance." But Riedel goes on to say, "Our home looked fine from without but was a nightmare within." The difference between the surface appearance of her new home and the abuse heaped on Riedel inside is dramatic. Use contrast to describe some family that you know whose exterior image differs from the reality they actually live day to day. Use a prewriting list to get you started, and then write a longer paper about this topic.

COLLABORATIVE LEARNING ACTIVITY

Analyzing Transitions

Because much of her essay is the story of her life, Riedel is careful to use transitional words and sentences to link the different parts of it:

> "My youth was a living hell at best."
> "My first mother . . ."
> "My second mother . . ."
> "But more than the beatings, I'll never forget the things she said."
> "Now, many years since Naomi's death and many miles from that home that was not a home . . ."

The essay uses other transitions too.

In your group, take turns reading the essay out loud and write down other transitions Riedel uses.

WRITING TIPS

The Circle Ending

Notice the "circle" ending of Riedel's essay. Her simple and dramatic conclusion "The village saved my life" brings us back to the beginning where she quotes the full proverb, "It takes a village to raise a child." At the end of your papers, always look back to the beginning for some unifying statement or idea that ties your work together.

REVIEW

The writer defines reality by giving details—the actions and words of real people.

STONE SOUP

Barbara Kingsolver

This piece is much longer than most of the readings in this text because it develops definitions about marriage and family by analyzing them in different stages of America's history. "Stone Soup" is an *extended* (long and detailed) definition of marriage and family life in our modern world.

VOCABULARY IN CONTEXT

"a *harbinger* of cultural ruin"—a sign, prediction

"a sweet *imperious* stare"—commanding, powerful

"vice versa"—the opposite, the other way around

"caprice"—changeable, illogical meaning

"irreconcilable differences"—can't be resolved

"specious"—deceptive; apparently true, but actually not

"straits"—waters of passage

"monogamy"—one spouse, one mate

"a child would *revel*"—enjoy

"unfathomably large"—difficult to understand

"tidy *symmetry*"—balance

"Its advantage may have been *resilience*"—strength, flexibility

"unprecedented numbers"—unheard of before, very large

"social historians *corroborate*"—support, confirm

"panacea"—cure-all

"sequestered suburbs"—secluded, hidden

"amorphous, adaptable structure"—shapeless, formless

"Olduvai Gorge"—site in Tanzania where some of the oldest human remains were discovered

"a pair of *beleaguered* soldiers"—tired, struggling

"a heck of a *bouillabaisse*"—chowder made up of different types of fish and seasonings

PREREADING

1. Read the title and the first two paragraphs. Predict what the full article will state.

Stone Soup

Barbara Kingsolver

1   In the catalog of family values, where do we rank an occasion like this? A curly-haired boy who wanted to run before he walked, age seven now, a soccer player scoring a winning goal. He turns to the bleachers with his fists in the air and a smile wide as a gap-toothed galaxy. His own cheering section of grown-ups and kids all leap to their feet and hug each other, delirious with love for this boy. He's Andy, my best friend's son. The cheering section includes his mother and her friends, his brother, his father and stepmother, a stepbrother and stepsister, and a grandparent. Lucky is the child with this many relatives on hand to hail a proud accomplishment. I'm there too, witnessing a family fortune. But in spite of myself, defensive words take shape in my head. I am thinking: I dare *anybody* to call this a broken home.

2   Families change, and remain the same. Why are our names for home so slow to catch up to the truth of where we live?

3   When I was a child, I had two parents who loved me without cease. One of them attended every excuse for attention I ever contrived, and the other made it to the ones with higher production values, like piano recitals and appendicitis. So I was a lucky child too. I played with a set of paper dolls called "The Family of Dolls," four in number, who came with the factory-assigned names of Dad, Mom, Sis, and Junior. I think you know what they looked like, at least before I loved them to death and their heads fell off.

4   Now I've replaced the dolls with a life. I knit my days around my daughter's survival and happiness, and am proud to say her head is still on. But we aren't the Family of Dolls. Maybe you're not, either. And if not, even though you are statistically no oddity, it's probably been suggested to you in a hundred ways that yours isn't exactly a real family, but an impostor family, a harbinger of cultural ruin, a slapdash substitute—something like counterfeit money. Here at the tail end of our century, most of us are up to our ears in the noisy business of trying to support and love a thing called family. But there's a current in the air with ferocious moral force that finds its way even into political campaigns, claiming there is only one right way to do it, the Way It Has Always Been.

5   In the face of a thriving, particolored world, this narrow view is so pickled and absurd I'm astonished that it gets airplay. And I'm astonished that it still stings.

6   Every parent has endured the arrogance of a child-unfriendly grump sitting in judgment, explaining what those kids of ours really need (for example, "a good licking"). If we're polite, we move our crew to another bench in the park. If we're forthright (as I am in my mind, only, for the rest of the day), we fix them with a sweet imperious stare and say, "Come back and let's talk about it after you've changed a thousand diapers."

7   But it's harder somehow to shrug off the Family-of-Dolls Family Values crew when they judge (from their safe distance) that divorced people, blended families, gay families, and single parents are failures. That our children are at risk, and the whole arrangement is messy and embarrassing. A marriage that ends is not called "finished," it's called *failed*. The children of this family may have been born to a happy union, but now they are called *the children of divorce*.

8   I had no idea how thoroughly these assumptions overlaid my culture until I went through divorce myself. I wrote to a friend: "This might be worse than being widowed. Overnight I've suffered the same losses—companionship, financial and practical support, my identity as a wife and partner, the future I'd taken for granted. I am lonely, grieving, and hard-pressed to take care of my household alone. But instead of bringing casseroles, people are acting like I had a fit and broke up the family china."

9   Once upon a time I held these beliefs about divorce: that everyone who does it could have chosen not to do it. That it's a lazy way out of marital problems. That it selfishly puts personal happiness ahead of family integrity. Now I tremble for my ignorance. It's easy, in fortunate times, to forget about the ambush that could leave your head reeling: serious mental or physical illness, death in the family, abandonment, financial calamity, humiliation, violence, despair.

10   I started out like any child, intent on being the Family of Dolls. I set upon young womanhood believing in most of the doctrines of my generation: I wore my skirts four inches above the knee. I had that Barbie with her zebra-striped swimsuit and a figure unlike anything found in nature. And I understood the Prince Charming Theory of Marriage, a quest for Mr. Right that ends smack dab where you find him. I did not completely understand that another whole story *begins* there, and no fairy tale prepared me for the combination of bad luck and persistent hope that would interrupt my dream and lead me to other arrangements. Like a cancer diagnosis, a dying marriage is a thing to fight, to deny, and finally, when there's no choice left, to dig in and survive. Casseroles would help. Likewise, I imagine it must be a painful reckoning in adolescence (or later on) to realize one's own true love will never look like the soft-focus fragrance ads because Prince charming (surprise!) is a princess. Or vice versa. Or has skin the color your parents didn't want you messing with, except in the Crayola box.

11   It's awfully easy to hold in contempt the straw broken home, and that mythical category of persons who toss away nuclear family for the sheer fun of it. Even the legal terms we use have a suggestion of caprice. I resent the phrase "irreconcilable differences," which suggests a stubborn refusal to accept a spouse's little quirks. This is specious. Every happily married couple I know has loads of irreconcilable differences. Negotiating where to set the thermostat is not the point. A nonfunctioning marriage is a slow asphyxiation. It is waking up despised each morn-

ing, listening to the pulse of your own loneliness before the radio begins to blare its raucous gospel that you're nothing if you aren't loved. It is sharing your airless house with the threat of suicide or other kinds of violence, while the ghost that whispers, "Leave here and destroy your children," has passed over every door and nailed it shut. Disassembling a marriage in these circumstances is as much *fun* as amputating your own gangrenous leg. You do it, if you can, to save a life—or two, or more.

12   I know of no one who really went looking to hoe the harder row, especially the daunting one of single parenthood. Yet it seems to be the most American of customs to blame the burdened for their destiny. We'd like so desperately to believe in freedom and justice for all, we can hardly name that rogue bad luck, even when he's a close enough snake to bite us. In the wake of my divorce, some friends (even a few close ones) chose to vanish, rather than linger within striking distance of misfortune.

13   But most stuck around, bless their hearts, and if I'm any the wiser for my trials, it's from having learned the worth of steadfast friendship. And also, what not to say. The least helpful question is: "Did you want the divorce, or didn't you?" Did I want to keep that gangrenous leg, or not? How to explain, in a culture that venerates choice: two terrifying options are much worse than none at all. Give me any day the quick hand of cruel fate that will leave me scarred but blameless. As it was, I kept thinking of that wicked third-grade joke in which some boy comes up behind you and grabs your ear, starts in with a prolonged tug, and asks, "Do you want this ear any longer?"

14   Still, the friend who holds your hand and says the wrong thing is made of dearer stuff than the one who stays away. And generally, through all of it, you live. My favorite fictional character, Kate Vaiden (in the novel by Reynolds Price), advises: "Strength just comes in one brand—you stand up at sunrise and meet what they send you and keep your hair combed."

15   Once you've weathered the straits, you get to cross the tricky juncture from casualty to survivor. If you're on your feet at the end of a year or two, and have begun putting together a happy new existence, those friends who were kind enough to feel sorry for you when you needed it must now accept you back to the ranks of the living. If you're truly blessed, they will dance at your second wedding. Everybody else, for heaven's sake, should stop throwing stones.

16   Arguing about whether nontraditional families deserve pity or tolerance is a little like the medieval debate about left-handedness as a mark of the devil. Divorce, remarriage, single parenthood, gay parents, and blended families simply are. They're facts of our time. Some of the reasons listed by sociologists for these family reconstructions are: the idea of marriage as a romantic partnership rather than a pragmatic one; a shift in women's expectations, from servility to self-respect and independence; and longevity (prior to antibiotics no marriage was expected to last many decades—in Colonial days the average couple lived to be married less than

twelve years). Add to all this, our growing sense of entitlement to happiness and safety from abuse. Most would agree these are all good things. Yet their result—a culture in which serial monogamy and the consequent reshaping of families are the norm—gets diagnosed as "failing."

17   For many of us, once we have put ourselves Humpty-Dumpty-wise back together again, the main problem with our reorganized family is that other people think we have a problem. My daughter tells me the only time she's uncomfortable about being the child of divorced parents is when her friends say they feel sorry for her. It's a bizarre sympathy, given that half the kids in her school and nation are in the same boat, pursuing childish happiness with the same energy as their married-parent peers. When anyone asks how *she* feels about it, she spontaneously lists the benefits: our house is in the country and we have a dog, but she can go to her dad's neighborhood for the urban thrills of a pool and sidewalks for roller-skating. What's more, she has three sets of grandparents!

18   Why is it surprising that a child would revel in a widened family and the right to feel at home in more than one house? Isn't it the opposite that should worry us—a child with no home at all, or too few resources to feel safe? The child at risk is the one whose parents are too immature themselves to guide wisely; too diminished by poverty to nurture; too far from opportunity to offer hope. The number of children in the U.S. living in poverty at this moment is almost unfathomably large: twenty percent. There are families among us that need help all right, and by no means are they new on the landscape. The rate at which teenage girls had babies in 1957 (ninety-six per thousand) was twice what it is now. That remarkable statistic is ignored by the religious right—probably because the teen birth rate was cut in half mainly by legalized abortion. In fact, the policy gatekeepers who coined the phrase "family values" have steadfastly ignored the desperation of too-small families, and since 1979 have steadily reduced the amount of financial support available to a single parent. But, this camp's most outspoken attacks seem aimed at the notion of families getting too complex, with add-ons and extras such as a gay parent's partner, or a remarried mother's new husband and his children.

19   To judge a family's value by its tidy symmetry is to purchase a book for its cover. There's no moral authority there. The famous family comprised of Dad, Mom, Sis, and Junior living as an isolated economic unit is not built on historical bedrock. In *The Way We Never Were,* Stephanie Coontz writes, "Whenever people propose that we go back to the traditional family, I always suggest that they pick a ballpark date for the family they have in mind." Colonial families were tidily disciplined, but their members (meaning everyone but infants) labored incessantly and died young. Then the Victorian family adopted a new division of labor, in which women's role was domestic and children were allowed time for study and play, but this was an upper-class construct supported by myriad slaves. Coontz writes, "For every nineteenth-century middle-class family that protected its wife and child within the family circle, there was

an Irish or German girl scrubbing floors . . . a Welsh boy mining coal to keep the home-baked goodies warm, a black girl doing the family laundry, a black mother and child picking cotton to be made into clothes for the family, and a Jewish or an Italian daughter in a sweatshop making 'ladies' dresses or artificial flowers for the family to purchase."

20   The abolition of slavery brought slightly more democratic arrangements, in which extended families were harnessed together in cottage industries; at the turn of the century came a steep rise in child labor in mines and sweatshops. Twenty percent of American children lived in orphanages at the time; their parents were not necessarily dead, but couldn't afford to keep them.

21   During the Depression and up to the end of World War II, many millions of U.S. households were more multigenerational than nuclear. Women my grandmother's age were likely to live with a fluid assortment of elderly relatives, in-laws, siblings, and children. In many cases they spent virtually every waking hour working in the company of other women—a companionable scenario in which it would be easier, I imagine, to tolerate an estranged or difficult spouse. I'm reluctant to idealize a life of so much hard work and so little spousal intimacy, but its advantage may have been resilience. A family so large and varied would not easily be brought down by a single blow: it could absorb a death, long illness, an abandonment here or there, and any number of irreconcilable differences.

22   The Family of Dolls came along midcentury as a great American experiment. A booming economy required a mobile labor force and demanded that women surrender jobs to returning soldiers. Families came to be defined by a single breadwinner. They struck out for single-family homes at an earlier age than ever before, and in unprecedented numbers they raised children in suburban isolation. The nuclear family was launched to sink or swim.

23   More than a few sank. Social historians corroborate that the suburban family of the postwar economic boom, which we have recently selected as our definition of "traditional," was no panacea. Twenty-five percent of Americans were poor in the mid-1950s, and as yet there were no food stamps. Sixty percent of the elderly lived on less than $1,000 a year, and most had no medical insurance. In the sequestered suburbs, alcoholism and sexual abuse of children were far more widespread than anyone imagined.

24   Expectations soared, and the economy sagged. It's hard to depend on one other adult for everything, come what may. In the last three decades, that amorphous, adaptable structure we call "family" has been reshaped once more by economic tides. Compared with fifties families, mothers are far more likely now to be employed. We are statistically more likely to divorce, and to live in blended families or other extranuclear arrangements. We are also more likely to plan and space our children, and to rate our marriages as "happy." We are less likely to suffer abuse without recourse, or to stare out at our lives through a glaze of prescription tran-

quilizers. Our aged parents are less likely to be destitute, and we're half as likely to have a teenage daughter turn up a mother herself. All in all, I would say that if "intact" in modern family-values jargon means living quietly desperate in the bell jar, then hip-hip-hooray for "broken." A neat family model constructed to service the Baby Boom economy seems to be returning gradually to a grand, lumpy shape that human families apparently have tended toward since they first took root in the Olduvai Gorge. We're social animals, deeply fond of companionship, and children love best to run in packs. If there is a *normal* for humans, at all, I expect it looks like two or three Families of Dolls, connected variously by kinship and passion, shuffled like cards and strewn over several shoeboxes.

25   The sooner we can let go the fairy tale of families functioning perfectly in isolation, the better we might embrace the relief of community. Even the admirable parents who've stayed married through thick and think are very likely, at present, to incorporate other adults into their families—household help and baby-sitters if they can afford them, or neighbors and grandparents if they can't. For single parents, this support is the rock-bottom definition of family. And most parents who have split apart, however painfully, still manage to maintain family continuity for their children, creating in many cases a boisterous phenomenon that Constance Ahrons in her book *The Good Divorce* calls the "binuclear family." Call it what you will—when ex-spouses beat swords into plowshares and jump up and down at a soccer game together, it makes for happy kids.

26   Cinderella, look, who needs her? All those evil stepsisters? That story always seemed like too much cotton-picking fuss over clothes. A childhood tale that fascinated me more was the one called "Stone Soup," and the gist of it is this: Once upon a time, a pair of beleaguered soldiers straggled home to a village empty-handed, in a land ruined by war. They were famished, but the villagers had so little they shouted evil words and slammed their doors. So the soldiers dragged out a big kettle, filled it with water, and put it on a fire to boil. They rolled a clean round stone into the pot, while the villagers peered through their curtains in amazement.

27   "What kind of soup is that?" they hooted.

28   "Stone soup," the soldiers replied. "Everybody can have some when it's done."

29   "Well, thanks," one matron grumbled, coming out with a shriveled carrot. "But it'd be better if you threw this in."

30   And so on, of course, a vegetable at a time, until the whole suspicious village managed to feed itself grandly.

31   Any family is a big empty pot, save for what gets thrown in. Each stew turns out different. Generosity, a resolve to turn bad luck into good, and respect for variety—these things will nourish a nation of children. Name-calling and suspicion will not. My soup contains a rock or two of hard times, and maybe yours does too. I expect it's a heck of a bouillabaise.

READING RESPONSE JOURNAL

1. Because "Stone Soup" is a long article, it may take a long paragraph or two to summarize.

2. What concerns about marriage and family does "Stone Soup" raise in you?

3. Does the reading give you any other food for thought?

4. How does this essay use the "sign of the cross" structure (see page 126) at the beginning?

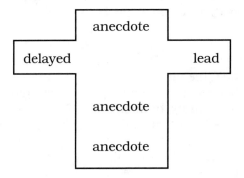

5. What was the "Family of Dolls"?

6. What did the writer learn about divorce going through it herself?

7. What is the "Prince Charming Theory of Marriage"?

8. What *benefit* from divorce does the writer's daughter point to?

9. Why does the essay cite the decline in teen pregnancy?

10. What insight does the essay draw from writer Stephanie Coontz?

11. According to the essay, how do today's marriages compare with those of the 1950s?

12. Why does the writer reject the Cinderella myth for the "Stone Soup" story?

WRITING FROM READING

The Definition Essay

The essay "Stone Soup" uses the child's story of the same name to argue for a new, modern definition of marriage and family. In her essay, the writer uses anecdotes, personal experience (her own divorce), and outside sources (statistics and writers such as Coontz and Ahrons) to build her definition.

1. Write a paper in which *you* define marriage and family life. Use examples, personal experiences, and outside sources if you wish. Consider using an anecdote or incident to begin your paper.

2. "Stone Soup" is in a sense a "definition paper" about the contemporary American family. The essay also uses the comparison and contrast method of development in studying marriages of the 1950s and other historical periods. You might wish to compare and contrast *your* thoughts on marriage with those of your parents or grandparents.

COLLABORATIVE LEARNING ACTIVITY

Using Clear Anecdotes

Listen for clear anecdotes in the papers from your group. Analyze the incidents for completeness. Do they have a beginning, a middle, and an end? Do they relate to the writer's definition?

WRITING TIPS

A Longer Thesis

Partway through the essay, the writer presents a clear thesis:

> Arguing about whether nontraditional families deserve pity or tolerance is a little like the medieval debate about left-handedness as a mark of the devil. Divorce, remarriage, single parenthood, gay parents, and blended families simply are. They're facts of our time.

Note that this thesis has three sentences because the writer believes her view cannot be expressed in just one sentence.

A longer essay often requires a longer thesis. In your definition essay, state your thesis clearly. A very long essay might need a thesis statement of more than one sentence.

REVIEW

Take note how the good writer uses many different kinds of sources, as well as anecdotes and personal experience, to build a good essay.

ENLIST HOLLYWOOD IN THE WAR ON TEEN PREGNANCY

Ellen Goodman

In this essay, Ellen Goodman argues that Hollywood sells images of unrealistic sex to impressionable teens.

VOCABULARY IN CONTEXT

"classic *paean*"—song of praise

"*euphemistically*"—saying a negative thing in a positive way

"*counterculture*"—opposition to mainstream culture

"*incessant* messages"—unending

"*conglomerate*"—huge corporate body

"say *unequivocally*"—with no doubt

"cultural *elite*"—special class or group

PREREADING

1. Read the title and the first two and the last two paragraphs. Predict some of what the essay will say.

Enlist Hollywood in the War on Teen Pregnancy

Ellen Goodman

1 When Kathleen Sylvester began researching welfare reform for the Progressive Policy Institute, she asked a Baltimore school principal the one thing she'd do to reduce the number of teenage pregnancies.

2 The principal had an immediate two-word answer for her: "Shoot Madonna."

3 This was not a serious attempt on this educator's part to cure sex with violence. The principal was not a character assassin.

4 She was probably thinking of the Madonna of the 1980s, the one who wrote the classic paean to teenage motherhood: "Papa Don't Preach." The Madonna of the '90s has a line in "Bedtime Stories" that sounds more like a paean to Joycelyn Elders: "Happiness lies in your own hand."

5 But the principal was speaking in a familiar vocabulary. It's a language shared by parents, teachers, policymakers, the whole range of

frustrated adults whose voices of reason are drowned out by a culture that sells kids sex as successfully as it sells them sneakers. Just Do It.

6   These messages that kids actually listen to ought to be piped into the hearing rooms where Congress is busy concocting a new welfare policy. The plan the House Ways and Means Committee is contemplating for teenage mothers is called euphemistically "tough love." But our culture offers something else. Sex without consequences.

7   "How many times do kids see sex on TV," says Sylvester, "in which no one gets pregnant, no one gets AIDS and no one has to get up in the middle of the night to feed a baby?"

8   In the face of the onslaught, the true counterculture in America is not the "McGovernik elite" or, for heaven's sakes, PBS. It's parents and reasonable adults who are left to literally counter the culture, to do combat with the incessant messages of mainstream films, music, television—the conglomerate known as Hollywood—as best we can.

9   Hollywood may not cause teen pregnancy. But Sylvester and others are convinced that any national campaign that goes to the heart and hardcore of the problem is going to have to engage these cultural message-makers.

10   We're going to have to do more than label them as villains. We need them as allies.

11   It will take all their creativity to make a successful pitch against irresponsible sex and teen pregnancy. "Just say no" won't do it. Teenagers are the most risk-taking part of the population. They're still being seduced by cigarette ads.

12   It will be harder to fashion a stand against sex than against smoking. After all, smoking is always bad for you, sex isn't. And hormones are even more powerful than nicotine addiction.

13   It will also be harder to campaign against unwed parenthood than against drunk driving. The campaign against drunk driving was successful in curbing dangerous behavior by creating a new social role: the designated driver. But a baby is a different sort of accident than a head-on collision.

14   If we can't preach, however much papa (and mama) may want to, we can say unequivocally in rhythm, rap or reel what Sylvester says in plain words: "It's wrong to bring a child into the world that you can't take care of." It's not cool, it's not manly, it's not womanly. It's wrong.

15   This goes beyond using Madonna for target practice. It even goes beyond lowering the sexual thermostat of the culture.

16   Entertainment executives like to say, on the one hand, that they are just reflecting reality and, on the other hand, that they're in the business of fantasy. With both hands, they wave furious charges of censorship at any critic.

17   But how about more reality? In an ad campaign, in soap operas, movies, music.

18   Not long ago, an outraged producer complained to Jay Winston, the public health guru who created the designated driver campaign: "Can you

imagine that people are lobbying to have Tom Cruise use a condom? Tom Cruise?" Why is that so hard to imagine?

19   At Harvard's Kennedy School of Government, a nervous Barbra Streisand recently offered a spirited defense of the artist as citizen. But the problem isn't that this "cultural elite" is too political, it's that it isn't political enough. As Winston says, "They ought to be powerful players in this process. They need to come to the table."

20   Let's begin with some sexual truth-in-advertising: one part passion to two parts diapers. Sex and consequences. Try humming a few bars.

READING RESPONSE JOURNAL

1. Write a one-paragraph summary of the article.

2. Prewrite about how the article might relate to your life.

3. Is there anything more for you to write on from this article?

4. Goodman claims that "our culture offers something else. Sex without consequences." If you think she is right, give some examples of your own from the media.

5. Asked what to do about teenage pregnancies, the principal replied, "Shoot Madonna." Why?

6. According to Goodman, some people think welfare reform is going to bring "tough love" to teenage mothers. What do you think this means?

7. Why does Goodman allege that teaching safe sex will be harder than warning about teen smoking or drunk driving?

8. What arguments do entertainment executives make against censorship of the media?

9. Why did the movie producer object to suggestions that Tom Cruise wear a condom?

10. Jay Winston, the public health expert, says, "They [media executives] ought to be powerful players in this process. They need to come to the table." What is Winston looking for from media big-shots?

11. What does Goodman's solution mean? "Let's begin with some sexual truth-in-advertising: one part passion to two parts diapers. Sex and consequences. Try humming a few bars."

12. Do you think Goodman's suggestions are realistic or not?

WRITING FROM READING

Problem-Solution Structure

Goodman's essay is written in a problem-solution pattern: She first defines the problems of permissive sex in the media and then points to some solutions like persuading the media to promote truth about sexual consequences.

1. Write a paper of your own about sex in the media. First, prewrite about the problems and then list some solutions. In the beginning of your paper, explain the problems, perhaps giving some real examples from the media. Then at the end of your paper, describe the possible solutions for the problems you've raised—keeping the same order from your explanation of problems.

2. Kathleen Sylvester has a strong message she wants the media to deliver to teens: "It's wrong to bring a child into the world that you can't take care of." Goodman then adds, "It's not cool, it's not manly, it's not womanly. It's wrong." Explain your thoughts about this message, framing your essay in the problem-solution pattern.

3. Imagine for a moment what Madonna would say to an interviewer after reading this essay. What does Madonna's own unwed pregnancy say to teens?

4. What if the media agreed with the ideas in this article? Can you suggest some positive ways in which the media could promote responsible sex? Again, write your essay in the pattern of organization Goodman uses: first problems and then their solutions.

COLLABORATIVE LEARNING ACTIVITY

Drafting a Group Paper

In your group, brainstorm about some possible solutions to the problems Goodman raises. See if you can put your ideas into a group paper.

WRITING TIPS

The Strong Ending

In her conclusion, Goodman wishes to leave something in the minds of her readers with her line about "sexual truth-in-advertising: one part passion to two parts diapers." This summarizes her plea for more reality in the media. In your essay, too, search for a strong last line.

REVIEW

The problem-solution structure is a natural one. Start by defining or explaining the problems and then suggest solutions to them in the same order that you introduced them.

"SUPERFLUOUS" DADS
A MENACE TO SOCIETY

William Raspberry

This article by William Raspberry analyzes the epidemic of fatherlessness in America today by defining what makes a "superfluous" dad.

VOCABULARY IN CONTEXT

"the *diminution* in the public mind"—lessening, shrinking

"this *marginalization*"—excluding, forcing outside

"this *phenomenon*"—unusual occurrence

"his *quandary*"—the difficulty, dilemma

"at some cost to their own *autonomy*"—independence

PREREADING

1. Check the definition of *superfluous* in a dictionary. Next, try to discover the meaning of the title: how a " 'superfluous' dad" can be a "menace to society." Then read the first and last paragraphs. Predict what the rest of the article will say.

"Superfluous" Dads a Menace to Society

William Raspberry

1 "A generation ago, an American child could reasonably expect to grow up with his or her father. Today, an American child can reasonably expect not to. . . . Never before in this country have so many children been voluntarily abandoned by their fathers. Never before have so many children grown up without knowing what it means to have a father."

2 Those words from the introduction to his new book, "Fatherless America," pretty much describe the culture change that David Blankenhorn believes is America's "most urgent social problem."

3 Blankenhorn believes (as I do) that the trend toward fatherlessness—the diminution in the public mind of the importance of fathers—is driving any number of America's social crises. The economic consequences are clear; fatherless households are statistically the poorest households in America. But I think the trend is also implicated in matters like crime and violence—both because boys who grow up without fathers are less likely

to get the discipline that can keep them straight and because the decline in the importance of marriage makes boys (and men) less valuable to their families and communities than they might otherwise be. This marginalization, I am convinced, feeds anti-social behavior.

4   Blankenhorn believes it too—believes, moreover, that there is a growing recognition that the trend toward fatherlessness has been overwhelmingly negative for children and for the society in general. His frustration is his—and the society's—inability to come up with a solution to the problem.

5   "People now recognize that there's an elephant in the room," he said in an interview from the Institute for American Values (which he founded) in New York City. "They know it's an elephant, not a mouse, and they know it's not OK to leave him there. They just don't know how to get him out."

6   The problem, he says, is that the trend toward fatherlessness has become rooted in the culture. "The conventional wisdom is that it was brought on by economic changes—industrialization, the loss of blue-collar jobs, that sort of thing," he says. "But I suspect it's deeper than that. It may involve the shift toward expressive individualism, the idea that your basic responsibility is to yourself, which means that your obligation to others becomes weaker. The mother-child bond remains the closest thing we have to an unbreakable bond, but the belief is growing that the father is not a necessary component of the family unit, that you don't really have to have a marriage. I don't think it really enhances the happiness of the adults, but it's been an unquestioned disaster for children."

7   And emphatically not just for **black** children. "This phenomenon never was confined to any race or class," he says, "but now it has really burst out. It's **us!**"

8   There are a couple of things Blankenhorn isn't saying. First, he's not proposing that single mothers could enhance their children's prospects by rushing out and marrying the first male they see. Second, he's not saying that existing marriages must be maintained at all cost. As to the first, he makes only the commonsense point that it's generally much better for children if their parents are committed to them and to one another—that is, married. As to the second: To say that children generally fare better if they live in homes is not to say that we shouldn't get them out if the house is on fire. Some marriages are on fire.

9   Still, Blankenhorn entertains no doubt that the trend toward what he calls the "superfluous father" has been a disaster for our society. His quandary, to repeat, is what to do about it.

10   He makes a number of recommendations in his book (including changing textbooks to be more supportive of the marriage idea), and he is using his book tour to try to get 10,000 men to take the pledge to try to become better fathers.

11   But he is frank to say that if all his ideas are implemented, it still may not be enough.

12   "We don't have much experience in knowing how to reverse cultural trends," he told me. "This isn't something that an institution can do, or the government can do. We are talking about how to get a huge number of individuals to change their minds, at some cost to their own autonomy. It's very hard to figure out."

13   And yet, he insists, we have to try. "The people who say we can't do anything about the trend may be right. Nobody knows. I do know that we'll never change the culture if we just sit around and say we can't."

READING RESPONSE JOURNAL

1. After reading the full article, summarize it in a paragraph.

2. What thoughts does the article provide that you can write about?

3. Are there any other ideas that occur to you from reading the article, for example, any personal views from your own life or from those close to you? If so, write your thoughts briefly.

4. Raspberry got many of the ideas he presents from a book written by David Blankenhorn and from a phone interview with the author. In his article, how does Raspberry give credit to Blankenhorn?

5. Raspberry's essay defines the "superfluous dad" from the title. From reading this piece, explain what Raspberry means by a "superfluous dad."

6. What "social crises" does Raspberry believe stem from fatherlessness?

7. Explain the analogy, or comparison, Blankenhorn makes between fatherlessness and "an elephant in the room." What is the point of the analogy?

8. What possible causes of fatherlessness does Blankenhorn think are *not* the main problem?

9. What does Blankenhorn pinpoint as the root cause of fatherlessness?

10. Why does Blankenhorn explain that fatherlessness is not just a "black" problem?

11. What does Raspberry mean by a "marriage on fire"?

12. What recommendations does Blankenhorn make to solve fatherlessness?

13. What does Blankenhorn mean when he says, "We are talking about how to get a huge number of individuals to change their minds, at some cost to their own autonomy"?

WRITING FROM READING

The Definition Essay Revisited

One strategy of Raspberry's essay is *definition*, that is, to define or explain the term *superfluous dad*. Definition is a rhetorical mode, or plan, for writing development, like description, problem-solution, cause and effect, and comparison and contrast. After reading this essay, we have a full definition of what it means to be a superfluous dad.

Fatherlessness may be a difficult topic for you to write about because it is so personal, but writing about such personal concerns and clarifying them in your own mind can also bring insight and peace.

1. Write a paper giving *your* definition of fatherhood, from a positive or a negative viewpoint.
2. Do you think Blankenhorn is correct when he suggests that the main reason for fatherlessness is men's "expressive individualism, the idea that your basic responsibility is to yourself, which means that your obligation to others becomes weaker"? In other words, has men's selfishness allowed them to neglect their children and the children's mothers? Write about your thoughts on this point.
3. Write about *your* father. Do any of the things Raspberry or Blankenhorn say apply to him? If your father has been a good father, write about those good qualities.
4. Write your thoughts about what kind of a father you are going to be (if you're a man) or what qualities you are looking for in the father of your children (if you're a woman).

COLLABORATIVE LEARNING ACTIVITY

Sharing a Sensitive Topic

In your groups, brainstorm about fatherlessness—and perhaps your fathers—and then share your writing with the group. Because this topic may be very personal, remember to be sensitive to what others say. This subject may be hard for you to write and talk about. If this is the case, take a pass and keep your thoughts to yourself.

WRITING TIPS

Citing Sources

Raspberry takes great pains to cite, or document, his reliance on Blankenhorn's ideas. To cite or document, as we've said before, means to tell where the ideas and words come from. Raspberry quotes from Blankenhorn's book (which he names), and he also quotes from a phone interview with Blankenhorn, telling us Blankenhorn's position and place of work. A writer uses quotations to give the exact words of his source. By doing this, Raspberry gives credit to Blankenhorn and avoids plagiarism, copying the ideas and/or words of another.

In your essay, you may wish to cite Raspberry (or through him, Blankenhorn) and that is fine. You give credibility to your own ideas by documenting the ideas of a respected columnist such as Raspberry and the author Blankenhorn.

Point out, if you wish, where you agree or disagree with Raspberry and his source. An essay is made up of your ideas, too, and they have value. On such important and complicated questions like fatherhood, no one has all the answers. In that sense, we are all experts.

REVIEW

Definition essays grope with key issues in our society, like parenthood and family.

KEEPER OF THE SEAL, from *MAAFA: WHEN NIGHT BECOMES A LION*

Martha Modena Vertreace

This is a short poem about family and gender roles that makes us work for its insights. To begin, try reading it out loud and then silently. You will read the poem many more times as you analyze it. In reading poetry, you must remember that the meaning *extends across line endings* as in lines 2–4:

> "my mother's eyes
> foretell my brother's fear
> years later"

As a unit of thought the line reads "my mother's eyes/foretell my brother's fear/years later." This thought about the "fear" passed on from mother to son is developed in the rest of the poem. When we read prose (all writing that is not poetry), the thought for a sentence ends at the period. Poetry requires us to read in a more concentrated way because the meaning may extend across several lines as in the example we've just seen.

VOCABULARY IN CONTEXT

> *"homo sapiens"*—humans, humanity

Keeper of the Seal, from *Maafa: When Night Becomes a Lion*

Martha Modena Vertreace

> *Modern Homo sapiens could have descended from a small group of male ancestors who lived fairly recently in evolutionary terms, about 270,000 years ago.*

> As if truth hung by a silk thread,
> the straight line lies: my mother's eyes
>   foretell my brother's fear
> 5   years later—that his son becomes
>   another young man
> with baggy pants splitting the crack of his butt,
>   sagging at the ankles;

another whose two pairs of boxers—one striped,
    the other spotted—show

10   through the armholes of his cut-away tee shirt.
    A tattoo. An earring.
A son who never chains white clover blooms,
    a necklace for someone
he loves; who never says

15   this binds us—you to me—us
    to whatever follows.

READING RESPONSE JOURNAL

1. Briefly summarize the poem.

2. What ideas does the poem raise in you?

3. What or who is a "Keeper of the Seal"?

4. How does the introductory quotation about the possible origin of humanity from male ancestors fit in with the ideas of the poem?

5. In the poem, what is "the straight line [that] lies"? Look to the quotation about humanity's origins.

6. The lines "my mother's eyes/foretell my brother's fear/years later" describe the worries of a mom about her son years before he, in turn, had "fears" for his own adolescent boy. Are the mom's concerns the universal fears all mothers have for their children?

7. Why does the father "fear" that his son will be "another" young man with "baggy pants," "tattoo," and "an earring"? What do these clothes and outward signs represent to the father?

8. Explain the meaning at the end of the poem, that the young son might be

   A son who never chains white clover blooms,
   >a necklace for someone
   he loves, who never says
   >this binds us—you to me—us
   >to whatever follows.

   When the father is afraid that the son won't make a daisy chain for his lover, what does the daisy chain represent to the father?

9. The poet presents a contrast between the particularities of the son's clothes, tattoo, and earring with the image of what the young man won't do and say—commit himself to a lover. Explain this contrast more fully.

10. Why does the poet separate her lines as in "a necklace for some-one/he loves"? It is important to remember again that in reading poetry you often have to look for meaning across lines because the sense is continued deliberately from one line to the next.

WRITING FROM READING

Thoughts from Poetry

1. After reading this poem by Martha Vertreace, prewrite about your initial reactions to it. Note that a poem can't be neatly summarized like a paragraph, so all you want to do is get your reactions down fast. The poet wants us to work through her poem, gathering meaning as we go.

2. A good poem is thought provoking, encouraging us to ask questions as we make our way through it. One such question from this poem may be about gender roles in a family. For example, why would the father want a son who makes flower necklaces for a lover, who commits himself "to whatever follows"? How does the father's worry about his son tie in with the introductory quote about the evolution of humanity, the "lie" that humanity originated from male ancestors? (Note that in "the straight line lies," the word *lies* may also have the meaning of "falls, leads to." The poet may intend both meanings here). Prewrite about this question for a while, perhaps thinking in terms of your own life; that is, what is expected of a son or daughter in *your* family? What do—or did—your father and mother want you to be like? Do you think that you have fulfilled their expectations? Why or why not?

3. Perhaps it would be interesting to you to write from another perspective—that of the parent, of the father in the poem. Assume the role (if you don't already have it) of a father or mother and describe *your* expectations for your son or daughter. What images of them do you hope for; what do you want them to be like? Prewrite about these questions and see what you come up with.

4. As a sequel to assignment 1 or 2, or to both if you like, do more prewriting and then write a longer paper about gender roles and their meaning in your family. One possibility for writing might be your thoughts on the current epidemic of fatherlessness in America, the phenomenon of "deadbeat Dads" who have abandoned their families. How do you view this problem? Has it affected you or any of your loved ones? This might be a powerful subject for you to write on.

COLLABORATIVE LEARNING ACTIVITY

Another Student Reads *Your* Paper to You

Share your prewriting with the other members of your group. For your final draft, switch papers and have another student read your paper back to you.

WRITING TIPS

Multiple Readings

What's called "close" reading requires you to read something carefully and multiple times. Poems and essays should be read in this way.

REVIEW

Notice how focused "Keeper of the Seal" is on family; every line of the poem develops the theme of the role of the son in the family. In your writing, too, keep focused and don't wander off.

Word Demons

WOMAN, WOMEN

Many students use the singular *woman* for both singular and plural. *Women* is the correct plural form of *woman;* for example, "One *woman*— Eleanor Roosevelt—stands out among many *women* as a trusted advisor to her husband the president."

Some of the confusion between these two words may stem from pronunciation. *Woman,* the singular, is pronounced "wuh man." The plural *women* is pronounced "wi men," very much like the singular. What may help in determining which word to use is thinking about the singular *man* and the plural *men.* The words *man* and *woman* are singular; the words *men* and *women* are plural.

Practice

Write a correct sentence for *woman* and one for *women.*

Complete the following sentences with either *woman* or *women:*

1. Eleanor Roosevelt was an activist _____, assuming a vital role for herself as an individual in her husband's administration.
2. Her husband's struggle with polio drove Mrs. Roosevelt to be much more than a wife; among _____ of her time, she was revered for her activism.
3. As a wife and mother, Mrs. Roosevelt was unhappy to learn of her husband's affair with another _____.
4. Hurt as she was, Mrs. Roosevelt faced the dilemma many _____ and men have—what to do with an unfaithful spouse.

5. Eleanor Roosevelt overcame her pain and continued to work for her husband and her country, a _____ not only for her time, but for all time.

WHEN, WENT

These words sound almost alike but have different spellings and meanings.

When has to do with time: "*When* the saints come marching in." *Went* is a verb, the past tense of "to go": "The soldiers *went* quickly through the night."

Practice

Write a sentence for *when* and a sentence for *went*.

Complete the following sentences with either *when* or *went:*

1. Hundreds of thousands of mourners _____ and saluted the train as it passed _____ the funeral train of President Lincoln made its way from Washington to Springfield, Illinois.
2. Andrew Johnson, a former opponent of Lincoln's, assumed the presidency _____ Lincoln was assassinated.
3. _____ Lincoln was killed, he was the first American president to be assassinated.
4. The Union _____ on and persisted, even after Lincoln's death.
5. It is always hard for us to imagine the loss of that great president _____ we look back at that time.

QUITE, QUIET

Although these words sound and look similar, they are very different. *Quite,* an adverb, means "very," as in "The patient was *quite* ill."

Quiet can be a noun, adjective, or verb with the meaning "silent, still" as in the sentence "The *quiet* crowd paid its last respects."

Practice

Write your own sentences for *quite* and *quiet.*

Complete the following sentences with either *quite* or *quiet*.

1. General Patton was _____ perceptive, realizing that after the Germans, we might have to fight the Russians.

2. Patton was rarely _____, but he was seldom wrong in his military judgments.

3. _____ taken with military history, Patton was a lifelong student.

4. When Patton gave orders, all around him were _____.

5. The German generals regarded Patton as a "pure warrior," _____ a compliment from the enemy.

MINI-HANDBOOK

Punctuation Basics

Before beginning this section on punctuation, you should realize that much of this work should come at the end—or editing phase—of the writing process. You work first in prewriting and writing to form ideas. Punctuation adds clearness to your writing after you have written your ideas.

Some of this same information about correcting fragments and run-on sentences is found in the text, but here we'll take another look at the fundamental rules and practice using them (though at times you probably are already doing so).

Rule 1: A comma and a coordinating conjunction join two ideas in one sentence. [Conjunctions are joining words, transitions, most often *and, but, yet, so, or, nor, for.*]

Examples

A. Immigration is a hotly disputed issue in America today, and no easy answers present themselves.

B. America must work to preserve its integrity, but we must also be mindful of the needs of others.

Notice that in these two examples the comma comes first, followed by the conjunction. It helps to remember the rule: A comma and a conjunction (in that order) join two ideas in one sentence. The conjunction (transition) you choose fits the meaning you want; for example, *and* adds ideas, *but* shows contrast.

The sentence examples given earlier are called *compound sentences* (more than one idea) and are *coordinated* (balanced in each part of the sentence).

Practice

Now write two compound sentences of your own, using words from the list of conjunctions *(and, but, yet, so, or, nor, for).*

Remember to read your sentences *out loud,* so you "hear" the two ideas in each sentence.

Rule 2: A semicolon (;) by itself joins two ideas in one sentence.

Examples

A. Immigration is a hotly debated issue in America today; no easy answers present themselves.

B. America must work to preserve its integrity; we must also be mindful of the needs of others. [Note that in using the semicolon here the sentence lacks the contrast it had with the comma and *but.*]

Notice that these two examples, as in Rule 1, are coordinated, compound sentences. Note also how the same ideas can be manipulated in different ways, depending on whether you want to use the comma and conjunction or vary your style with a semicolon.

Practice

Now write two sentences using the semicolon correctly. Again, be sure to "hear" each sentence by reading it out loud to yourself.

A word of caution about the semicolon: Some teachers prefer you to use the comma and conjunction, fearing you may use the semicolon incorrectly. Check with your teacher on this point.

Rule 3: When a sentence begins with a subordinate clause (introduced by *after, before, when, until, since, because, if, though, although*), put a comma after the subordinate clause. When these subordinate clauses come at the end of the sentence, no punctuation precedes them.

Examples

A. *Although* immigration is a hotly disputed issue in America today, no easy answers present themselves.

B. *Because* America is a land of integrity, we must be mindful of the needs of others.

C. We must be mindful of the needs of others *because* America is a land of integrity.

These three sentences are called "complex sentences" because they have one subordinate clause (beginning with the words listed earlier) and one main idea.

Practice

Now you try it. Write four complex sentences using four different subordinating words from our list. Vary the placement of the subordinate clause, putting it at the beginning or end of the sentence.

Like the coordinating conjunctions (and, or, nor, for, so, but, yet), subordinating conjunctions are transitions that indicate relationships: for example, *because* shows cause and effect, as in example B, "*Because* America is a land of integrity"; *when, until, after, since, before* describe a time relationship; *if* and *although* describe a relationship that sets up conditions—"*although* immigration is a hotly disputed issue in America today."

Note that when you use different kinds of sentences (simple—one main idea; compound—two or more main ideas; complex—one subordinate and one main idea), you achieve variety in your writing style. Variety keeps you—and your reader—interested.

We have already covered three sentence punctuation rules:

1. A comma and a coordinating conjunction *(and, but, yet, so, or, nor, for)* join two ideas in one sentence. Sample sentence: Immigration is a hotly disputed issue in America today<u>, and</u> no easy answers present themselves.
2. A semicolon (;) by itself joins two ideas in one sentence. Sample sentence: Immigration is a hotly disputed issue in America today; no easy answers present themselves.
3. When a sentence begins with a subordinate clause (introduced by *after, before, when, until, since, because, if, though, although,* put a comma after the subordinate clause.

   Sample sentence: Although immigration is a hotly disputed issue in America today, no easy answers present themselves.

Bear in mind again that punctuation is secondary to meaning. Writing and ideas come first. Checking for correct punctuation should be one of the last steps of your writing process.

Let's now turn to some more punctuation rules:

Rule 4: Commas set off, or surround, subordinate (dependent) clauses beginning with *who* and *which.*

Examples

A. The international controversy over land mines, <u>which have been used in many Third-World nations</u>, continues to simmer.
B. Many American soldiers, <u>who were themselves injured seriously by land mines in Vietnam</u>, have spoken out against their use.

Practice

Now you write a sentence for *who* and one for *which.* Remember to surround the *who* and *which* subordinate clauses with commas.

A related point: *who* refers to humans; *which* to things.

Example

Any international ban on land mines, <u>which</u> have destroyed thousands of lives, must be approved by the President, <u>who</u> has been slow to take up this cause.

Rule 5:   Commas are used to set off (surround—front and back) appositives, which are nouns or groups of words that rename or identify further a preceding noun or pronoun.

Example

A. General Westmoreland, commander of the army, was heavily criticized for America's defeat in Vietnam.
B. Tom Stack, a professor, was a Vietnam War hero.

In these sentences, "commander of the army" and "a professor," are appositives identifying, or telling more about, the preceding nouns, General Westmoreland and Tom Stack.

Practice

Write an appositive, a noun or group of words, about a preceding noun or pronoun. Here's a start:

A. Richard Nixon, _____, was impeached for conspiracy.

Now write two sentences of your own, remembering to set off each appositive with commas.

Rule 6:   Commas are used to separate words in a series (three or more).

Example

America has been involved in four major conflicts during the twentieth century: the First World War<u>,</u> the Second World War<u>,</u> the Korean War<u>,</u> and the Vietnam War.

Note that a comma precedes the *and* before the last item of the series. Sometimes this last comma is considered optional, but be safe and always use it. Also, notice that there must be a series, three or more, to use commas. In the phrase "peanut butter and jelly," there is no comma because *and* by itself joins the *two* items.

Practice

Write a sentence in which you use commas to separate words in a series.

Rule 7: A colon (:) sets off a list.

Examples

A. The American Civil War had many interrelated causes<u>:</u> slavery, secession, economics, and regional pride. [Note how the colon here prepares the reader for the list of "causes."]
B. The Civil War lashed the country with terrible cruelties: the loss of sons, husbands, and fathers; the destruction of villages, towns, farmland, and railroads; and the residue of hatred between North and South. [The colon sets off the explanation of "cruelties" to follow.]

Practice

Now you try using the colon. Remember that it comes before a list, usually at the end of a sentence, as in the earlier examples.

ACKNOWLEDGMENTS

Maya Angelou, "Momma Confronts the Dentist" from *I Know Why the Caged Bird Sings*. Copyright © 1969 by Maya Angelou. Reprinted with the permission of Random House, Inc.

Anonymous, "Do Immigrants Ruin America?" Reprinted with the permission of the author.

Dave Barry, "Are Guys Smart or What?" from *The Miami Herald* (November 23, 1997). Originally titled *A Superior Intelligence*. Reprinted with the permission of the author.

John Boslough, "Against All Odds" from *Stephen Hawking's Universe*. Copyright © 1985 by John Boslough. Reprinted with the permission of William Morrow & Company.

Sandra Cisneros, "Geraldo No Last Name" from *The House on Mango Street* (New York: Alfred A. Knopf, 1984). Copyright © 1984 by Sandra Cisneros. Reprinted with the permission of Susan Bergholz Literary Services.

Ellis Cose, "Memories in Blood" from *Newsweek* (December 8, 1997). Copyright © 1997 by Newsweek, Inc. Reprinted with the permission of *Newsweek*. All rights reserved.

Andrea J. Fine, "Dropping Back In: Mother gives up dead-end life, returns to school, and writes the book on how to get off welfare" from *The Chicago Tribune*. Reprinted with the permission of the author.

Michelle Genz, "Getting Pucked." Reprinted with the permission of the author.

Ellen Goodman, "Enlist Hollywood in the War on Teen Pregnancy" from *The Chicago Tribune* (February 21, 1995). Reprinted with the permission of Knight Ridder/Tribune Media Services.

Bob Greene, "Words, Good or Bad, Can Echo Through a Lifetime" from *The Chicago Tribune* (November 10, 1997). Copyright © 1997 by Tribune Media Services, Inc. All rights reserved. Reprinted with permission.

Bob Greene, "Two Words —'I Do'—Speak Volumes about Bob Love" from *The Chicago Tribune* (December 13, 1995). Copyright © 1995 by Tribune Media Services, Inc. All rights reserved. Reprinted with permission.

Elia Herrera, "Monika Teaches Me to Walk" from *The Daley Express*. Reprinted with the permission of the author.

Roger Hoffman, "The Dare" from *The New York Times* (March 22, 1986). Copyright © 1986 by The New York Times Company. Reprinted with permission.

Abbie Jones, "Yes I Can': Shy woman overcomes double set of obstacles" from *The Chicago Tribune* (March 23, 1997). Reprinted with the permission of Knight Ridder/Tribune Information Services.

Barbara Kingsolver, "Stone Soup" from *High Tide in Tucson*. Copyright ©1995 by Barbara Kingsolver. Reprinted with the permission of HarperCollins Publishers, Inc.

Alex Kotlowitz, "The Quiet Riot Next Door" from *The Chicago Tribune* (August 27, 1996). Reprinted with the permission of Knight Ridder/Tribune Information Services.

William Least Heat Moon, "Native American Prejudices" [editor's title] from *Blue Highways*. Copyright © 1982 by William Least Heat Moon. Reprinted with the permission of Little, Brown & Company, Inc.

Brian Manning, "The Thirsty Animal" from *The New York Times* (October 15, 1985). Copyright © 1985 by The New York Times Company. Reprinted with permission.

Elvia Martinez, "Should Immigrants Be Welcomed or Repudiated?" Reprinted with the permission of the author.

James McBride, excerpt from *The Color of Water: A Black Man's Tribute to His White Mother*. Copyright ©1996 by James McBride. Reprinted with the permission of Putnam Berkeley, a division of Penguin Putnam, Inc.

Violet A. Mieleulis, "A Song Unsung." Reprinted with the permission of the author.

Kathleen Parker, "Fathers Provide Bridge Over the 'River of Goo'" from *The Chicago Tribune* (August 19, 1998). Copyright © 1998 by Tribune Media Services, Inc. All rights reserved. Reprinted with permission.

William Raspberry, "Offensive Words" from *The Chicago Tribune* (June 4, 1996). Reprinted with the permission of The Washington Post Writers Group.

William Raspberry, "Superfluous Dads a Menace to Society" from *The Washington Post*. Reprinted with the permission of The Washington Post Writers Group.

David Raymond, "On Being 17, Bright, and Unable to Read" from *The New York Times* (April 25, 1976). Copyright © 1976 by The New York Times Company. Reprinted with permission.

Bunnie Riedel, " 'Had It Not Been for the Village . . .': The Story of a Successful Single Mom." Reprinted with permission.

Mike Rose, excerpts from *Lives on the Boundary: The Struggles and Achievements of America's Underprepared*. Copyright ©1989 by Mike Rose. Reprinted with the permission of The Free Press, a division of Simon & Schuster, Inc.

Mike Royko, "Schools May Have Problems, But They Begin at Home" from *The Chicago Tribune* (November 15, 1996). Copyright ©1996 by The Chicago Tribune Company. Reprinted with permission.

Leslie Marmon Silko, excerpts from "Fences Against Freedom" from *Yellow Woman and a Beauty of the Spirit*. Copyright © 1996 by Leslie Marmon Silko. Reprinted with the permission of Simon & Schuster, Inc.

Kate Simon, "Jimmy and Death" from *Bronx Primitive*. Copyright © 1982 by Kate Simon. Reprinted with the permission of Viking Penguin, a division of Penguin Putnam Inc.

Gary Soto, "The Locket" from *A Summer Life*. Copyright © 1990 by Gary Soto. Reprinted with the permission of University Press of New England.

Brent Staples, "Just Walk On By: A Black Man Ponders His Power to Alter Public Space" from *Ms. Magazine* (September 1986). Copyright © 1986 by Brent Staples. Reprinted with the permission of the author.

Martha Modena Vertreace, "Keeper of the Seal" from *Maafa: When Night Becomes a Lion*. Copyright ©1996 by Martha Modena Vertreace. Reprinted with the permission of the author.

INDEX

INDEX BY AUTHOR